Inside the Colonels' Greece

By
'ATHENIAN'

TRANSLATED AND
WITH AN INTRODUCTION BY
Richard Clogg

W · W · NORTON & COMPANY · INC ·
New York

Originally published in French under the title
Vérité sur la Grèce by La Cité, Éditeur, Lausanne

Library of Congress Cataloging in Publication Data
Main entry under title:

Inside the colonels' Greece.

    Translation of Vérité sur la Grèce.
    Includes biblographical references.
    1. Greece, Modern—Politics and government—1935–
I. 'Athenian.'
DF852.V4513 1972   320.9'495'07   75–173629
ISBN 0–393–05466–7

PRINTED IN THE UNITED STATES OF AMERICA

1 2 3 4 5 6 7 8 9 0

Contents

INSIDE THE COLONELS' GREECE

Translator's Introduction

THE author of this book is a Greek intellectual who is still living in Greece today. For this reason he clearly cannot write under his own name, but this enforced anonymity in no way detracts from the book's authenticity, for the author has been able to support his assertions with abundant documentation.

The work was originally written in French and published in Lausanne in 1970. It has fortunately been possible, since then, to obtain from the author himself some corrections, as well as some additional material concerning the period from March 1970 to April 1971. However, a number of major developments during this period are not covered in his text and the purpose of this introduction is to give a brief account of them. The author's general analysis is in no way affected by these later developments; most of them, in fact, confirm his conclusions.

No significant changes occurred in the political situation in Greece during this period. Martial law remained in force four years after the coup, which must in itself be something of a record. In April 1970 Prime Minister George Papadopoulos claimed that martial law was 'moribund' and in April 1971 that it had been 'reduced to a mere shadow'. Sedition and attempts to overthrow the existing social order by force, covered by Law 509 of 1947, were in future no longer to be tried by military courts. But a number of specific offences ranging from rebellion, forming armed bands, and causing an explosion, to conspiracy to commit a felony or misdemeanour, breach of the peace, spreading false rumours and selling the records of Melina Mercouri remained subject to the military courts.

During the course of the year a number of purported measures of 'liberalisation' were introduced. These included implementation of Article 10 of the 1968 Constitution which, among other things, guarantees freedom from arrest without charge, although this provision was in fact systematically violated during the course of the year. In April 1970 the Council of State pronounced that passports could not be withheld or annulled without sufficient reason being given to the applicant, and in July Deputy Prime Minister Pattakos announced the removal of passport restrictions for former M.P.s, except those belonging to the left-wing E.D.Λ. But passports were still withheld from a number of Greeks for unspecified reasons of 'public order'.

In November a 'mini-parliament' came into being. Ninety-two candidates were elected by a very limited electorate of 1240, drawn mainly from the trade unions and professional associations. Of these, forty-six were selected by the Prime Minister, who added ten of his own nominees. Half of the candidates were aged between 25 and 40, the remainder between 41 and 50. The successful nominees, who were to enjoy an annual salary of £4200, were regarded by Papadopoulos as constituting the future political leadership of the country, although it was made quite clear that the 'mini-parliament' was to be a purely advisory body, with no legislative functions. When early in the new year this assembly showed some inclination to deviate from complete acquiescence, it was sharply put in its place by Pattakos.

Also in November the regime published a draft of the institutional law relating to the future working of political parties. But at the same time the regime made it quite clear that any talk of elections in the near future was out of the question. The regime's newly appointed chief spokesman, George Georgalas, a former communist whose appointment and considerable influence were resented by some of the junta's strongest supporters, announced that there could be no talk of elections until the annual income per head had risen from 800 dollars to 1100 dollars. Papadopoulos himself further emphasised the remoteness of elections when he stated in December that there would be no change in the constitutional order during 1971. He had, moreover, earlier promised to give one year's notice before holding elections. Pattakos further stressed in March 1971, that no major changes were envisaged in the near future and no announcement on the subject could be expected before Papadopoulos' 'state of the nation' speech due to be made in December 1971. But the regime's confident rejection of foreign pressures for elections could not disguise the signs of internal dissension within the regime, and of tension between the inner élite of Papadopoulos' immediate circle and the formerly influential members of the 'revolutionary council'.

The regime's new press law had come into force on 1 January 1970, but the *Ethnos* trial in March-April of the same year soon clearly indicated the fate that awaited those newspapers and journalists that took seriously even its limited freedoms. Five of the publishers and editors of *Ethnos* were tried for publishing 'false reports likely to cause anxiety among the public'. Also on trial was Ioannis Zighdis, a former Centre Union minister, who in an interview with the newspaper had called for a government of national unity to deal with the Cyprus situation. Prison sentences of up to five years were passed and fines totalling £18,750 were imposed, resulting in the immediate closure of the paper. While Zighdis was serving his sentence efforts were made by the authorities to foreclose on his house to pay off his fine. A further threat to press freedom was contained in a statement by the regime in early December 1970 that foreign correspondents in Greece, irrespective of nationality, would be subject to Greek law and thus liable to lengthy prison sentences and substantial fines for filing 'false reports'. The Minister of Justice later stated that the decree did not apply to non-Greek nationals and that the misunderstanding was due to a 'printer's error'. But it appeared that the decree still applied to the many correspondents of foreign newspapers and agencies who were Greek nationals.

Despite these measures of 'liberalisation', arrests and trials of opponents of the regime continued throughout the year. The most significant of these trials was that which came to be known as the Trial of the Thirty-Four, held in March-April 1971. The thirty-four defendants were alleged to have been members of the resistance organisation Democratic Defence, and were mostly charged under Law 509 of 1947 which makes advocacy of the violent overthrow of the existing social system punishable by death. A further twenty were indicted but not tried as they were abroad. Those on trial included a number of distinguished intellectuals and professional men, among them Professor Dionysios Karayorgas of the Panteios School of Economic and Political Studies, Professor George Mangakis, professor elect of criminal law in the University of Athens, and General George Iordanidis, a former Greek representative to NATO. A number of the accused made statements that their confessions had been extracted under torture, and a number of these depositions were published in the Greek press before the president of the court intervened to prevent any more going into the court record. This was the first time since the coup that allegations of torture had been reported in the Greek press.

One of those indicted but not tried was the American film director and husband of Melina Mercouri, Jules Dassin. In the indictment he was described as 'an American Jew' and it was alleged in the trial that he had sent 900 dollars to Democratic Defence. When the defence queried a suggestion that this was money belonging to the organisation, the crown prosecutor Major Liapis replied, 'That's obvious. Can a Jew ever part with his own money?' Eight distinguished foreign jurists were refused entry to the trial on the grounds that their presence constituted 'an insult to the dignity of Greek justice'.

The trial assumed considerable political significance as the defence witnesses included a number of leading pre-coup politicians, notably Panayotis Kanellopoulos, the leader of the right-wing E.R.E., and George Mavros, a leading Centre Union politician. Kanellopoulos in his testimony declared that 'under certain conditions it became an honour to use violence for the purposes of restoring freedom'. One of the witnesses for the defence, a university professor, was subsequently suspended by the regime. Towards the end of the trial, Papadopoulos announced that the judges would be regarded as 'criminals' if they allowed their humanitarian feelings to influence them. There were fears that death sentences might be passed, but this was not the case. Professor Karayorgas, who had blown off part of a hand and injured an eye while handling bombs in his own home, was sentenced to life imprisonment, and nineteen others to gaol terms ranging from one to eighteen years. Fourteen others were released, seven with suspended sentences.

Further trials of those accused of resistance activities continued throughout the year. A notable one was that in July of some leading members of the illegal Greek Communist Party. Among these were Nikolaos Kaloudis, one of the members of the seven man Politburo of the Communist Party, and Zenon Zorzovilis, a member of the Party's Central Committee. Both were sentenced to life imprisonment. Nine of the eleven defendants had renounced their lawyers for their own protection after one of the defence lawyers, Constantine Kiziridis, was given a one-year sentence for contempt of court for questioning the impartiality of military judges in a trial concerned with sedition against the regime.

In late November, a number of Greeks, estimated at between 40 and 160, were arrested after a bomb had exploded near the Truman statue in Athens, one of a number of bomb incidents during the course of the year. They were held without charge despite the purported implementation of Article 10 of the Constitution, which required an arrested person to be taken before an examining magistrate with twenty-four hours. Later arrests included those of Christos Sartzetakis, the examining magistrate in the Lambrakis murder case, Professor Dimitrios Maronitis, formerly of the University of Thessaloniki, George Romaios, editor-in-chief of the Athens daily *Vima*, Dimitrios Papaefstratiou, manager of American Express in Athens, and retired Air Commodore George Papadonikolakis. In early May 1971 a number of those held in the earlier round-up were eventually charged with offences concerning conspiracy and explosives, which remained under the jurisdiction of the military courts. Earlier official statements had implied that they would eventually be charged with sedition, which had been removed from martial law jurisdiction the previous month. Those charged included Sartzetakis, the Centre Union deputy Talbot Kefallinos, retired Brigadier Christos Rougheris and Evangelos Yannopoulos, who had been one of the defence lawyers at the Trial of the Thirty-Four. A sinister new development during the course of the year was the tendency of E.S.A., the military police, to take over from the civilian security police (*Asfaleia*) and gendarmerie the function of arresting and interrogating suspected opponents of the regime.

Alongside these new arrests and trials, releases of prisoners and those in exile continued throughout the year, culminating shortly before the fourth anniversary of the coup in April 1971 in the release of all those held in administrative detention since the coup, with the exception of fifty 'dangerous and unrepentant communists' who were now to be exiled. A number of non-communists were also kept in exile. The detention camps of Partheni on Leros and Skala Oropou were closed down. In a speech during the previous December Papadopoulos had promised that all those detained without charge or in exile would be released within the next four months provided that there was no change in the existing situation regarding internal security. This promise had been repeated by Georgalas in a press conference as late as 17 March 1971.

Perhaps the best known of these released in the course of the year was the composer and former left-wing deputy Mikis Theodorakis. He was allowed to leave Greece in April 1970 after the personal intervention of the French radical politician Jean-Jacques Servan-Schreiber. This, together with the implementation of Article 10 of the Constitution, appeared to have been done in anticipation of a meeting in May of the Committee of Ministers of the Council of Europe, from which Greece had withdrawn under pressure in December 1969. The Greek regime was particularly anxious that the report of the European Commission of Human Rights, which had already been circulated among member governments, should not be made public.

The Committee of Ministers did however decide to publish the report, the substance of which had been leaked in the *Sunday Times* the previous November. The massively documented four-volume report was a severe indictment of the regime and the way in which it treats its political opponents. The Commission found it 'established beyond doubt that torture or ill-treatment contrary to Article 3 (of the European Convention for the Protection of Human Rights and Fundamental Freedoms) has been inflicted in a number of cases'(ii, 417) and that the general failure of the Greek govenment 'to order enquiries, either administrative or judicial, into numerous allegations of torture or ill-treatment, where both victim and offender have been named and other circumstantial evidence provided, is remarkable'. 'No Government could', the Report continued, '. . . allow such allegations to stand unchallenged by proper enquiry without the inference being drawn that it is generally indifferent to them and therefore tolerates any torture or ill-treatment that does in fact take place' (ii, 419). The large number of complaints received by the Commission was in itself 'a strong indication that acts of torture or ill treatment are not isolated or exceptional, nor limited to one place' (ii, 418).

The Commission stated that it 'has not found that the evidence adduced by the respondent Government shows a displacement of the lawful Government by force of arms by the Communists and their allies was imminent on 21st April, 1967; indeed there is evidence indicating that it was neither planned at that time, nor seriously anticipated by either the military or police authorities' (i, para. 159). Nor did it accept 'that the street demonstrations, strikes and work stoppages in the first months of 1967 attained the magnitude of a public emergency' (i, para. 160). 'The picture of strikes and work stoppages', it noted, 'does not differ markedly from that in many other countries in Europe over a similar period; indeed, as regards the length of strikes and stoppages it is more favourable than in some' (i, para. 161). In conclusion, the Greek government had not satisfied the Commission 'that there was on 21st April, 1967, a public emergency threatening the life of the Greek nation' (i, para. 165).

After Greece's withdrawal from the Council of Europe and the publication of the Human Rights Commission report, the regime showed signs of less sensitivity to foreign opinion. One symptom of this was its failure to renew its agreement with the International Red Cross, whereby representatives of the latter were allowed to visit all places of detention, both police stations and prisons. This had been signed shortly after the European Commission of Human Rights' report had been distributed to member governments of the Council of Europe in the autumn of 1969.

The regime's relations with the E.E.C. also became increasingly strained during the course of the year. In April the Common Market Commission announced that it would 'reconsider' the agreement of association signed between Greece and the Common Market in 1962, because of its increasing anxiety about the situation in Greece. The association agreement had already been frozen soon after the coup but there was some doubt whether it could be actually terminated. Certainly in January 1971, Makarezos, the Minister of Co-ordination, confidently declared that he expected Greece to be a full member of the Common Market by 1984, as the agreement had originally provided. The regime came in for further censure from the International Labour Organisation in November 1970. A commission chaired by Lord Devlin found that the Greek regime had breached a number of I.L.O. conventions on freedom of association and collective bargaining. Faced with exclusion from the I.L.O., the regime was forced to prepare a new law concerning the functioning of trade unions. A further blow to Greece's international effort came with the death in July 1970 of the regime's able Foreign Minister, Panayotis Pipinelis, virtually the only one of the pre-coup politicians of note who had chosen to collaborate with the regime.

But despite these setbacks the regime received a considerable boost to its prestige with the announcement by the U.S. State Department on 9 September 1970, after persistent rumours and a reportedly stormy meeting of the National Security Council, that heavy arms shipments, which had been suspended after the coup, would be resumed. When the resumption was announced the State Department spokesman, Robert McCloskey, stated that although the United State administration had hoped for a more rapid return to representative government 'the trend toward a constitutional order is established. Major sections of the Constitution have been implemented, and partial restoration of civil rights has been accomplished.' The resumption of arms shipments was said to be conditional on the regime's honouring its timetable for a return to constitutional rule.

In earlier hearings in June before the Sub-Committee on United States Security Agreements and Commitments Abroad of the Senate Foreign Relations Committee it had already become apparent that the United States administration had decided that it was going to learn to live with the colonels. Rodger Davies, Deputy Assistant Secretary for Near Eastern and South Asian Affairs, stated that he believed that the Constitution 'would be implemented by the end of this calendar year' (i.e. 1970). He declared that 'his impression' was that there had been 'some excesses' in Greece and 'that the regime has not been conscious of its public relations responsibilities, and its responsibilities as a government to publicly dissociate itself from these excesses'. Davies maintained that the regime had undertaken certain reforms 'of an egalitarian nature, which have been welcomed in rural communities'. 'One that I particularly recall', he added, 'was the abolishment of church fees by which the wealthy could get first-class funerals and the poor would have to make do with whatever the minimum service was.'

The Senate Foreign Relations Committee was clearly unhappy about the direction taken by U.S. policy in Greece and in February of 1971 it sent two investigators, James Lowenstein and Richard Moose, to Greece. The main task of this mission was to reconcile the increasingly glaring discrepancy between the State Department's apparent conviction that a 'trend towards a constitutional order' had been established and Papadopoulos' explicit declaration that no political or constitutional changes were envisaged in 1971. On their return in February, Moose and Lowenstein gave a private briefing to the Senate Foreign Relations Committee. After the briefing Senator Fulbright stated that their report indicated that 'there has been no real movement towards democracy in Greece'. The quality of the political intelligence supplied by the U.S. Embassy in Athens was clearly of some concern and predictably was the target of some severe criticism in the investigators' report. Their doubts were confirmed with the publication of a letter written by the U.S. Ambassador in Athens, Henry Tasca, to an American academic who had enquired about the welfare of an activitist in the Centre Union youth movement E.D.I.N. Tasca wrote that the individual concerned had 'a record of having been a member of a United Democratic Left (E.D.A.) Youth Group (E.D.I.N.)'. E.D.I.N., of course, had no connection whatsoever with E.D.A., which had its own youth movement, the Lambrakis Youth. Tasca's gaffe betrayed an alarming ignorance of the basic facts of pre-coup politics in Greece.

There was some sign of a more realistic appraisal of the situation tion by the American administration when towards the end of March 1971 William Rogers, the Secretary of State, declared his 'disappointment' that the Greek government had not done more 'to move towards the restoration of representative democracy'. This brought an immediate rebuke from Pattakos, who claimed that the 'revolution' had put an end to foreign interference in Greece's internal affairs.

However, it was not long before the American administration reverted to its more normal position. A few weeks later, in April 1971, Maurice Stans, the Secretary of Commerce, at an official luncheon in Athens, was reported as saying, 'I am particularly complimented by the fact that there are nine ministers and deputy ministers of the government who hear me address you today. It is a compliment to the government of the United States and to the wonderfully close relations that exist today between our two countries.' The regime's communiqué on his visit stated that Stans had conveyed President Nixon's 'warm love to the Greek government and the Greek people'. The American Embassy later suggested that Stans had spoken instead of 'warmth and confidence'.

The other significant trend in the regime's foreign relations was the strengthening of ties with the Eastern bloc countries. A trade agreement was signed with Albania, with whom Greece was still technically in a state of war, and Foreign Minister Pipinelis declared that the Albanians had shown 'understanding' by returning Greek fugitives. This presaged the opening of diplomatic relations between the two countries. The Bulgarian Foreign Minister visited Athens in May 1970, and in February 1971 Bulgaria proposed a far-ranging plan for economic co-operation with Greece, while negotiations were initiated for a trade agreement with Red China.

Early in 1971 Greek foreign policy took an unusual turn with the enunciation of a new policy of an 'opening to Africa' or, in another variant, a 'Mediterranean Commonwealth'. In February Pattakos visited Egypt and Ethiopia at the invitation of President Sadat and the Emperor Haile Selassie. On his return Pattakos declared that Egypt and Ethiopia both 'respond absolutely to the universal, peace-loving and humanitarian message of Greece'. This visit was followed up in March by Pattakos' visit to Libya. These new initiatives appeared to be part of a crude attempt to warn the regime's foreign critics that Greece could seek new friends outside the Western alliance.

On the economic front the return to the high growth rate of pre-coup years was maintained following the slump of 1967-68. During 1970 the gross national product rose by 7·1 per cent. But at the same time the very high level of liquidity and the adverse balance of payments, with a predicted deficit of 420 million dollars in 1970 against 343 million in 1969, gave rise to serious doubts about the long-term soundness of the Greek economy. Despite this foreign banks, including British merchant banks, were prepared to make substantial loans at undisclosed rates of interest. In a speech in January 1971, Makarezos claimed foreign investments totalling 921 million dollars which, he asserted, was more than had been made in the whole of the preceding seven years. However, in this total were included the 800 million dollars of investments promised in package deals concluded with the ship-owners Aristotle Onassis and Stavros Niarchos early in 1970. These deals envisaged the construction of a number of heavy industrial enterprises. Onassis, in return for the concession to supply a large quantity of crude oil to Greece, undertook to build an oil refinery, an aluminium plant and an electrical generating plant, part of an investment package totalling 600 million dollars. In a smaller deal Niarchos undertook to introduce investments totalling 200 million. By November, however, Onassis was seeking a major revision of his contract, including a demand for officially backed guarantees for foreign investors. This demand is said to have provoked serious differences between Papadopoulos and Makarezos. No agreement was reached on the question of revision, and Onassis submitted his dispute with the regime to international arbitration. It was later reported that Onassis was trying to retreat from his investment commitment by asking that if the contract were upheld after arbitration he should be compensated for losses, which were estimated at 1400 million dollars over the ten-year life of the contract. He was also asking for the reimbursement of expenses so far incurred, nearly 20 million dollars.

In a striking departure from their earlier silence, a number of distinguished Greek intellectuals decided to exploit the margin of freedom allowed by the regime's abolition of preventive censorship and the new press law. In the summer of 1970 the *Dekaokto Keimena (Eighteen Texts)* appeared, containing poems, essays and short stories, a number of which consisted of thinly veiled allegorical attacks on the regime set in a mythical Latin American dictatorship 'Boliguay'. Within six months it had sold nine thousand copies, a remarkably high sale by Greek standards. In the spring of 1971 this was followed by the *Nea Keimena (New Texts)*, consisting mainly of literary texts but with a number of essays on sensitive topics such as democracy and economic development and the problems of the intellectual under a tyranny. The contributors represented a broad spectrum of political opinion, and three of them were actually behind bars for their opposition to the regime.

It was inevitable that the regime should seek to exploit the 150th anniversary of the Greek War of Independence in March 1971 for the purposes of its own propaganda. But the regime's opponents were also not slow to link their country's struggle for independence with the struggle now being waged to restore those political freedoms for which the protagonists of 1821 fought.

Shortly before 25 March the leaders of the two main political parties in pre-coup Greece, which between them shared over 80 per cent of the votes cast at the last elections, issued a joint statement urging the return of democratic institutions. The statement was signed by Panayotis Kanellopoulos for E.R.E., and George Mavros and Ioannis Zighdis for the Centre Union. This was the first time since the coup that leaders of E.R.E. and the Centre Union had pledged to work together for the 'restoration of democracy through free institutions'. Statements were also issued by Dimitrios Papaspyrou, president of the last Parliament, and Stefanos Stefanopoulos, a former Prime Minister. At the same time another statement was issued by about 130 leading Greek intellectuals and others, including George Seferis, the poet and Nobel prize winner. This declaration's principal message was that during the one hundred and fifty years of Greece's independence almost all major reforms were achieved 'under democratic institutions and parliamentary government'.

In a New Year message Panayotis Kanellopoulos had expressed the hope that in the anniversary year 1971 Greece would once again obtain its freedom. This was not to be the case, however, and 1971 saw Greece enter on the longest period of dictatorial rule in its modern history, with no sign of change in the near future.

London, April 1971   RICHARD CLOGG

Author's Preface

MOST Europeans feel an instinctive revulsion towards the military dictatorship which was established in Greece in April 1967. This reflex is certainly healthy. But it is important to know more exactly the kind of regime that has provoked it. It is essential to understand the nature of the illness, its causes, its symptoms, the chances of a cure, if the patient is to receive the correct treatment, or if the infection is to be prevented from spreading. There also exists a minority who either approve of what has happened in Greece or choose to suspend judgment. In so far as they are not neo-fascists, these people are clearly badly informed.

Both groups ask, or should ask, a variety of questions about the past, and how and why all this has happened. What was the situation in Greece before the coup? Was its parliamentary system as inefficient and as corrupt as it has been made out to be? Was there any real danger of anarchy, leading to a civil war and a communist take over? Then come the questions about the present. What kind of dictatorship is this? Who are these colonels and how do they exercise their power? How do the Greeks themselves see the situation, and how do they react to it? What truth is there in the reports of resistance and police terror? Finally, there are queries about the future. When and how will the dictatorship end? What will follow it? Should Western Europe take a stand on the Greek question, and if so, what should it be?

Despite the abundant literature on Greece which has already appeared, it seems to me that there is still room for an attempt at a systematic answer to all these questions, particularly if this comes from a Greek actually living in the colonels' Greece. This is the justification for the present book. Although written by a single individual, it none the less reflects the opinions of a whole group of opponents of the regime. Lawyers, journalists, economists, and former officers have contributed to gathering the necessary documentation. They include moderate conservatives, liberals, and democratic socialists. They have one thing in common: faith in freedom and in dialogue, and an uncompromising opposition to all forms of totalitarianism, whether of the right or of the left. They are fighting against the military dictatorship so as to be

13

free to disagree with each other openly, and to settle their differences by civilised discussion, persuasion, and free elections. A vast gulf separates them from the present regime and from all those who envisage some kind of compromise or collaboration with it. No less vast a gulf separates them from those who may eventually fight against the present totalitarian regime, but simply wish to replace it by another, of the kind which has twice been thrust upon Czechoslovakia.

An attempt to answer the questions posed above forms the basic framework of the book. The first part, dealing with the background to the putsch, in fact forms a brief political history of modern Greece. For a knowledge of Greece's past is essential to any attempt to understand the present situation, and to speculate about its possible outcome. And this historical background is little understood abroad, where propaganda of various kinds has helped to distort the true picture.[1] In this historical sketch, which is more or less chronological, I have not attempted to analyse the socio-economic infrastructure underlying Greek politics. This type of analysis needs to be done either meticulously or not at all. And in any case, it would have required a disproportionate amount of research and space.[2] In the following section I have abandoned the chronological framework and have attempted a descriptive analysis of the dictatorship, area by area. But pressures of space have forced me to be selective, and there are inevitable omissions. I shall try to justify these.

I have deliberately omitted any account of the putsch itself, as well as the King's attempted counter-coup. Others have written accounts of 21 April and 13 December 1967, and the technical minutiae of these military operations have little relevance to the real problems facing the country.

In general, I have tried to avoid burdening the text with detailed references which will not be of great interest to the general reader. This has enabled me to give more space to examples, and to accounts of actual experiences, sometimes tinged with a black humour, which illustrate the atmosphere in which we live more graphically than a long lecture.

Some of the omissions have been forced upon me. These result from the great difficulties experienced in trying to document certain subjects. Special precautions must be taken even to consult some issues of the *Official Gazette*. There is no way of obtaining exact information on the number of civil servants who have been purged, or the number of political detainees, or the privileges bestowed on the new military élite. The true figures on the state of the economy have now become jealously guarded state secrets.

Very few people have access to them before they are doctored for publication. Every time information of this type has been leaked, civil servants with access to the true figures have been hauled before the security police, accused of 'having supplied information to the enemies of the regime'.

The third part of the book is devoted to a consideration of future prospects, and attempts to outline what appears to me a realistic strategy to hasten the return of democracy to Greece.

The need for security has obliged me to remain anonymous and to hide the identity of almost all those opposed to the regime, except of course those who have acted openly or whose activities have subsequently become publicly known. Similar considerations have kept me from utilising certain information which would discredit the regime but at the same time would endanger the position of some of its opponents.

So much for omissions, intended or imposed. I only hope that the actual contents of the present work will seem to the reader to justify the difficulties and dangers of its composition.

Athens, March 1970

POSTSCRIPT FOR THE ENGLISH LANGUAGE EDITION

I am particularly gratified to see my book translated into English, the more so since it is going to be published in the United States as well as in Great Britain. In fact, had I been given the choice, English would have been the first language in which it would have appeared. There is a specific and cogent reason for this, which will become abundantly clear in the sections entitled 'The Utopia of the Ideal Revolution' and 'A Realistic Strategy'. To put it briefly here, the solution of the Greek problem depends on the U.S.A. more than on any other single country. One of the few things Western Europeans can do about it (and which I urge them to do at the end of my book) is to press Washington to reconsider the misguided policy it has been following in Greece over the last four years.

There is no time to lose. America has become very unpopular in my country, even in the most traditionally pro-Western moderate and conservative circles. For this the U.S. has only its present leadership, or lack of such, to blame; you cannot support a hateful dictatorial regime and at the same time retain the good will of the people oppressed by it. The result has been the rapid decline of a valuable friendship, originally founded on a common faith in democratic freedom.

And yet there is still hope. Decent and intelligent Americans are becoming increasingly uneasy about their government's tolerant, or even friendly, attitude towards the Greek colonels. May this book help them to see how right they are to worry, and encourage them to fight for a policy both worthier of the best American traditions and more in keeping with true American interests—before it is too late.

Athens, July 1971

PART ONE
The Past, or how it all came about

1. THE ROOTS OF LIBERTY: UNTIL 1936

WHEN writing about their own history, the French rarely go further back than 1789, or the Napoleonic period, in seeking the roots of the present. The Greeks however, without the slightest hesitation, look as far back as Justinian, or even Alexander the Great. While not going to these extremes, anyone wishing to understand present-day Greece must bear in mind that the country was under Ottoman rule from the middle of the fifteenth century until the beginning of the nineteenth century. During this period Greece was cut off from the Western world and experienced neither the Renaissance, nor Enlightened Despotism, nor urban civilisation. The break with classical antiquity, already advanced during the Byzantine epoch, was completed under the Turks. Ancient Greek was now understood by only a handful of educated people, mainly priests. The people sang the praises of their folk heroes in the 'demotic'. or spoken language. Thanks to the influence of the Orthodox Church, which remained the sole repository of national consciousness, the Christian Byzantine tradition virtually effaced the pagan tradition of classical antiquity.

Under Ottoman rule, the Greeks were *rayas*, that is vassals or slaves. A certain number of the educated, by collaborating with the Turks, were able to achieve a comfortable social and economic status as diplomats or administrators. These *Phanariots*, so called because they lived mainly in the Phanar quarter of Constantinople, nevertheless found themselves, like other *rayas*, in a precarious position, at the mercy of the whims of the Sultan or the Grand Vizier. This forced them to master the intrigues of the seraglio, to hide their feelings of solidarity towards their oppressed fellow-countrymen and to become, as a condition of survival, distrustful and two-faced. Covering their hatred with an obsequious smile, they protested their loyalty to the Sultan and took care not to flaunt their wealth. It was not always easy to define the borderline between prudent collaboration, which sometimes rendered great services to the Greek nation, and treason pure and simple. The Phanariot lived on a tightrope: one false step could lead to his execution by order of the Porte, or to rejection by his fellow-countrymen.

17

The Phanariots were entrenched in the very heart of the Empire. A very different type of Greek grew up in the provinces which make up the Greece of today, and in which the Turks were only a minority. This was the *klepht*, who refused to submit to Turkish rule and took to resistance in the mountains. Half brigand, for the word 'klepht' means 'thief', half legendary hero, his real or imagined exploits against the Turk inspired a whole genre of folk ballads. The klepht formed a striking contrast to the Phanariot. He was unlettered but straightforward; uncouth but jealous of his honour; ignorant of fine phrases but an expert marksman.

Falling between these two extremes, the great mass of the Greeks, organised in small, semi-autonomous communities, lived as best they could, sometimes with the servility that befitted the raya, sometimes in revolt after the example of the klepht. They were torn between prudence and bravery. They detested and at the same time submitted to the backward Ottoman administration, which was as oppressive as it was inefficient. During the eighteenth century a bourgeoisie consisting of Greek merchants and shipowners came into being and spread throughout the Mediterranean world. It was these men who, having in some cases amassed substantial fortunes, founded in the early years of the nineteenth century the *Filiki Etairia* (literally the 'Society of Friends'), and taking their example from the Italian *carbonari* began to work in secret for a national uprising.

The War of Independence in 1821-1829 brought to the surface the internal tensions in Greek society. The educated notables, the frock-coated Phanariots who claimed the right to direct the war, clashed with the kilted former klephts, who had no time for discipline on the European model. The first insurgent assemblies adopted democratic constitutions. These, inspired by the principles of 1789, were, however, a dead letter amidst the conflict between islanders and mountaineers, between Peloponnesians and Roumeliots. Soon, in the very midst of the holy war against the Turks, there was civil war among the Greeks. Then the Great Powers intervened and the Greeks became divided into enthusiastic champions of England, of France, and of Russia. Each faction believed that the country's salvation and liberty would come exclusively from one of these countries. Eventually the Allied fleet destroyed by mistake the Turkish-Egyptian fleet at Navarino and the southern part of Greece, now liberated, was created an independent state.

This short historical sketch is necessary to understand several tendencies in Greek public life which have persisted right up to the present day. Indeed, the very factors which had enabled the nation to survive during the centuries of servitude soon appeared to be obstacles to the progress of the independent state. These included a narrow local patriotism, a mistrust of all central power, a naïve faith in the Great Powers, a tendency to circumvent civic obligations by means of deception and bakhshish, an alternation of heroic gestures with a fatalistic submission to the powers that be, the prodigies sometimes accomplished by individuals and the inability to co-operate, a trust in good connections and personal favours rather than in abstract principles. All these traits date from the period of Ottoman rule.

The beginnings of the new state were not easy. Ignoring the democratic and liberal tendencies which had emerged during the first constitutional assemblies and which had been, it is true, somewhat discredited by the ensuing anarchy, the Powers made Greece an absolute monarchy with a sovereign chosen from the royal house of Bavaria. The young King Otto came to the throne flanked by Bavarian advisers. These set about organising a modern state based on models with which they were already familiar, without stopping to consider the character and wishes of the local inhabitants. Deeply attached to their own communities, for which they were ready to make any sacrifice, the Greeks took very badly to a highly centralised government, and they directed their old antipathy towards the Turks against the new government. At the same time, the Phanariots and the educated middle class ensured that their own cultural ideal, a return to ultra-classicism, prevailed. This had a disastrous effect on the language. The only living language, the 'demotic', which the great poet Solomos had already employed, was barred from the schools and polite usage. To take its place the so-called 'katharevousa', or purist language, was devised. The work of a number of grammarians, the artificial katharevousa became the only acceptable language. To appreciate what this involved one has only to imagine France in the sixteenth century turning its back on French and, under the pretext of honouring Cicero, adopting a corrupt form of mediaeval Latin.

In 1843, a revolution forced the King to grant a constitution and the Greeks came to experience parliamentary institutions. In 1862, another revolution drove out Otto, who was succeeded by a member of the royal house of Denmark, George I, the great-grandfather of the present King. The Constitution of 1864 gave the sovereign no greater prerogatives than those enjoyed by the kings of England. This was particularly so from 1875 onwards when the convention of summoning the leader of the majority party to head the government was firmly established. It is worth remembering that Greece enjoyed universal suffrage at this period, even before Britain, and subsequently experienced almost half a century of internal peace and unimpeded political life. For foreigners, who know little about Greek history, are too ready to fall for the myth that the Greeks 'have never known democracy'. True, there was ballot rigging, but not on a wide enough scale to prevent the parties alternating in power. It is also the case that these parties, centred entirely around personalities, considered the offices of state as fiefs to be distributed among their own supporters, and that favouritism and influence peddling were rife. There was, however, no corruption in the financial sense of the word, and no politician became rich out of the proceeds of office.

The people themselves got by as well as they could. They struggled to understand the purist language and rallied for or against whichever foreign power was considered to favour or to frustrate, by turns, the national aspirations of the Greeks. These aspirations were unashamedly irredentist, and on a grandiose scale. They aimed at nothing less than the liberation of those territories regarded by the Greeks as theirs by right because they had been, or were still, inhabited by a Greek majority. These embraced, besides Epirus, Macedonia and Thrace, which were gradually incorporated into Greece after independence, areas now belonging to Albania, Yugoslavia, and Bulgaria, as well as all the islands of the eastern Mediterranean and the coastal region of Turkish Asia Minor. The summit of this dream of 'Great Greece', inculcated in all Greeks through schooling, tradition, literature, and the press, was of course Constantinople, once the splendid capital of the Byzantine Empire which was again to be restored.

On several occasions during the nineteenth century, the small kingdom attempted to fulfil this dream by attacking the Ottoman Empire. On each occasion Greece was prudently held in check by the Great Powers. On one occasion, in 1897, it was not held back, and a brief war with Turkey resulted in a shameful fiasco for the Greeks. At last they were forced to appreciate the distance between the dream and the reality, between their aspirations and their true potential. For decades the political parties had indulged in bellicose rhetoric, but had failed to prepare the country for war: the 'klephtic' spirit had naïvely assumed that bravery by itself would be enough. Only one politician, of Phanariot origin, tried to oppose this naïve optimism, and argued that the country should equip itself with a proper state structure and solid finances before embarking on foreign adventures. This was Kharilaos Trikoupis, who died before the disaster which his political opponents brought down upon the nation.

The humiliation of 1897 and the ensuing national bankruptcy resulted, during the years that followed, in the discrediting of the political parties and of the royal family. In 1909, this malaise assumed a concrete form in a revolt by young army officers. These officers, inspired by a vague desire for national revival, and disquieted by the progress made by Greece's neighbours, had no real ideology or political programme. Fortunately they had the sense not to try to govern themselves. Instead they called in the Cretan Eleftherios Venizelos, a statesman of genius who combined the dash and idealism of the klepht with the prudent good sense of the Phanariot. Venizelos founded the Liberal Party, won a crushing electoral victory and, surrounded by a team of remarkable young politicians, undertook the wholesale restructuring of the country. An indefatigable reformer, an incomparable leader, and a virtuoso diplomat, he manœuvred so well during the Balkan wars of 1912-13 that Greece emerged from them victorious, with her boundaries greatly enlarged and with aspirations to Mediterranean power, which in the future would have to be taken into account.

The war of 1914 led to a very serious constitutional crisis. Venizelos was a convinced supporter of the Entente, and wished to side with it. As such he came up against the stubborn neutrality of King Constantine, the son of George I. Constantine admired the German military machine and had faith in the ultimate victory of his brother-in-law Kaiser Wilhelm II. Hounded from office despite his parliamentary majority, Venizelos rebelled and, regaining power with the backing of the Entente in 1917, brought Greece into the war. In the elections of 1920, however, Venizelos suffered a crushing defeat, despite his remarkable record in foreign policy. The elections brought Constantine back to his throne, and it was now Venizelos who went into exile. Greece was then engaged in a new war against Turkey for the mastery of the west coast of Asia Minor, which was inhabited by a million and a half Greeks. Exhausted and abandoned by its erstwhile allies, Greece suffered the debâcle of 1922. This, by the Treaty of Lausanne in 1923, resulted in the permanent influx of more than a million Greek refugees from Asia Minor.

The dream of 'Great Greece' had finally collapsed, and it was also the end of an epoch. Modern Greece can be said to date from the inter-war period. Wrangles about foreign policy and the best means to achieve the irredentist dream were succeeded by the more prosaic social problems created by the refugee influx, the beginnings of industrialisation, and the founding of the Communist Party. Constitutional order, which had appeared so solidly established during the reign of George I, had difficulty in reviving after the battering which it had received during World War I. In 1922 a revolt by the defeated army drove Constantine from the throne once again. A republic was proclaimed in 1924, and it was endowed with a constitution in 1927. Meanwhile, a military putsch had installed a comic opera dictatorship which sought to regulate the length of women's skirts, but this was overthrown the following year by yet another putsch. The danger of Greek political life sliding into the South American pattern was temporarily averted by the return of Venizelos to politics. He won the elections of 1928 and governed uneventfully for four years. But when his opponents won the elections in 1933, there were two abortive military coups attempting to dislodge them from power. Venizelos himself had assumed responsibility for the second of these, in 1935, and was forced into permanent exile. He died the following year, while his political opponents restored the monarchy, in the person of George II, son of Constantine, and revived the old constitution.

2. LIBERTY STIFLED: 1936-1944

During the first century of their independence the Greeks had expended a great deal of energy in creating a state from scratch, in doubling their territory, in increasing their population almost tenfold, in fighting against their neighbours, and in absorbing an influx of refugees equalling almost a third of their previous population. Taking all this into account, not to mention the effort expended on revolutions, *coups d'état*, and plots, one is forcibly struck with the country's progress. Greece by 1936 had carried out a very successful land reform, which had created what was essentially a country of small proprietors. It had acquired roads, railways, harbours, railroads, universities, and a passable civil service. An educational reform, carried out by George Papandreou while a minister under Venizelos, had made primary education free and compulsory, and introduced the demotic language into education. From the very first stages of industrialisation, modern and humane social legislation had spared the working classes the horrors of primitive capitalist exploitation.

Political life centred around two principal movements whose origins, and whose differences, had been moulded by the personality of Venizelos between 1910 and 1920. These were a conservative and royalist movement, represented principally by the Populist

Party, and a republican movement centred mainly in the Liberal Party. This had been Venizelos' party, while the Populist Party was that of his opponents, who had no objection to describing themselves, in the absence of a more concrete political programme, as 'anti-Venizelists'. There were also parties of lesser importance, which usually formed alliances with whichever of the two major parties they had most in common.

Although party strife was characterised by an unscrupulous fanaticism, political life had none the less made some progress in comparison with the pre-war period. To begin with, the civil service had stood apart from these squabbles; civil servants no longer changed with each government. Secondly, the Council of State, founded in 1928 and modelled on the French pattern, gave protection from abuse by the executive to the citizen as to the civil servant. Thirdly, the parties were no longer the mouthpieces of foreign powers. To appreciate the progress that had been made, it should be remembered that under King Otto the parties had openly declared themselves to be 'anglophile', 'francophile', or 'russophile'. 'Russophilia' had given way to 'germanophilia' towards the end of the nineteenth century. For Russian openly supported the nationalistic demands of the Serbs and the Bulgarians, which clashed with those of the Greeks and gave birth to a fear of and hatred for 'panslavism'. This was considered a threat to Greek Macedonia, and a new and much more serious menace than the declining Ottoman Empire. In contrast, the Kaiser's Germany had become a power of the first rank. It commanded respect and much was expected of it. The dissensions between royalists and liberals during World War I had been in effect one long quarrel between 'germanophiles' and 'ententophiles', the latter being a word coined in Greek to describe the supporters of both France and England.

By 1935, however, the positions of these two great political movements had evolved considerably. In 1933 the Populists concluded an alliance with Yugoslavia and Rumania, who were traditional allies of the Western powers, while Venizelos' own sympathies veered towards Italy. Curiously, 'russophilia' was reborn with the Greek Communist Party (K.K.E.), founded in 1920. Numerically rather weak, the party showed itself very turbulent and was regarded by its opponents as the thin end of a panslavic wedge, an accusation which was given substance by the party's position on the Macedonian question. For the K.K.E. sought autonomy for Greek Macedonia, thus for all practical purposes aligning itself with the traditional policies of Serbia and Bulgaria. This inexcusable error, which the K.K.E. was subsequently forced to disclaim, although for tactical reasons it was later repeated, has ever since been the source of a great deal of trouble to the party. To say to the Greeks, who had fought to liberate Macedonia from the Turks, that it should be handed on a plate to their Slav neighbours (for an autonomous Macedonia would inevitably be annexed by one or the other of them) appeared, and still appears, to be high treason. It was this issue, perhaps more than the working class unrest that was attributed to the communists, which impelled the Liberal Venizelos in 1929 to enact a special law aimed at combating their subversive activities. It was from 1936 onwards, however, that fear of communism became a decisive factor in Greek political life.

The result of the 1936 elections, the first since the restoration of the monarchy, was so close that the communists, with only fifteen out of three hundred seats, held the balance between the two great parties. With the situation in Parliament uncertain, the King entrusted the formation of provisional governments first to Demertzis, and then, after his death, to Metaxas, a veteran royalist and leader of a minuscule party. The major parties, absorbed in their horse trading, failed to see any danger in this. The impasse in Parliament continued. And then an agreement was concluded between the Liberals, now led by Sofoulis, and the Communist Party, whereby the latter was to give parliamentary backing Sofoulis in exchange for certain concessions. Also authorised Metaxas to dissolve Parliament a government into a dictatorship. This was do being fired, on 4 August 1936. The army   liberal elements as a result of the abortive republican co   ..e previous year, supported the new regime. The operation received the blessing of Great Britain which, exercising a preponderant influence on the palace and in military circles, sought to assure a 'tranquil' and disciplined Greece, capable, if need be, of serving as an ally.

The British government's choice of George II and Metaxas as instruments of their policy may at first sight appear odd. The former was the son of Constantine and a nephew of the ex-Kaiser. The latter had shown himself to be a notorious germanophile during World War I. But the British knew what they were doing. The royal family, as well as Metaxas, had learned a salutary lesson from the events of 1915-1922, from defeat and from the downfall of the monarchy. They had woken up to the fact that political survival in Greece was impossible without British support. These former German sympathisers now came to rival their liberal opponents in their loyalty towards the Western powers. And the British well knew that there was not the slightest danger that the

Liberals, however indignant they might be over the treatment they had received, would opt for the Axis powers.

Metaxas was 66 when he became ruler of Greece. Offspring of a noble family, he had been tormented in his youth by a feeling of inferiority engendered by his poverty and his small stature. Ambitious and hard working, he followed a military career, distinguishing himself in the General Staff where he alone in 1915 predicted the failure of the costly campaign launched by the Allies against the Dardanelles. He was later exiled by Venizelos, and on his return he attempted a coup in 1923 to re-establish Constantine, but failed. Later he had founded a royalist party which never succeeded in broadening its base or in supplanting the Populists. Above all he admired discipline on the German model, and his preference in antiquity, for he was a reasonably cultured man, was for Sparta, a silent and militaristic oligarchy, rather than for the brilliant and turbulent Athenian republic.

All the protagonists of the revolutions and *coups d'état* that had buffeted the country between 1909 and 1935 had claimed to be, and to a greater or lesser extent were, devoted to free institutions. If they rebelled it was for or against the King, or to rectify an electoral result they considered to be unjust. Liberty rapidly returned. There was only one exception, the dictatorship of Pangalos in 1925-26, which was of the South American type. Metaxas was the first openly to scorn democratic principles and to be clearly inspired by the totalitarian models of his time. It must be remembered that criticism of parliamentary government and even of democracy itself was then fashionable almost everywhere. In France, for example, André Tardieu published his indictment of 'the parliamentary profession'. Fascist or quasi-fascist dictatorships seemed to many bourgeois, distraught by the growing social unrest following the great slump of 1929, to be a vigorous, modern and dynamic alternative to the 'decadent and corrupt democracies'. These dictatorships occasioned little surprise in a Europe in which they were almost becoming the norm.

The dictatorship of Metaxas was for the most part relatively benign, closer to the Italian than to the German model. There were no executions, no military courts, no purges. A thousand communist internees represented the bulk of repression against individuals. To this must be added the deportation of a couple of dozen politicians including George Papandreou and Panayotis Kanellopoulos, a young sociology professor who had recently founded a party with a moderately progressive platform. The government, wholly composed of civilians, did not prove to be less capable than any other. It built schools, organised social security schemes, adopted a new civil code and encouraged the demotic language. The reorganisation of the armed forces included a screening on entry to the Military Academy, followed by a training which assured the homogeneity of an officer corps which was now exclusively royalist and conservative.

The most alarming aspect of the regime concerned indoctrination, propaganda, and mass demonstrations. The admiration of Metaxas for Hitler's Germany, thwarted in matters of foreign policy by the close surveillance exercised by the King on behalf of the British, was given free reign domestically in the imitation of nazi and fascist institutions. All young people were compulsorily enrolled in a 'National Youth Movement' which paraded in uniform and gave the fascist salute. The slogan of a 'Third Hellenic Civilization' was the theme of numerous speeches, military parades, and mass jamborees held at the taxpayer's expense. The weakness of Metaxas as a man lay in his lack of a sense of the ridiculous, which his education should have given him. He authorised and even encouraged a personality cult of Stalinist proportions, allowing such sonorous titles as 'first worker', 'first peasant', etc., to be conferred on him, while his photograph adorned all public offices alongside that of the King.

Between 1936 and 1940, Greek democrats once again assumed the attitudes of raya and Phanariot. With sadness or cynicism, they bowed their heads in the not very optimistic expectation of better days. A number of plots were uncovered in time. Andreas, the son of George Papandreou and at this time a student, was arrested as a Trotskyite, but was allowed to leave the country for the United States. On the surface all appeared calm.

In the initial stages of World War II, Metaxas pursued a policy of prudent neutrality, which did not prevent his performing some small favours for the Allies. In October 1940, however, Italy, already the master of Albania, attacked Greece. Greece thus found herself on the side of the British, and her sole ally during the most difficult period of the war. At that moment it was a sacred union. The entire country, without regard to politics, threw itself with enthusiasm behind Metaxas in the struggle against the invader. The Greeks could at last bring into the open their hatred of fascism, their sympathy for the Western democracies and, more discreetly, their hopes of regaining their own freedom after victory. The Phanariot was eclipsed. It was the klepht who drove the armies of Mussolini into retreat.

Metaxas died in January 1941, and the King replaced him by Koryzis, a former banker. In April the German armies invaded

Greece, by way of Bulgaria, to come to the rescue of their dis-
comfited Italian allies. The Greeks, caught in a pincer, succumbed, and the army of Epirus surrendered. Koryzis, blaming
himself for the defeat, committed suicide. The King replaced him
with another former banker of liberal tendencies, Tsouderos, with
whom he fled to the Middle East to continue the fight.

The shock of the German occupation, combined with the break-
down of all the familiar institutions of public life and the collapse
of the economy, unleashed among the majority of Greeks a
reaction against the Metaxas government as violent as it was over-
due. This reaction embraced the King who had backed the dictatorship, as well as the royalist and conservative faction that had
supported it. The fact that the collaborationist governments which
followed between 1941 and 1944 were composed of men who had
belonged to this faction only served to exacerbate popular hatred.
The fact that other members of this same right wing, including the
royal family and the majority of officers, had shown themselves to
be loyal patriots, and had continued the fight outside the country,
was overlooked. The will to resist the occupiers was accompanied
by a general swing towards the left which might have prepared
the way, after the war, for a renewal of the country's political life
with the establishment of a modern and forward-looking democracy. Almost all the resistance organisations claimed to be aiming
at such an ideal. That it proved impossible to attain was the fault
of the Communist Party.

The Greek Communist Party had been the only party, at the
moment of the Greek army's victorious advance into Albania,
to protest against this 'imperialist war' and to demand, by underground channels, an end to hostilities and request Soviet arbitration between Greece and Italy. The German occupation
authorities had noted this, and one of their first acts was to free a
number of communist detainees who opposed any idea of resistance until Hitler had attacked the Soviet Union.

Overnight the K.K.E. assumed an ultra-patriotic posture. In
September 1941 it founded, with the co-operation of a number of
small and fairly nominal groups, the resistance organisation
E.A.M. (National Liberation Front), and the following year the
guerilla army E.L.A.S. (Greek Popular Army of Liberation).

These organisations, generously subsidised by the British,
enjoyed striking success and greatly surpassed in membership, as
well as in power, the non-communist resistance organisations.
This success was due, above all, to the communists' experience
in clandestine activities, an experience for which courage and
devotion, which the non-communist resistance showed in equal

measure, did not prove an adequate substitute. The communists, moreover, knew how to exploit to the full popular resentment against the King, his officers, and the whole of the right, while other resistance groups preferred to postpone domestic reckonings until after victory, so as not to disrupt the common front against the common enemy.

Here we must dwell on a subject often discussed abroad but very little understood. According to a cleverly propagated myth, there was in Greece only one resistance group. This, it is claimed, was E.A.M., in which communists participated on the same basis as others. But this is quite untrue. Firstly, there were several independent resistance organisations. Though E.A.M. was undeniably the most important of these, other organisations enjoyed important successes, organising armed resistance and bearing their share of the casualties. Secondly, although it is true that E.A.M. had many non-communist militants among its members, especially in its initial stages, its leadership and cadres were always firmly under the control of the Communist Party, which missed no opportunity to indoctrinate new non-communist recruits in a subtle and skilful manner. In this way E.A.M. as a resistance organisation served the Communist Party both as a suitable façade for attracting patriots and as a nursery for new recruits to the party.

The monopoly of resistance which the K.K.E. and E.A.M. claimed after the event was in fact an objective tenaciously pursued by the communists, who saw in it the best means of assuming power at the moment of liberation. To ensure this monopoly, what can only be described as a reign of terror against the other resistance organisations was instigated from the winter of 1942-43 onwards. Denouncing members of rival groups as 'traitors' and as 'agents of the Gestapo', they did not shrink from allowing them to fall into the hands of occupying troops when necessary. Nor did they shrink from assassinating non-communist resistance fighters whose successes or popularity were a source of embarrassment to them: one need only mention the murder of the heroic Colonel Psarros and the destruction of his resistance band, or the surprise attack on General Zervas' rear while he was leading his guerillas against the Germans.

This tactic, which was applied with increasing ferocity as liberation approached, had consequences whose seriousness can scarcely be exaggerated. First of all, it provoked a fratricidal struggle amongst Greeks which distracted effort from the common struggle against the enemy. This of course played directly into the hands of the Germans, who soon found that they no longer needed to undertake major offensives against their opponents, as these virtually cancelled each other out. Besides, the, communists' excesses resulted in pushing a number of Greeks, who could in no sense be described as born traitors, into the arms of the Germans, or at least into those of the collaborationist governments. Thus there were former supporters of Psarros who, hounded by the communists and seeking both to survive and to avenge their murdered comrades, enrolled in the 'Security Battalions' formed by the collaborationist governments to fight the communists with German weapons.

The Communist Party did not concern itself with these consequences. In 1944 it thought only in terms of seizing power once the war had ended. Believing the end to be near, it sought only to preserve its forces intact and practically ceased fighting the Germans. The Red Army was descending on the Balkans. The Greek communists, loud in its praise, awaited it in a kind of mystic exaltation. Were they ignorant of the Churchill-Stalin agreement, which placed Greece within the British sphere of influence, or did they hope to present the world with a *fait accompli*? We simply do not know. Be this as it may be, the Communist Party adopted a more moderate attitude shortly before the liberation. It agreed that its representatives should take part in a government of national unity, formed in exile by George Papandreou and of which Panayotis Kanellopoulos was also a member.

This government arrived in Athens in October 1944, on the heels of the retreating Germans, although it did not have any military power at its command. There certainly had been crack Greek units in the Middle East, which had distinguished themselves in Africa and Italy, as well as a not inconsiderable naval force. But the British had not permitted these to return home with the new government, for fear of antagonising the communists, whom London still hoped to appease. The Communist Party had in fact done its best through a series of mutinies, fomented by its agents in 1943 and 1944, to create disaffection among the Greek forces in the Middle East, simply because they had fought on the orders of the government in exile. For this reason the communists described them as a 'praetorian guard' and opposed their return to liberated Greece.

3. LIBERTY THREATENED: 1944-1949

We come now to the most critical time of the whole period, and one which was to determine the political future of Greece for many years. If, on liberation, the Communist Party had checked its immediate ambitions, it would have helped the country on to the path of reconciliation, of a genuine democracy and of an eventual evolution, by peaceful means, towards the left.

But it did not want this. Confident of its own strength, despising the lack of strength of its Greek opponents, and mistaking British moderation for weakness, it decided on a once and for all gamble. Despite an earlier agreement, it refused to disband E.L.A.S., which controlled the greater part of the country. It withdrew its representatives from the government and took up arms against it. This was the terrible uprising of December 1944, whose very mention is enough to revive fearful memories for those who lived through it. The fighting took place in Athens, where the communists were faced with a government which had neither territory nor army, and was supported only by a handful of gendarmes and volunteers. The Communist Party was very near victory when, at the last minute, the British decided on military intervention. Their intervention necessitated rushing in troops from Italy, thus weakening their forces on the Italian front.

Few decisions have provoked so much recrimination, not only from the communist side, which is understandable, but also from people as well meaning as they are ignorant. It has been argued then and since that it was a question of the 'people' rising up for 'liberty' and against 'the King' and 'the collaborators'. This has served to perpetuate the myth assiduously propagated by the Communist Party. The British intervention has even been compared with that of the Soviet Union in Budapest or in Prague. All of these claims and comparisons are most misleading. It was not an uprising of the people or of the 'resistance', which, as we have seen, did not exist as a single entity, but was purely and simply an armed coup undertaken by the communists alone. Their objective was not the defence of freedom, which was threatened by no one, but the establishment of a dictatorship similar to those against which first the Hungarians and then the Czechs have since rebelled. The communists had no reason to rise up against the collaborators, who at this moment were either dead or in prison, nor against the King, who had remained abroad, awaiting the plebiscite which would decide his fate. As for the British intervention, it limited itself to preventing the communists from using weapons, which had been supplied for resistance against the Germans, to overthrow the only government able to claim a provisional legitimacy until elections could be held. The communists understandably did not want these elections, for they realised that while they would get a respectable number of seats, they would obtain neither a majority nor power. All the resistance organisations except E.A.M. backed the Papandreou government, which could not possibly be described as fascist. Its leader and several of its members had in fact been persecuted as liberals during the Metaxas period.

If we insist on a correct understanding of these unfortunate events, it is because Greece to this day suffers from their consequences. The civil war was ended in February 1945 by an agreement by which the communists had to disband E.L.A.S. and surrender all their arms, which in fact they did not do. In return, on the insistence of the British, they benefited from an amnesty for all but murderers. And there had been an enormous number of murders: in Athens alone thousands of corpses were discovered in mass graves. These people had been murdered, with or without being tortured, by the communist 'people's militia'. The victims were no 'collaborators', but people known for their moderate opinions, relatives of members of the non-communist resistance, women, the aged and the adolescent, of all social classes. Moreover, the communists had led away another several thousand citizens, seized by chance as 'hostages' when they evacuated Athens under British pressure. Many of these had died during forced marches in the snow, often in bare feet, with stragglers being summarily shot.

These atrocities were detailed in the report compiled by a group of British public figures, under the leadership of the trade unionist Walter Citrine. They arrived to carry out an on-the-spot investigation following Labour protests against Churchill's intervention. The report remains a chilling document to this day. It is not difficult to imagine the reaction of the Greeks at the time, when the details of what had happened became known. There was an explosion of hatred against the communists, which the authorities restrained only with difficulty. Inevitably there were reprisals. Amnestied communists returning home were sometimes set upon, maltreated, or even killed by furious relatives of the victims or by members of extreme right-wing groups. This 'white terror', however, which the forces of order suppressed with kid gloves, never reached the proportions of the red terror. Its victims could be counted in tens rather than thousands. Those communists who were not amnestied were tried, and a number of them, for the most part convicted of multiple murders, went before the firing squad. But these were too few in the eyes of the public.

When we speak of 'the public' we do mean Greeks of all shades of political opinion. Royalists and liberals, right wingers and progressives were unanimous in condemning communist atrocities and in calling for their punishment. And the Communist Party itself, belatedly realising how badly savage terrorism had injured its cause, engaged in solemn self-criticism. It attributed 'a number of regrettable excesses' to fictitious leftist deviationists, and emphasised that terrorism is not in the true nature of communism. As a proof of its sincerity it organised the assassination of the former head of E.L.A.S., Aris Veloukhiotis, the foremost hero of the left who had rejected the agreements and remained in the mountains.

This was of little concern to those who had lost relatives as a result of the erroneous application of Leninist principles. Their hatred, and the hatred of the vast majority of the Greeks, against the party and the ideology that had drenched the country in blood remained unshaken. The elections of 1946, the first for ten years, were to prove this.

The communists resumed their activities soon after the amnesty, benefiting from the freedoms they had sought to destroy. They gave the impression that they represented a large proportion of the population. Nevertheless, the Communist Party boycotted the elections on the grounds that there was no guarantee of a free vote. One of the numerous provisional governments that had succeeded Papandreou invited the four great powers to send observers to the elections. The Soviet Union refused, but observers from the United States, France, and Great Britain took part. It should be remembered that British policy in Greece, unpopular in Britain itself, had also been vigorously criticised in France and America, where there was a tendency to consider the Greek communists simply as unfortunate oppressed democrats. There was thus no reason for the observers to be ill disposed towards them. These observers watched the elections, and conscientiously compiled their report. This concluded that the elections had been free, and that about 25 per cent of the voters had abstained. Taking into account normal abstention, the percentage of 'political' abstentions, that is to say those who had followed the orders of the Communist Party, did not exceed 10 per cent.

The figure appears very modest indeed. However, it is not far different from the percentages obtained by the extreme left in the elections which have taken place since, percentages which have always, with only one exception, been in the order of 10 to 15 per cent. This is far from an 'uprising of the people'. The communists after the war were revealed to be a small minority which through its zeal, its discipline, its courage, and its arms, had succeeded in creating the illusion of being sizeable. This illusion was now destroyed.

Although reliable statistics are lacking, it is almost certain that E.A.M. had been supported by a much higher percentage of the population in 1943-44. Its diminished support could only be accounted for by the extremist policies of the Communist Party. A good number of those who had been attracted by the ideals of resistance and of renewal which E.A.M.'s slogans seemed to promise gradually drifted away as the movement was seen to be conducting a struggle which was becoming increasingly fratricidal and progressively less anti-German. Moreover, the Party had during the occupation repeated its old error by signing an agreement with the Bulgarian communists, the terms of which once again jeopardised the integrity of Greek territory. This alienated many a staunch patriot who had joined E.A.M. but who objected to the handing over of Macedonia to Greece's neighbours. For others the moment of truth came with the insurrection of December 1944 and its ensuing horrors.

The result was that Greece, which in 1941 seemed ready to turn towards a liberal and democratic left, found itself in 1946 in full reaction. And reaction against communism led to reaction pure and simple, to a narrow and obscurantist conservatism. This was an unfortunate but, none the less, predictable reflex. The very word 'left' became suspect, the word 'communist' a term of abuse. The right, represented by the revived Populist Party, triumphed in the elections of 1946, and reorganised the state machine with anti-communism as its principal objective. All those suspected of communist opinions, or even of sympathy towards them, were purged from the public service and from education. The King returned after a plebiscite in which royalist votes, assisted by a little ballot rigging, easily prevailed. Even liberal republicans, although clearly opposed to communism, seemed suspect in the eyes of the public.

This same psychological climate also benefited those who had collaborated with the Germans. They were treated with a tolerance that would have been unthinkable had the occupation not been followed by civil war. Public hatred was centred on the Communist Party, and there was little left for collaborators. Indeed, those who claimed that their collaboration had been inspired solely by a desire to defeat communism became almost popular. The purging and punishment of collaborators was handled with kid gloves or overlooked, and only a small number of them were convicted by the courts. The communists have made much of this leniency, without considering their own responsibility for it.

But the Communist Party during these years was not distinguished by an ability to learn from its mistakes. Despite its self-criticism, which was limited to tactical details, the party never openly disowned its policy in 1943 and 1944. Even worse, it was soon to re-introduce a policy which had already failed. From the end of 1946, using as a pretext police harassment of its members, the Party once again resorted to violent underground activity, organising partisan bands which attacked isolated police posts and massacred gendarmes. In 1947 its activities were stepped up. Arms illicitly retained in 1945 were dug up from their hiding-places, and others were supplied by neighbouring communist countries, whose territory served as supply and training bases for Greek guerillas, and as a refuge whenever they found themselves in trouble. Government repression increased accordingly. The Communist Party was banned, and its official newspaper was suppressed. The assassination of the Minister of Justice by a communist militant was countered by the execution of a hundred communists who had previously been sentenced to death. The police and the gendarmerie could no longer control the situation, and the army had to be brought in. Pitched battles, with artillery and air support, were needed before the insurrection was finally ended in 1949.

There were thousands of casualties during this second civil war, with atrocities on both sides. More than a million peasants were forced to leave their devastated or threatened villages. The economy of the country, which had not yet begun to recover from the war and occupation, now fell victim to a new and terrible recession. This was so extreme that Greece, even with American aid, found the task of reconstruction very difficult, and did not enter upon the path of prosperity until four or five years after other European countries.

But it is the political consequences of this second civil war that should particularly be noted. For international communism had shown its true colours in the assistance given to the Greek rebels by her northern neighbours. In foreign policy the fear of communism meant that all the other Greek parties agreed that Greece should associate as closely as possible with NATO and the United States which, since the proclamation of the 'Truman doctrine' in 1947, had taken over Britain's role as protector of Greece. In domestic policy, the mechanism of repression was strengthened. Any progressive movement found itself hampered and was automatically suspected of pro-communist sympathies. Despite all this, the remarkable and almost miraculous fact is that basic democratic institutions survived. Even at the height of the civil war, when communist guerillas controlled practically the whole of the countryside, and were attacking and even temporarily occupying towns, no one considered a military dictatorship necessary. Parliament functioned normally. Individual liberties were only slightly restricted, when this was necessary for military operations. Inevitably several thousand communist militants were interned. But apart from this, people were perfectly free to criticise the government openly, and the opportunity to do this was frequently taken. Justice remained independent and there was no censorship of the press.

For this was not a kind of Spanish civil war, a clash between progressives and reactionaries. It was a war between the communists, isolated on the one side, and all the rest of Greece on the other. The two great parties were reconciled, and were united in coalition governments which succeeded each other between 1947 and 1949. The elderly liberal Sofoulis led one of them. For all democrats and liberals, however much they disliked the reactionary right which had a majority in Parliament, accepted the rules of the game and rejected communist insurrection, which sought for the second time to impose the will of a minority on the country. Everyone fought on the side of legality. The totalitarian onslaught was rebuffed and finally overcome by democracy.

4. LIBERTY IN TUTELAGE: 1950-1963

After the trials of the 1940's, the 'fifties were for Greece a period of convalescence on a special diet: a regime which was basically a democracy but which discriminated against communists. While they could be criticised, these rules would have been intelligible —given the upheaval that had given rise to them—had their extent and duration been kept to the strict minimum demanded by state security. The country dared not risk a third civil war.

Unfortunately, this was not the case. The right, which remained in power almost without interruption, inflated the communist bogey well beyond its true dimensions. In this way it was able to perpetuate its own power and to smear its liberal opponents by calling them 'fellow-travellers'. The 'national spirit', i.e. anti-communism, was, in the absence of any other political programme, its only slogan, its sole rallying cry, its one criterion of worth.

This right wing, like the Divinity of the mystics, sometimes changed its name but never its substance. In 1951 the Populist Party reappeared as the 'Greek Rally' of Marshal Papagos, the former commander of the armed forces. On the death of Papagos in 1955, Karamanlis took over the leadership of the party which now became the 'National Radical Union' (E.R.E.). Its electoral supporters, its leaders, and its power base in the army, the palace, and the state machine remained the same. The right wing normally obtained between 40 and 50 per cent of the votes at elections, a percentage which, thanks to the complexities of the electoral law and the lack of unity among its opponents, assured it a comfortable parliamentary majority. It is true that elections were rarely held without some pressure being exerted on the electorate by a right-wing administration. None the less, it would be wrong to talk of an electoral farce. The manipulation of votes by these more or less illicit pressures was not on a scale sufficient to have reversed a true shift in opinion had it occurred. Besides, pressures were only possible in the villages and small towns where it was difficult to maintain the secrecy of the ballot. Here the gendarmerie could let certain individuals know that if they did not co-operate they would be refused a passport to emigrate, a hunting permit, an agricultural loan, or a certificate of 'civic reliability'. This police certificate, testifying to the absence of any communist affiliations, was essential for entry into the public service, education, local government, and certain other professions. The electoral propaganda of the right claimed repeatedly that the communist threat was more serious than ever, that the communists were massing on the borders, armed to the teeth, and awaiting the moment to recross the frontiers, that the liberals failed to recognise this danger, and that only the 'party of national spirit'—whatever its exact title at the moment—was capable of facing up to it. From time to time, to back up these claims, communist spies and saboteurs coming from Eastern Europe were arrested. By coincidence this always happened just before elections were due, and of course had the desired effect.

On the economic front, the 'fifties saw the beginning of a boom which was soon to give Greece one of the highest growth rates in Europe. Industrial investment was far outstripped by the development of tourism: roads, hotels, and resorts sprouted like mushrooms under a prudent administration which was firmly committed to orthodoxy and shunned anything that could be construed as inflationary, for inflation was a nightmare from which the Greeks had continually suffered between 1941 and 1953. The drachma became a stable and respected currency.

The moving spirit behind this boom from 1955 onwards was Constantine Karamanlis. A brusque and efficient man of action, he was personally tolerant towards ideologies which he despised.

Nor did he shrink to the great disgust of his party's backwoods-
men, from employing liberals, or even former communists, if he
considered them the right people to fill particular posts. Not
given to discussion or abstract ideas, he thought highly of men
who knew 'how to get things done'. Some of his ministers proved
quite able. Gradually this led, if not to a depoliticisation of the
country (that would be too much to expect of the Greeks), at
least to a defusing of the charged political atmosphere. The
attractions of a consumer society and increasing prosperity molli-
fied the old hatreds. One of the last political executions took place
in 1952. This was of the communist Beloyannis, who headed a
clandestine network and was accused of espionage. Slowly the
number of communist detainees and exiles diminished.

Although he possessed undeniable qualities as an administrator and had a number of successes to his credit, Karamanlis
somewhat lacked that broad vision which distinguishes the statesman. Essentially a pragmatist, and inclined to appreciate only
visible investments in asphalt and concrete (he had earlier been an
excellent Minister of Public Works), he neglected less tangible
and more long term but extremely important matters such as the
restructuring of the civil service and the reform of education. And
he would have had the time for such radical reforms, for he ruled
Greece for eight consecutive years, a national record. Finally,
although he was personally devoid of fanaticism, his collaborators
included a number of intolerant bullies who delighted in harass-
ing communists. These men indulged in witch hunts, and kept
in being emergency measures such as the infamous Law 509
long after their initial justification had disappeared. This law,
enacted at the very height of the civil war, provided rigorous
penalties, including death, for 'belonging to an organisation seeking to overthrow the established social system'.

If E.R.E. was the most recent parliamentary expression, and
the civil service and the army the permanent props, of the right
wing, its unofficial focus was the crown. During the civil war and
immediately afterwards, King Paul, who had succeeded his
brother George II in 1947, and Queen Frederika had shown themselves to be impeccably democratic and constitutional monarchs.
They had enjoyed a brief honeymoon with former republicans
such as Sofoulis, who for their part had loyally accepted the
monarchy. Later, however, as in ancient tragedies, an excess of
confidence engendered *hubris*. The royal couple, believing their
position to be above control, began to indulge in partisan inter-
ventions. One of the guiding principles of the crown's policy seems
to have been to avoid having a head of government who was too

independent, for this would deprive the King of chances to meddle in politics.

Thus the palace strongly opposed the candidature of Marshal Papagos, despite the fact that he was a veteran royalist. And for the same reason the King appointed Karamanlis, previously a rather obscure figure, as Papagos' successor. It was thought that, owing all to the crown, he would continue to be its humble and obedient servant. For the crown liked to intervene in all public matters, and it also liked to be obeyed. The Queen had her favourites among ministers and intervened even in the appointment of hospital directors, while the King regarded military matters as his own private preserve. He showed a detailed interest in the armed forces and had his own favourites among senior officers. He wished to be their effective, and not merely honorary, leader. A good man, but badly advised, he did not realise the extent to which he offended liberal opinion by referring in his speeches to 'my army'. All this, together with a series of notable gaffes, such as organising royal cruises paid for by the wealthy Greek shipowner Niarchos, slowly whittled away the sympathy which the royal couple had undeniably commanded at the beginning of their reign. The expenses of the civil list, and the royal family's acquisition of a number of estates in different parts of Greece, provoked an increasing number of complaints. And from 1955 onwards there was much talk in liberal circles of the favour which the right appeared to enjoy with the palace, to the detriment of other parties.

During these same years a major evolution was occurring within the left. The Communist Party had been banned, the partisan bands finally crushed, and their surviving members had fled to the East, which meant that the Greek communists were deprived of their most hardened militants. They at last had the sense not to try to resume revolutionary activity. In 1952 they founded a new party, the United Democratic Left (E.D.A.) whose overt leaders and parliamentary candidates had been carefully selected for their inoffensive past. To these they added a certain number of non-communist personalities with unblemished police records, who had no objection to playing the decorative role assigned to them in return for a seat in Parliament.

E.D.A. took care to operate strictly within the law. Its parliamentarians displayed an altogether British moderation and correctness. All its activities—and one can imagine how closely these were scrutinised by the authorities—were as scrupulously innocent as its official programme. This included a complete liberalisation on the domestic front, and in foreign affairs a neutralism which aimed at keeping the Western powers at a distance. To a liberal unfamiliar with the past, E.D.A. would have appeared a very acceptable party. But it was precisely the very recent past which prevented its acceptance by a public athirst for complete democracy, peace, and progress. The links between E.D.A. and the Communist Party remained too apparent. E.D.A., which was the beneficiary of all the communist votes and dependent on them, could not detach itself from the K.K.E., whose revolutionary and terrorist past it had never disowned. Its programme was generally no more than a thinly disguised regurgitation of instructions from behind the Iron Curtain. The neutrality which E.D.A. claimed, and which was seasoned with continuous attacks against the West, did not mask its unconditional attachment to the Soviet Union, which was never criticised in the party's publications. And the suspicious viewed their demands for total liberalisation as a manœuvre aimed at permitting exiled communists to return home *en masse*, to join forces with those in the detention camps and then resume the violent struggle.

E.D.A's opponents were justified in refusing to take it at its own estimation as a left-wing democratic party akin to those in the Western democracies. But it would be a mistake simply to identify it with the Communist Party, as did the right. The acceptance of parliamentary democracy and the concern for legality in the beginning may well have been a mere sham designed to pull the wool over the eyes of the bourgeoisie. But with the passage of time, with the old militant cadres in exile, and with the coming of age of a new generation, E.D.A. gradually became more bourgeois and more democratic, as did most Western communist parties. Growing prosperity weakened the implacable hatreds born of war, misery, and hunger. Parliamentarianism, initially a façade, gradually acquired real roots within the Greek left. On top of this there was an unspoken disillusionment with the Soviet Union, which had twice let its Greek admirers down. A third assault on the right became less attractive as the left came to realise it could expect no outside help. It became used to debating with its opponents, instead of summarily massacring them. This in itself was a major step forward.

This, then, was the background against which E.D.A. entered the electoral stakes. The only time it significantly exceeded its usual share of the vote, which was, as we have seen, between 10 and 15 per cent, was in the 1958 election. Then, to the great alarm of its opponents, it won almost 25 per cent of the votes. There were two major reasons for this brief upswing in E.D.A. support, which soon subsided. Firstly, popular anger against the West, and more particularly the NATO countries, because of their attitude over the then acute Cyprus question; and secondly, the ineffectiveness of the centre parties. At this time these were more fragmented than ever. Many democrats who were disillusioned by the centre switched their vote to E.D.A. It was during this period that thinking Greeks had most cause to regret the absence of a genuinely democratic party of the left, with no special links with the Eastern bloc. This might have served to canalise popular resentment into a constructive direction.

It is sometimes claimed that this 25 per cent vote in the 1958 election indicates E.D.A.'s true electoral strength. For there were fewer charges of fraud in this election than in earlier ones or in the following one, in 1961. But this fails to account for the fact that in the elections of 1963 and 1964, which were generally regarded as completely free, E.D.A. received no more than 14 and 12 per cent of the vote respectively. The essential difference between the 1958 and the 1963-64 elections was that by the time of the latter the forces of the centre had regrouped and offered the protest voter the viable alternative which had been absent in 1958.

The right and the left, each in its own way, had remained united and disciplined during the 'fifties, but the reverse was the case with the centre. After the death of Sofoulis, the centre parties splintered even more than before. For a time, the fragments formed a coalition under the more or less nominal direction of ex-General Plastiras. Plastiras was a courageous soldier, a hero of the Asia Minor campaign, the leader of the republican revolution of 1922, the protagonist of the failed coup of 1933, and the successor to Papandreou in December 1944, when the English considered him better equipped to deal with the insurgent communists. Of humble origins, and with the best of intentions, Plastiras loved the small man, and in turn was loved by him. But his political views were of the most nebulous sort and he had no kind of concrete programme. There was also considerable friction between his associates, George Papandreou and Sophocles Venizelos, the son of the great statesman. A liberal by tradition but a dilettante by inclination, Venizelos was in fact very close to the right and to the court in his outlook.

Between 1950 and 1952, the country was governed in turn by centre coalitions and centre-right coalitions, none of which had any permanent impact. Plastiras and his associates did nothing to democratise the country. In the clutches of a reactionary bureaucracy, they succumbed to the blandishments of the palace. These men, whom the propaganda of the right had long depicted as dangerous fellow-travellers, seemed to have been mainly concerned to prove that they were quite as 'nationally minded' as the right. Most serious of all, they did not interfere with the status quo in the armed forces, and even went so far as to allow the controlling clique in the air force to arrest, torture, and then condemn as 'communist saboteurs' a number of perfectly loyal officers. This affair sparked off such a scandal in Parliament and in the press that the right-wing government which succeeded was forced to decree a general amnesty. This applied to all those involved in the affair, not only the victims but also the torturers, of whom the foremost was called Skarmaliorakis.

The centre in effect had only continued the policy of the right in an atmosphere of demagogic confusion. It was not surprising that the electorate quickly tired of it and in 1952 turned again to the right, which at least had the honesty to speak its mind. The right was now led by Marshal Papagos, the respected Commander-in-Chief of the Armed Forces in 1940-41 and 1948-49. A man of few words, Papagos, in contrast to his predecessors, inspired confidence. He won an electoral landslide. The right was now to be in power for eleven years without a break.

This unfortunate experience had highlighted the weaknesses of the centre: a lack of cohesion, the absence of a concrete reform programme, and an oscillation between progressive slogans and conservative practice. Its foreign policy was identical with that of the right, and it was under a centre government that Greece joined the NATO alliance in 1952. There remained the explosive issue of domestic liberalisation. If the centre had shown too much zeal in abolishing restrictive measures and in releasing the remaining imprisoned communists, it would have met with opposition from the palace and the army. If, on the other hand, it merely carried on with right-wing policies it had no *raison d'être*. Its leaders for a long time vacillated between these two policies, indulging in verbal gymnastics and compromises which ended up convincing no one. In 1958, the centre seemed truly moribund, and it was E.D.A. which became the principal parliamentary opposition. This polarisation of political forces satisfied both extremes. The right and the left were not in the least perturbed to be considered as the sole alternative to each other. Both gained from the absence of a moderating force which would have robbed them of marginal votes.

When, in 1961, there was a fresh attempt to regroup the ranks of the centre, it seemed doomed from the start. The Centre Union, with Papandreou as leader and Venizelos as his principal henchman, appeared to have no greater chance of achieving power than had its ideological predecessors. None the less, Papandreou, already a septuagenarian, threw himself into the fight with tremendous panache, and quickly breathed new life into the moribund aspirations of moderate democrats. Defeated at the 1961 elections, the Centre Union none the less obtained a good share of the vote, and emerged as a serious rival to the right. It also challenged the validity of the election, claiming that it had been fraudulent, and embarked on a vigorous campaign for a new election.

It does seem that there was ballot rigging and illegal pressure in the 1961 election, but not to the extent of radically affecting the results. E.R.E. obtained probably 2, 3, possibly even 4 per cent more votes than it should have. Even without this boost E.R.E. would have had a parliamentary majority. At the very most its majority might have been relative rather than absolute, forcing it to compromise with the Centre Union by offering it a number of ministries.

Although these electoral frauds did not have a decisive influence on the results, their political consequences were of the highest importance. The storm that they provoked was a sign that Greece's political conscience was becoming more mature. People were no longer prepared to tolerate skulduggery of that sort. The results in the army were particularly scandalous. The percentage obtained by E.R.E. could not be reconciled with its overall average of 50 per cent. This could only be explained by very considerable pressures being brought to bear on young conscripts who statistically might have been expected to vote in much the same way as other Greeks. Much later indeed it became known that the General Staff had set up a secret committee to organise this electoral fraud. Its secretary and guiding spirit was a certain Major Papadopoulos.

Despite this victory at the polls Karamanlis' difficulties mounted during the two following years. The target of violent attacks by the centre, he no longer enjoyed unswerving support from the palace, with which his relations became increasingly tense. As the leader of a majority which had long derived its power from the ballot box and not from the good pleasure of the court, he had tried on several occasions to foil royal initiatives which were not compatible with the Constitution. This was held against him no less than his vain efforts to revise the Constitution (already revised in 1952) so as to define the royal prerogatives more closely.

An unexpected event sparked off the crisis which was brewing. The E.D.A. deputy Lambrakis was assassinated in May 1963 by members of an extreme right-wing terrorist organisation which had direct and disturbing links with senior officers in the gendarmerie.

There was a storm of protest throughout the country. A month later Karamanlis advised against a royal state visit to Great Britain. The King ignored the protests of his Prime Minister and the break was total. Karamanlis resigned, designating as his successor Pipinelis, a member of his cabinet, known to be a supporter of absolute monarchy. No one for a moment believed that the question of the royal visit was anything other than a pretext. The court wanted to get rid of Karamanlis, who had become too independent for its liking, and also too compromised by the assassination of Lambrakis. For although no one seriously claimed that the Prime Minister had inspired the assassination, he could not escape responsibility for the fact that, under his government, the security forces were in league with assassins.

Karamanlis had the good grace in the eyes of his supporters, the weakness in the eyes of his opponents, not to protest about his forced resignation, which had little constitutional basis. This precedent was regrettable, as subsequent events were to demonstrate. The Centre Union itself made the mistake of greeting the downfall of its main opponent as a victory, and failed to realise that it struck a blow against the whole parliamentary system. A victory brought about by the King rather than the electorate was apt to undermine the position of all succeeding governments.

5. TOWARDS COMPLETE LIBERTY: 1963-1965

But for the moment the centre was all jubilation. The palace, aware of the advantages of alternating the parties in power, seemed ready to welcome the Centre Union with open arms. In November 1963 scrupulously honest elections resulted in a relative majority for the Centre Union: 138 seats out of 300. Papandreou was invited to form a government. To govern effectively, however, he had to rely for support on either the right or the left, both of which hastened to offer him parliamentary support. Wisely, he refused any deal that would have made him the prisoner of either. Throughout the election campaign he had stuck to his slogan of 'the battle on two fronts', against both authoritarianism of the right and totalitarianism of the left. Trusting in his mounting popularity, which he had nourished during his brief term in office by a series of pay rises to different sections of the population (which prompted taunts of demagogy by the right), he sought new elections. These were granted by the King.

This time the Centre Union had nothing to fear from the redoubtable Karamanlis who, disheartened by his defeat, or sulking as his opponents put it, had abandoned politics and gone abroad. The leadership of E.R.E. fell to Panayotis Kanellopoulos. We last mentioned Kanellopoulos as a member of Papandreou's liberation government. Since then he had moved to the right and become Karamanlis' principal lieutenant. A distinguished intellectual and a man of liberal temperament, his loathing of communism had pushed him into a more extreme position than came naturally to him. After ten years of associating with uncouth and quasi-fascist military men (he was for long Minister of Defence) his courtesy and humanity continued to stand out in these circles. He had never gained the confidence of the military or of the hardliners on the right who poked fun at this progressive intellectual. The parliamentary party elected him leader in the absence of any other figure who could command general respect, but his electoral campaign lacked spirit. Defeat was in the air. And indeed, the elections of February 1964 were a real triumph for the Centre Union, which won 53 per cent of the votes, against 35 per cent for E.R.E. and 12 per cent for E.D.A. Despite the gloomy prognostications of those who regarded a struggle on two fronts as political suicide, the party of moderation had gained power. With 171 seats out of 300, and well regarded by the court, it looked like being able to carry out its programme of liberalisation, of educational reform, of ending the sinister activities of the para-state groups such as those which had planned the assassination of Lambrakis, and of pursuing a more independent foreign policy.

George Papandreou's political style was reminiscent of the Third French Republic, where his oratorical talents would surely have been appreciated. At 76 he was still a man of astonishing vitality and broad vision. Manœuvres in the corridors of power held no secrets for him. He had, moreover, a number of able subordinates. Despite all this, less than a year and a half after reaching office he had fallen and his party was split wide open. How did this unprecedented setback occur?

To his committed supporters, Papandreou was simply the victim of a reactionary plot, hatched by the palace, the army and the right, and abetted by the treachery of a fraction of the Centre Union. To his right-wing opponents, his troubles were of his own making and his culpable indulgence towards the left and towards his own son had substantially contributed to them. To his adversaries on the left Papandreou had made the mistake of behaving too softly towards the forces of reaction, and of playing their game instead of creating a common front with the left.

These interpretations, although radically different, have at least one thing in common. They all hinge on the personality of George Papandreou, on his character and on his political judgment. This is significant, for although allegedly a party based on principle, the Centre Union was in fact a party centred around the personality of its leader, and was indeed almost unthinkable without him. The lack of cohesion and the internal quarrels, which had for long been the norm in centre circles, had by no means disappeared with the formation of the Centre Union or with its victory at the polls. Varied in its make-up, the Centre Union had no party discipline enabling it to surmount major crises and assuring continuity in its leadership. What unity it did have was due solely to the personal authority of George Papandreou. It was he who had led it to victory; it was he who suffered personal defeat in July 1965.

The general level of Centre Union deputies was far from satisfactory. Papandreou was aware of this, and counted on the next elections when, with his own personal popularity well established, he would run with a reconstructed party containing men of better quality. Putting off the decision on elections, he tried to govern but showed himself to be too authoritarian in his attitude to the party's parliamentary group, which inevitably created friction. On the other hand, in his choice of a cabinet he was less concerned with individual worth than with the necessity to appease the various factions that made up the Centre Union, each of which had as its principal objective to look after its own supporters and to fight off rival factions.

In these circumstances, it was not long before the new government began to disillusion some of its warmest supporters. True, the spectacle of ministers spending most of their time procuring favours for their friends was nothing new in Greece, and the right had certainly not shrunk from such practices. But now the pace quickened. The centre policitians, long absent from power, had considerable ground to make up. Moreover, the Centre Union had raised expectations among those, especially the young, who expected reforms in every sector, a.id insisted on a high standard of honesty in government.

This high standard of honesty was particularly in evidence when it came to denouncing the previous administration of E.R.E., towards which the Centre Union was merciless. Used to being in opposition, Papandreou and his supporters continued to act like an opposition even when they were in power. No doubt on certain points their criticisms were justified. But the most convincing criticism would have been some positive achievement, surpassing those of the right. In its accusations of embezzlement against Karamanlis and his colleagues, the Centre Union was right off the mark. But instead of recognising its mistake with a good grace, the party allowed doubts to linger, papering over the lack of proof with a kind of amnesty which was voted in Parliament, and which deprived its opponents of a chance to clear themselves fully. This provoked bitter resentment on the part of E.R.E. and contributed in large measure to the souring of the political climate.

George Papandreou had the defects of his qualities. His gift for the apposite phrase often led him to mistake rhetoric for reality. His oratorical talents inflamed popular passions with promises which were often unrealisable, and from which he would then extricate himself by a display of further rhetoric. His broad vision was exercised at the expense of administrative detail, which he tended to ignore or to despise. He saw no reason for party leaders to draw up a cogent and detailed programme, and he depended too much upon day-to-day improvisation.

On top of all this there was the controversial question of Andreas Papandreou, the son of the leader. It should be remembered that he had left Greece for the United States as a young student. There he had become an American citizen and a distinguished professor of economics. About 1960 Karamanlis offered Andreas the directorship of the recently founded Centre for Economic Research. Andreas Papandreou accepted, but at the end of 1963 resigned and, taking up Greek nationality again, plunged into politics at his father's side. Elected a deputy in 1964, he straight away became Minister to the Prime Minister, and later alternate Minister of Co-ordination. His rapid rise provoked envy among some veterans of the centre. They considered that their hard struggle over the years gave them more right to high office than this new arrival who without apparent effort (and, it was openly suggested, solely because he was the son of the party leader) had immediately reached the highest echelons of government. The Finance Minister Mitsotakis, a clever politician, in particular felt profoundly bitter towards him.

Andreas Papandreou appeared to be a more up-to-date version of his father. An able theoretician, quick to grasp and flatter the desires of his electors, he proved inadequate as an administrator. He was also highly aggressive. Influenced by Kennedy-style liberalism, he denounced without hesitation whatever he found to be unjust or outmoded, without always troubling to verify his facts. And above all, after an absence of twenty years, he lacked knowledge and experience of various aspects of Greek life. He had not

lived through the traumatic years of the 'forties and as a consequence he little understood the widespread fear of communism.
In this he saw only an obsession, artificially whipped up by the
right as a smokescreen for its own authoritarian ambitions. Now,
although the right had indeed exploited this fear and done its best
to foster it, it is a fact that this anti-communism had for long been
perfectly justified, and that it still had deep roots in large sections
of the population. Rationally, this fear could be considered un-
justified in 1964. But a politician could ignore it only at his peril.
This, nevertheless, is exactly what Andreas Papandreou proceeded
to do. In contrast to his father, who had always taken care to wage
war on both fronts, Andreas saw only one serious adversary,
namely the right. This, he felt, had to be crushed if Greece were
to become a modern and progressive democracy. He threw himself into this task with more energy than discretion, making no
distinction between Kanellopoulos, the moderate and courteous
leader of the opposition, and the most sinister conspirators of the
extreme right.

The antipathy was mutual. From the very beginning of Andreas
Papandreou's political career, the right-wing press had singled him
out as a scapegoat, attacking his qualities as well as his faults, his
achievements as well as his mistakes, his private as well as his
public life. This campaign, conducted on a level unusually low
even by Greek political standards, doubtless explains the growing
vehemence of Andreas' counter-attacks. At the same time he made
enemies at the United States Embassy by insisting on the immediate recall of the American official responsible for certain broadcasts by the 'Voice of America' which had been considered hostile
to Greece.

These broadcasts had been on the Cyprus question, which was
critical throughout the period when the Centre Union was in
power, creating additional problems and absorbing a great deal
of the government's energy. The Western powers, and notably the
United States, had urged what Greece regarded as an unacceptable compromise with Turkey. George Papandreou, who had
previously criticised as unwarranted certain concessions made by
the Karamanlis government, sought to prove himself more determined than Karamanlis. His long resistance to American pressures,
and his sending units of the army to Cyprus, did not make him
popular with the American administration. And certain opposition circles took the opportunity to whisper into American ears
that a more right-wing government might prove more flexible.

Despite these weaknesses, the Centre Union scored at least two
major successes. It liberalised public life, and set about the reform

of education. For the second time (the first had been under the Venizelos government of 1928-1932) George Papandreou injected a new spirit into the educational system. This delighted all those who cared for the living culture of the country. The period of compulsory schooling was raised from six to nine years, education at all levels became free, school textbooks were brought up to date, new universities were founded in the provinces, a Higher Education Institute was set up to improve the quality of teachers, and the use of the spoken language at last penetrated secondary education. So as to ensure school attendance and the health of rural children, who often lived far from their nearest school, free school meals were made available in primary schools in rural areas. During the first year some 300,000 children were fed in this way, and the number was to have risen progressively. The educational reform can certainly be criticised in points of detail, but the urgent need for reform and the generous inspiration that lay behind it cannot be denied. Nevertheless, the opposition, carried away by partisan passion, proceeded to do precisely this. Although Kanellopoulos' objections in Parliament were measured, the right-wing press raged against a reform which, it claimed, was designed to destroy the country's cultural heritage in order to appease the government's communist allies.

These vituperations may seem astonishing to the foreign reader. They were however, typical of the style of opposition adopted by an important section of the right. During the election campaign the right had played the apparently inexhaustible card of 'the communist danger'. After its defeat at the polls, it continued to argue, against all the evidence, that the new rulers were virtually communist stooges. George Papandreou might endlessly reiterate his faith in democracy, which his entire career in fact confirmed. He might refuse the parliamentary support of E.D.A. or any form of collaboration with it. It made not the slightest difference. The figures had clearly shown that the Centre Union's gains between 1961 and 1964 had been mainly at the expense of the right, whose share of the vote fell from 51 to 35 per cent, rather than from the left, which had lost only about 3 per cent. Yet the right insisted that George Papandreou had come to power with the help of communist votes. The economy might well prosper, as did the balance of payments, despite the heavy cost of keeping Greek troops in Cyprus. Yet the right loudly proclaimed that the Centre Union was leading the country to ruin, and bitterly denounced as demagogic the measures taken on behalf of certain underprivileged groups, such as the farmers.

Liberalisation was clearly the most burning issue which faced the Papandreou government. By 'liberalisation' is meant all the measures necessary to make Greece truly democratic, in the Western sense of the word. That is to say, to make it a country where all citizens would be equal before the law, in practice as well as in theory; where the civil service would be free of political interference; where everyone would have to respect the law but not be called to account for his opinions, his vote, or his political past; where the emergency legislation would finally be lifted, and political detainees released; where the crown would conform strictly to its constitutional rights and duties; where the army would cease to be the instrument, or even the covert source, of a policy distinct from that of the legally elected government.

This was a great deal. George Papandreou, who had no wish to offend the sensibilities of the court, showed himself to be cautious without, however, lapsing into the inertia of earlier centre politicians. If the apparatus of repression was not completely dismantled, it was at least placed partly in abeyance. The gendarmerie in the countryside no longer behaved like local satraps, bullying those who bought dissenting newspapers. The left was able to exercise its rights of meeting and association, and to organise 'peace marches'. The certificate of 'civic reliability' was not abolished completely, but it was no longer required for certain jobs or official business. For the first time in twenty-eight years, all Greeks could again breathe and speak freely. On the other hand, the emergency laws, and notably Law 509, remained in force. Only some of the political detainees, who it is true totalled less than one hundred, were released. Permission to return to Greece was only occasionally granted to former communist militants who had fled to the Eastern bloc. The ban on the Communist Party remained in force.

Despite the Prime Minister's prudence, which was bitterly attacked by the left, the right continued to proclaim a communist stranglehold on the state as imminent. When Tsirimokos, a former socialist who had belonged to E.A.M. twenty years before, was appointed Minister of the Interior, there was uproar. As indeed there was when the Attorney-General Kollias was disciplined for trying to exert pressure on Christos Sartzetakis, the examining magistrate in the Lambrakis affair, in an attempt to prevent the questioning of certain suspected senior gendarmerie officers.

It is undeniable that, during the first few months of this liberalisation, the left almost daily organised public demonstrations, marches and meetings, on a variety of issues. These demonstrations were generally peaceable, however, resulting only in obstruction, and the police rarely needed to intervene. It is also true that there was a rather childish reaction against the forces of order which had previously commanded such exaggerated respect. Many citizens took a malign pleasure in trivial acts of disobedience: motorists, for example, blew their horns to their hearts' content. But all this was only a temporary and harmless way of letting off steam which soon died down of its own accord. Only hysterical conservatives could see in all this a premonition of anarchy, which would somehow lead inexorably to massacres. The right, accustomed for almost twenty years to a respectful, timid left, could not get used to the idea that the communists had once again become citizens, enjoying the same rights as everyone else. And this way of thinking was fully shared by the court.

The honeymoon between the court and George Papandreou was of short duration. The young King Constantine, who had succeeded his father soon after the Centre Union came to power, possessed neither the experience nor the authority of the late King Paul. He was also said to be very much under the influence of the Queen Mother, Frederika. The latter was very annoyed with the criticism the centre press aimed at her, and she let the Prime Minister know that she held him responsible for the disrespectful attacks against her by the journalists of his party, those upstarts who dared to discuss the size of her pension, or to carp at the dowry granted to her eldest daughter by the Treasury.

The court's displeasure also had other and less frivolous causes. It could not get used to a Prime Minister who rarely asked for an audience, who neglected to report back to the palace, and seemed to think that he was responsible to the electors alone. Karamanlis, who latterly had considered himself the true head of the executive, had not been sacked only to be replaced by a Papandreou who held to this view just as firmly. The premature death, shortly before the elections of February 1964, of Sophocles Venizelos was deplored; for the palace felt he would have been able to keep the Centre Union suitably respectful towards the Sovereign. But what aroused more indignation and alarm than anything was Papandreou's intention, which gradually became clear, of involving himself in the affairs of the armed forces.

By the beginning of 1965 it became clear that the vast antigovernment propaganda campaign, which fed on some truth and much falsehood, did not originate in the official parliamentary opposition. Kanellopoulos, stampeded by the hard liners in his own party, merely followed the herd: the strings were being pulled by others. Secret army and police reports, painting the 'communist peril' in the most alarming colours, were leaked to the right-wing press even before they reached the ministers for whom they were intended. A vile 'communist plot' was sensationally 'unmasked' in this way. This concerned an armoured unit in which tanks were said to have been sabotaged. The enquiry which followed proved that no such plot had existed. The whole furore had been stirred up in the interests of right-wing propaganda by the commander of the unit, a certain Lieutenant-Colonel Papadopoulos, the same Papadopoulos who had organised the electoral fraud in 1961. It is said that the Prime Minister, on looking at his dossier, decided not to take any serious action. 'Democracy', he is said to have declared, 'has nothing to fear from a colonel.' An excellent theory which has since been contradicted by the facts. The future was to show the extent to which this complacency was misplaced.

There were increasing indications that the Army General Staff was behind the conspiracy. The army had for long constituted a state within a state, even to the extent of running its own radio station, whose programmes alternated between popular music and primitive, nationalistic slogans, heavily tinged with a crude anti-communist propaganda. The great majority of the officer corps was composed of men who were royalist by tradition and reactionary by training. Possessing the military strength, and trusting in royal protection, they scarcely concealed their contempt for the government. The latter contented itself by removing a number of particularly hostile officers from key positions, such as the intelligence service and the units stationed near the capital. Out of deference to the King the government had not touched the crux of the problem. The Minister of Defence, Petros Garoufalias unconditionally loyal to the palace, effectively blocked all attempts to subordinate the army to the civil power. The centre press warned of military conspiracies and of a 'junta', and demanded energetic counter-measures. The right-wing press denounced in advance any government interference in the armed forces as an attack on national security.

It was in this tense atmosphere that the ASPIDA affair broke in May 1965. ASPIDA (literally 'Shield') was the name of a clandestine group, of centre-left leanings which the military authorities claimed to have uncovered in the army. There were some arrests. The right triumphantly claimed that its worst fears had been justified, that government supporters and communists were plotting to subvert the army. Centre supporters assumed that the reactionaries were simply trying to cover up their own plans for a *coup d'état*.

This last theory, although still without direct proof, remains the most plausible. Only one fact emerged clearly from the protracted trial which took place after the fall of the Centre Union, and which was conducted with an obvious bias against the accused by the presiding judge, Kamberis. This was that a dozen junior officers had signed an 'oath' as vague as it was pompous, very similar in fact to the style of the present junta's own declarations. Were these absurdities the work of *agents provocateurs*? Be this as it may, it is impossible to extract any kind of political line from remarks about 'saving the country', or ensuring that 'the best are in command', and so on. It was nevertheless on this basis that the intelligence services and the legal branch of the army, all right wing in outlook, had erected a fantastic edifice seeking to incriminate several senior officers. These particular officers were among the few known for their democratic outlook, and as such were seen by their fascist-minded colleagues as possible stumbling-blocks to their future plans. Finally, only one senior officer was found guilty, though without anything remotely like serious proof, and he was given a prison sentence along with several junior officers: this was Colonel Papaterpos, deputy head of the Central Intelligence Service (K.Y.P.) and a former resistance hero. We shall see later the probable causes of this attack against him.

The instigators of the plot implied that Andreas Papandreou was implicated in the 'ASPIDA conspiracy', and indeed that he was its secret leader. They were, however, in no hurry to produce their evidence, and allowed the preliminary enquiries to drag on for more than two years. This was part of a deliberate policy of prolonging the suspense so as to increase political tension. Once the real conspirators had achieved their objective, when the present junta had seized power, they preferred to decree an amnesty, which relieved them from any need to furnish proof. It is difficult to believe that if this proof had in fact existed, the junta would not have used it to blacken its enemies and to justify its own actions.

We have anticipated events a little, so as to show that the intrinsic importance of the ASPIDA case was minimal. But on the other hand, the political importance of this affair at the time should not be underestimated. Gullible right wingers believed that the country was in danger, threatened by a formidable conspiracy embracing hundreds of officers and led by the Prime Minister's son. The young King in particular swallowed this gigantic fantasy unquestioningly.

George Papandreou was now seriously worried by all this, and wished to replace the Chief of the Defence Staff, General Ghennimatas, who was close to the palace and whom he considered responsible for the machinations. He met with opposition, however, from the Defence Minister, Garoufalias, who moreover refused to resign. The Prime Minister decided to remove him and to assume the defence portfolio himself. The right protested that this was unacceptable and was simply a manœuvre to cover up his son's involvement in the ASPIDA affair. The King refused to agree to the Prime Minister's becoming Defence Minister as well, and sent him three very harsh letters in rapid succession. These Papandreou showed to no one for the moment. The crisis became protracted and public opinion became daily more agitated, while the incredibly violent polemics of the press scarcely helped to calm an increasingly worried public.

The King meanwhile had been making secret contact with right-wing members of the Centre Union. Among them were some senior members of the cabinet, such as Mitsotakis, Kostopoulos, and Melas, as well as the President of Parliament, Athanassiadis-Novas. These, prompted by their conservative outlook, by loyalty to the palace, or by ambition, agreed to side with the King in the coming showdown. It seems likely that some of them promised to bring with them quite a sizeable fraction of the Centre Union parliamentary group, which would have deprived George Papandreou of his majority. E.R.E. for its part, together with a minuscule right-wing independent group led by Spyros Markezinis, undertook to support a cabinet composed of centre dissidents.

The fateful day was 15 July 1965. On that day the King summoned George Papandreou and, by again curtly refusing to accept him as Defence Minister, obliged him to resign. The plotters, who until then had given no indication to the Prime Minister that they disagreed with him, were ready and waiting in an antechamber, having donned the frock coat demanded by protocol. A few minutes after Papandreou had left, the King swore in Athanassiadis-Novas as Prime Minister, and the other conspirators as ministers. As there were so few involved each had to take charge of several ministries. The same evening, the palace had broadcast the texts of the letters in which the sovereign of 25 had addressed his nearly octogenarian Prime Minister in insufferably patronising terms. At the same time, the armed forces were placed on the alert, to crush the uprising of the centre and of the left that was said to be imminent.

6. LIBERTY CONDEMNED: 1965-1967

The right was overjoyed: the country had been saved. Its relief was openly shared by the United States Embassy, which appeared to have encouraged the royal initiative. The centre raged against the 'apostates', as the dissident Centre Union M.P.s were called, and protested that the Constitution had been violated. The left followed suit, delighted to find itself for once on the side of constitutional legality. Opinion was divided, however, as to the legality of the existing situation. The revised Constitution of 1952 left a loophole which was to be filled by convention. Apologists for the King's intervention argued that he had adhered to the letter of this Constitution, according to which 'the King appoints and dismisses ministers'. His opponents pointed out that he had infringed its spirit.

The real struggle was begun in Parliament. The essential question was whether the new government would obtain a vote of confidence and thus gain retrospective legality. Each individual centre deputy was subject to pressures and counter-pressures. In order to survive politically, the 'apostates' had to win over about fifty Centre Union deputies, whose votes, with those of E.R.E., would assure them a majority in Parliament. Every deputy who was prepared to defect was promised at least a ministerial portfolio. Rumour had it that certain of the people's representatives allowed themselves to be swayed by more material inducements. All these rumours, whether true or not, scarcely helped to improve the prestige of parliamentary institutions.

The Athanassiadis-Novas cabinet was defeated in Parliament and the centre was jubilant. The King, refusing to be disconcerted, entrusted the formation of another new cabinet to Tsirimokos, who had meanwhile allowed himself to be won over. The right, in congratulating him, conveniently forgot that a year earlier they had considered it nothing short of scandalous that the Ministry of the Interior had been given to such a dangerous leftist. Tsirimokos was defeated in his turn, but by a smaller majority. Little by little the parliamentary group of the Centre Union began to disintegrate. Its members, whose quality we have already alluded to, succumbed one after the other to the various temptations which power offered. At the third effort its opponents succeeded, and in September a cabinet presided over by Stefanopoulos, Deputy Prime Minister under Papandreou, narrowly scraped a vote of confidence.

The immediate objective of the conspiracy had been achieved: George Papandreou had been removed from power. The court once again ruled the roost, and the army remained firmly under right-wing control. By a stroke of good luck force had not proved necessary; parliamentary sleight of hand had been enough. A breathing-space of two and a half years had been gained before there need be new elections. By this time, the theory ran, an electoral majority would be achieved which would retrospectively justify the royal initiative. The unchanging order which had existed before would then be restored.

This was where the calculations proved faulty. The people could not be bought off as easily as a few deputies had been. The circumstances of George Papandreou's fall from power brought him an enormous gain in popularity. The many mistakes of his government were forgotten. His lack of decisiveness and of political finesse in handling the crisis was overlooked. The average Greek, even if he did not like Papandreou, was indignant at his opponents' tactics, and thought the King had no right to meddle in the party struggle, nor to dismiss the people's elected representative.

One profoundly unhappy man during the months that followed was Kanellopoulos. He had only reluctantly allowed himself to be persuaded into supporting the succession of 'apostate' cabinets imposed by the court. His struggle against communism had for long blinded him to dangers coming from the other extreme, but his democratic conscience was painfully reawakened in 1965. It is wholly to his credit that he alone on the right spoke of elections, even though the hard liners in his party soon forced him to retract. But perhaps his temporary acceptance of an irregular situation was due to a recognition that the 'apostasy' had at least spared Greece a palace coup, which he would have been unable to prevent. (This argument was advanced publicly, in justification of his own defection, by Mitsotakis, who had been the moving spirit behind the dissident Centre Union faction.)

Between July and September there were street demonstrations which on several occasions disturbed public order. Crowds of young centre supporters and left wingers booed the King and the 'apostates', clashed with the police, and sometimes erected barricades. Once or twice they smashed the windows of shops and damaged cars. The right, alarmed, cried anarchy and demanded energetic measures. The security forces fortunately kept calm, however, and altogether the clashes resulted in fewer victims and less damage than those which have since shaken France and Italy.[1]

Andreas Papandreou had become the hero of this turbulent youth movement. He now appeared as leader of the radical wing of the Centre Union, soon to be called, without much justification, the 'centre-left'. The right denounced his inflammatory speeches, his refusal to disown acts of violence, and especially what it described as collaboration with E.D.A. In fact, Andreas Papandreou cared little for E.D.A. It could even be said that he deliberately ignored the left, for he never spoke of it. It has been appositely asserted that 'he was neither pro-communist nor anti-communist—he was a-communist'.[2] At this time it was Andreas who gave the lead and E.D.A. which followed, paradoxically showing more moderation than he did in its language and policies. Moreover, the leaders of the left had little sympathy for Andreas Papandreou, whom one faction in the Greek Communist Party has since described as an 'adventurer'. His abrasiveness and growing popularity were making him a serious rival for the votes of E.D.A. supporters.

The moderates in the Centre Union urged greater restraint, fearing that extravagant language and threats would only serve to frighten the bourgeoisie and drive them into the arms of the right who, together with the 'apostates', posed as the 'party of order'. There were also fears that this type of behaviour might serve as a pretext for extreme right wingers thinking in terms of coups. For two months these moderates were scarcely heeded, for as long as the democratic opposition believed itself able to defeat the government in Parliament. The radical wing considered street demonstrations a legitimate means of applying pressure to wavering deputies and newspapers. George Papandreou seemed no longer able to control his son, who had made enemies throughout the establishment, in the army, the Ministry of Justice, and the diplomatic service, by accusing them all of being bastions of reaction and in promising to reform them from top to bottom.

Once the Stefanopoulos government was well established, however, the demostrations practically ceased and daily life returned to normal. The opposition resigned itself to waiting patiently for the next elections, contenting itself for the moment with violent speeches and virulent newspaper polemics, to which the right responded in kind. Strong emotions were given free reign in Parliament, where the deputies slanged each other with vigour and sometimes came to blows. This was nothing new in Greece, where political passions run as high as feelings about football or bull-fighting do elsewhere.

It is necessary to stress all this, for the period 1965-1967 has been described in retrospect as an anarchic, almost revolutionary period. This is absolutely false. With the exception of these rather tumultuous months, the rest of the period was completely normal. Except for the palace's sleight of hand in Parliament, life was free. The fundamental rights of citizens had not been touched. One is faced here with the same misunderstanding that existed under the Papandreou government. For the right, accustomed to police controls which kept the left in its place, the fact that the left could legally demonstrate was an intolerable scandal. Partial strikes, and small incidents which pass unnoticed in any Mediterranean country, seemed to the conservatives, who read inflated accounts of them in their newspapers, to be the portents of doomsday. The best proof of the normality of life in Greece between 1965 and 1967 is the uninterrupted development of the economy. The annual income per head continued to increase on average between 7 and 8 per cent, as it had under Karamanlis. Indexes of industrial expansion and of investment presented the same picture. And with the exception of the ASPIDA trial, which inflamed public opinion, political life was marked by no event of importance. A possible exception was the opposition's lively reaction to the royal message on 1 January 1966, a message that was clearly political, and in which communism was labelled as 'filth'. Stefanopoulos' government was marked by an unprecedented level of nepotism, if not of corruption. Its members, conscious of their lack of popularity and of the elections to come, did their utmost to attract a political following by giving favours of dubious legality.

The right looked on with growing concern. True, the 'apostate' government took its orders on every important issue from the court and E.R.E., which kept it under close surveillance. But E.R.E. began to question whether it was sensible in the long run to identify themselves with an unpopular government, supporting it in Parliament without sharing in the spoils of office. For the following which the 'apostates' were so desperately trying to create would be at the expense of the right. Kanellopoulos' viewpoint was increasingly accepted.

Towards Christmas 1966, the E.R.E. leader reached an understanding with George Papandreou, with whom he had always been on good personal terms. The two major parties decided to oust the 'apostates', and to replace them by a caretaker government to organise elections, which were planned for the spring of 1967. And the King, belatedly realising that he had made a mistake in 1965, gave his blessing to this project, which alone could breathe new life into politics by giving a say to the electors. As a result, the Stefanopoulos government was defeated and replaced by a cabinet whose members enjoyed the confidence of the court, without being too compromised by party allegiances. The colourless Prime Minister was Paraskevopoulos, deputy governor of the National Bank of Greece.

The moderate majority of the two main parties welcomed this agreement, for it opened the way for a restoration of democratic processes. Inevitably, however, the hard liners within E.R.E., led by Pipinelis, condemned it for the very same reason. They found an unexpected ally in Andreas Papandreou, who criticised it with equal severity, arguing that it entailed unnecessary concessions to the right. Relations between the Papandreous, father and son, became strained, and about forty deputies sided with Andreas. A further split within the Centre Union seemed possible. At the last minute, however, the radical wing accepted the lead of the majority of the parliamentary party.

What were the conditions which Andreas Papandreou objected to? It is widely known that the agreement included a secret clause, by which the centre undertook to stop attacking the King, so that the monarchy would not become an election issue. It was the price which the Centre Union had to pay in order to get the elections which it had ceaselessly demanded since 1965. This may have smacked of blackmail, but the Centre Union had no option but to accept it. It is naïve to imagine that it would ever have been allowed to win an election on an anti-monarchist platform. By refusing the agreement the party would have forced the King into unconstitutional measures, and would have lost any hope of achieving power.

Andreas Papandreou let it be understood that his father had also secretly agreed to respect the status quo in the armed forces if he were to win the elections. This clearly would have been a far more serious concession. The government would then have been permanently at the mercy of extreme right-wing officers, supposedly owing allegiance to the King. Such a parody of democracy would certainly have been highly objectionable, but it might have stood a chance of being modified. The alternative in the short term was a royal coup backed by the army, which the opposition was scarcely well enough organised to resist. But whatever the facts of the matter, George Papandreou opted for moderation, and his son, as we have seen, seemed to have accepted this decision.

The extremist groups who led an independent existence on the fringes of the official right were disconcerted by the announcement of elections. A whole world of intriguers, of professional anti-communists, and of police informers felt its privileges, even its livelihood threatened. They were finished if the Centre Union returned to office, for it would take its revenge on all those who had conspired against it in 1965. The 'apostates' themselves did not take the news well and loudly deplored the gross ingratitude of the King, for whom they had sacrificed so much and who was now prepared to condemn them to political death; for they were under no illusions as to their electoral prospects.

The most uneasy and the most dangerous of all were the officers who had staked everything on a once and for all defeat of the Centre Union, and thought that they had carried it off. Now serious observers were predicting an electoral triumph for the Centre Union that would make its 1964 victory pale into insignificance. Its fanatical opponents attached no importance to the concessions and promises which the party might have made before the elections. Once in office, with a crushing majority, what would prevent it from turning against its enemies, whose morale would be broken? At all costs the elections had to be forestalled and the King had to be persuaded to change his mind. For a start, friction between the two main parties had to be stirred up and the communist threat resurrected once again. The means were at hand: Andreas Papandreou must be needled.

The ex-professor of economics fell into the trap. Playing his opponents' game, he answered press attacks in an increasingly violent manner. Despite his father's undertakings, he did not spare the monarchy. His enemies riposted by reviving the ASPIDA affair. The public prosecutor tried to have Andreas Papandreou's parliamentary immunity lifted so that he could be charged. Even if Parliament were to refuse the request, his immunity would cease with its imminent dissolution, and he could find himself in custody during the electoral campaign. The Centre Union tried to parry this move by submitting a draft law prolonging parliamentary immunity for the duration of the campaign. Angered by Andreas' aggressiveness, the hard liners in E.R.E. gained ground at the expense of Kanellopoulos, and their party refused to vote for the proposed law. This led to the collapse of the temporary coalition, and the Paraskevopoulos government resigned.

This occurred at the beginning of April 1967. The new governmental crisis caused serious concern. The chances of a *coup d'état* by extreme right-wing officers were being openly discussed, for under the Stefanopoulos and Paraskevopoulos governments these officers had again taken over all the key army posts. This had been done with the King's approval. He trusted in their absolute loyalty and thought that he could control them through his secretary and confidant, Major Arnaoutis. Those in the know considered talk of the forthcoming elections as naïve.   .

The King asked Kanellopoulos to form a new government to oversee the elections. Normally in Greece elections take place under caretaker governments which are meant to be impartial; this is to obviate the advantage which the party holding office just before and during an election is considered to have over other parties. This time, however, the E.R.E. leader did not seem to have been motivated by considerations of party advantage.

Anxious to preserve constitutional procedures, he considered that an interim E.R.E. government would calm the military and forestall some desperate move on their part. They would scarcely rebel against the party of order.

George Papandreou understood the reasons for his opponent's unusual move and made only a routine protest against this breach of convention. He trusted Kanellopoulos, and also believed that his own party would enjoy an electoral landslide. Parliament was dissolved and elections were announced for 28 May. The electoral campaign was to be inaugurated on 27 April by George Papandreou in Thessaloniki, where his supporters were preparing a massive reception. Everything was going well. It was clear that Kanellopoulos would have the sense to forbid any judicial harassment of Andreas Papandreou during the campaign.

The Prime Minister was almost the only one in the E.R.E. camp to believe, or to pretend to believe, in the possibility of victory. With each day that passed, the prospects became more gloomy for the right. The military conspirators, solidly entrenched in the intelligence services, saw that ever more alarming reports were sent to the government and the palace. A disorderly demonstration of building workers in Athens and a student riot in Thessaloniki were spotlighted, and their importance exaggerated out of all proportion.

Those in authority were not impressed by these manœuvres. About 20 April Kanellopoulos and his Defence Minister, Papaligouras, met with the heads of the armed forces and the commanders of army corps in Athens. An armed coup would present no technical difficulties. Military units had sealed orders in accordance with a plan drawn up in conjunction with NATO in case of war or revolution. Only a button had to be pressed to set the operation in motion. The Prime Minister forbade the button to be pressed, pointing out that there was no reason to depart from constitutional procedures. Small-scale disorders, easily put down by the police, were not enough to justify even a temporary dictatorship. The country would go to the polls. It was understood that if serious disorders were to break out the campaign, or even immediately after the election, or if a victorious Centre Union proved unwilling to be reasonable, there would still be time to deal with the situation before handing over power.

The generals promised to respect these orders, which were also approved by the King, and solemnly undertook not to act on their own initiative. After this they were sent away. Papaligouras retired to bed on the night of 20 April, confident that the government had the situation well in hand, and that it could count on the loyalty of the generals, and in particular that of Brigadier Pattakos, the commander of the tank units stationed near the capital.

Someone else who was getting ready to pass an untroubled night was Andreas Papandreou. During recent weeks he had moderated his language, belatedly following the advice of those who knew the Greek right better than he, for he had been reliably informed that something serious was brewing in the army. Expecting an imminent coup, he had not slept at home for some time. On that evening, however, when he was told by friends of the King's and the government's decision to respect constitutional procedures, he considered the danger past, and returned for the first time to his house.

At two o'clock in the morning, on 21 April 1967, the coup took place, catching the King, the government, the opposition and the generals alike off balance and all in the same unsuspecting sleep. It was the colonels who had pressed the fatal button, bypassing those who thought they commanded them.

7. WHO WAS RESPONSIBLE?

Explanations of historic events differ, even when the historian has been able to gather all available documentation, and to analyse it dispassionately. No wonder then there is divergence in the analysis of more recent events, many aspects of which are still cloaked in mystery and which still provoke emotional reactions. Simplistic explanations tend to prevail, a result both of the law of the least intellectual effort, that mental laziness which is so widespread and which gladly seizes on any interpretation that obviates more nuanced thought, and of partisan passion which hastens to throw the blame on its adversaries.

It is not only irresponsible journalists who have erred in their analysis of the dictatorship established in Greece on 21 April 1967. Political leaders, no less than distinguished academics, have sometimes put forward hasty interpretations based on ideological prejudices rather than on established fact.

First of all, there is that very small minority which accepted the explanation for the coup put out by its protagonists, i.e. that it was an 'army intervention to ward off the imminent danger of a civil war and of a communist seizure of power'. It is scarcely necessary to refute these absurdities. We have seen, in the preceding sections, the extent to which the left had become a constitutional party. The way in which it was caught napping by the coup, and the absence of any attempt to fight back, showed how little it expected, or desired, a trial by force. Most of its leaders were arrested on the night of 20-21 April without offering the slightest resistance, and its archives were found intact in E.D.A.'s official headquarters. The putschists announced, it is true, that they had seized sensational documents which proved the revolutionary objectives and preparations of the left. It was also leaked that they had discovered arms depots and bogus gendarmerie uniforms intended to disguise 'communist cut-throats' as the guardians of law and order when the day of revolution came. A number of gullible conservatives shuddered in anticipation of the promised revelations. They are still waiting for them. Not a pistol, not a single cartridge, not even a button from a gendarmerie uniform has been presented by way of evidence. The junta has merely published a few documents. This published material—which one assumes to be a careful selection of the most compromising items —only goes to demonstrate that all of E.D.A.'s activities were perfectly legal. One looks in vain for a single document which betrays revolutionary objectives. No political party would have disowned this humdrum ragbag of membership and subscription lists, notes on trade union organisation and electoral tactics, which could just as well have belonged to the British Labour Party. In any case, the 'communist threat' justification for the putsch was so flimsy that the junta has gradually abandoned it in favour of other more complex rationalisations, which we will examine later. In other words, the junta deliberately lied to the entire world, and particularly to the Council of Europe, for almost two years. This lie about the 'red peril' was not the only one. As we shall see, it was just as misleading to speak of the 'intervention of the army'.

Although those who believed in the first explanation put forward by the putschists were few, another explanation, diametrically opposed to the first, found a much larger audience, especially abroad. There are variants, but basically it goes something like this: 'The putsch was the work of the King, the army, the Americans, and the great monopolists.' This interpretation clearly conforms to the rather doctrinaire historical viewpoint of a certain section of the left, just as evoking the 'communist peril' never fails to provoke a reaction in certain right-wing quarters. But it is altogether a more serious thesis than the first one and thus merits a closer scrutiny.

Let us begin by clarifying certain concepts which could give rise to confusion. When a military putsch is said to be the work of X, this could mean one or more of the following: (a) that X decided on it and ordered it; (b) that X gave it decisive encouragement;

(c) that X was not opposed to it, although he could have prevented it; (d) that X contributed to creating the conditions which made it possible. These are very different degrees of responsibility, ranged in descending order. In the cases of (a) and (b) it is a matter of direct responsibility, subdivided into primary and secondary responsibility. In the case of (c) it is a negative responsibility, and in the case of (d) it is an indirect responsibility.

There is no doubt that much of the indirect responsibility falls on the King, the army leaders and the Americans, as well as on the politicians and the right-wing press. The colonels were their creatures, their protégés. The key posts which they held, and which enabled them to seize power, had been given them above all during the 'apostate' government, by the generals with the blessing of the palace and under the benevolent eye of the Pentagon's representatives. The right still cultivated a climate of hysterical distrust towards every dissident viewpoint. It proclaimed that the return of the Centre Union to power would be a national catastrophe. Papandreou was cast in the role of 'Kerensky', paving the way for the communists. Besides, the events of 1965 had gravely diminished the prestige of Parliament.

To all this, moderate anti-regime right-wingers now reply by invoking first the left's revolutionary terrorism during the 'forties, which in their view fully justifies their subsequent suspicion. And secondly they point to the Centre Union's mistakes and notably Andreas Papandreou's, whose language alone was enough to alarm the party's conservative opponents. There is an element of truth in all this, particularly in the second argument. It is clearly unwise to threaten unscrupulous opponents when one does not have the means necessary to keep them in check. Even the humblest peasant knows that if he cannot squash a wasp by a single blow, it is better not to irritate it. However, these mitigating circumstances are rather slender and do not substantially decrease the direct responsibility of the King and the army chiefs, together with the Americans who supported them.

The King. The King can certainly be cleared of all direct responsibility for the coup. He neither initiated it nor backed it. He was taken by surprise when the rebel colonels burst into his palace on the night of 20-21 April, and was at first extremely angry, refusing to sign the proclamation of martial law. He gave in only towards the middle of the following morning, 'to avoid bloodshed', as he later explained. This is where the question of his negative responsibility comes in: his constitutional duty was to refuse any compromise whatsoever with the putschists; and he did not carry out this duty.

The argument put forward by those who approve of the King's conduct runs something like this. If he had resisted when he was isolated and without any physical force to fall back on, he would have lost his throne and thus any chance of influencing the future course of events. On the other hand, by prevaricating and accepting a temporary co-existence with the junta, he retained the option of taking action at a more propitious moment. Besides, he consulted the chiefs of the armed forces and the legal Prime Minister, under arrest, before reaching a decision, and only Kanellopoulos and Admiral Engolfopoulos, chief of the naval staff, advised him to resist; all the generals counselled him to accept the *fait accompli*. Besides, his defenders add, he did sucessfully insist that the new cabinet was not to be composed exclusively of army officers, and that it was to be presided over by a man whom he trusted, the former Attorney-General Kollias.[1] Finally, they add, by remaining at his post, the King prevented a number of important loyalist officers from being retired. And with their aid he tried, in December of the same year, to overthrow the junta. The fact that he failed does not alter the picture.

So much for the defence. His critics reply that if this were the case, putting the best possible interpretation on his behaviour, he made a series of serious errors of judgment, as subsequent events have shown. Kollias' prime ministership and the appointment of several more or less senile members of the Court of Appeal to unimportant ministries in no way changed the nature or policy of the dictatorial regime, for all effective power remained in the colonels' hands. At the same time, the King's capitulation lent the regime a more respectable façade and helped to secure its recognition abroad. Furthermore, the royal example served as an excuse for most of the country's leaders, civil servants, judges, ambassadors, academics, and all official bodies to submit in turn. If the King had refused to submit, his critics maintain, if he had appealed for resistance, then the majority of the armed forces would undoubtedly have obeyed him. The putsch was in its initial stages a gigantic bluff, supported only by a few army units. There would perhaps have been a bloody confrontation, but this would have been short, and would have been much less of a catastrophe for the country than the establishment of a fascist dictatorship.

Besides, by what logic had the country fought to defend itself against communist insurrection, only to succumb later to a handful of officers? In compromising with the junta, the King formally made himself a party to all its illegalities, to all its tyrannical measures. It was in his name that prisoners were tortured. If by remaining on the throne he had at least made a success of his counter-coup in December 1967, and if it had in fact led to the re-establishment of democracy, he could have been excused his other mistakes. But here also he erred in every possible way. Not only had secrecy not been maintained but the handling of the operation itself was deplorable. Able to count on the support of the best armoured units of the army of the north, with Thessaloniki, the capital of the north, within his grasp and free of government troops, and with the entire navy and air force at his command, the King forbade his loyal generals to advance, once again to 'prevent bloodshed'. There is no future in organising a military coup with the firm resolve not to fire a shot in anger, particularly if your adversary does not share your scruples. At the first setback, the King packed his bags and fled to Italy, abandoning his loyal officers to the enemy.

We still lack knowledge of certain factors which would help us assess the exact measure of King Constantine's responsibility. Why, for instance, did he issue the unfortunate proclamation with which he began his December coup? This extraordinarily inept text, which is open to the interpretation that the King intended to substitute his personal dictatorship for that of the colonels, did nothing for his public image, nor have other statements which he has since made in exile. One factor, however, is in his favour: he has refused to return to Greece on the colonels' terms, and he appears to be insisting on the setting of an election timetable as an essential pre-condition of his return.

The Army. We have seen that the putschists claim to represent the 'army'. They stress this point in their proclamation, in their speeches, even in the new school textbooks. Curiously, this myth has also been given equal credence for propaganda purposes by some of their left-wing opponents. This matter is highly important, not only for an understanding of the past but also for the future.

What exactly do we mean by the 'army'? In peace time, the army is composed principally of career officers on the one hand and conscripts on the other. Accepting that the conscripts represent a cross-section of the population at large, the statistical probability is that the army contained a majority of centre supporters in 1967. The anti-fascist majority within the army becomes overwhelming if one adds the left wingers to the centre supporters, not to mention that part of the traditional right which is opposed to dictatorship. But no one asked the enlisted men's opinion. It was the officers who decided everything. In the French army in Algeria, the attitude of the conscripts at the time of the general's putsch in 1961 was decisive for the failure of the coup. In that case, however, the head of state had the opportunity to address them by radio, and to make his appeal for disobedience of orders heard. Nothing similar was possible in Greece, where the great majority of the armed forces did not realise what was happening until it was too late. And when we say the great majority, we include the career officers.

This was because the operation was based on a fraud as outrageous as it was clever. Assured of control of communications throughout the country, the conspirators succeeded in persuading the King that the entire army was behind them, and the rest of the army—notably the units stationed in the provinces—that their orders originated with the King. In fact, the conspirators had at their disposal only a few crack units near Athens, namely the tank corps, the L.O.K. commandos, the cadets of the Military School and the Military Police. None of the conspiracy's leaders was of a rank higher than that of colonel, except for the tank commander, Brigadier Pattakos. For the first stage of the operation, however, they needed a more impressive façade. They woke General Spandidakis, chief of the Army General Staff, in the middle of the night, and summoned him to join them. Spandidakis was supposed to be loyal to the palace. Being a characterless opportunist, however, and perhaps seeing a chance to achieve his personal ambitions, he accepted. The only other generals who were in on the secret were Anghelis, who later became Chief of the Defence Staff, and Zoitakis. The latter commanded the Third Army Corps, which was stationed in the north, and included some of the most powerful units in the army. His co-operation was of the greatest importance—and he received his reward later when he was made regent after the King's flight.

All the other generals, who remained loyal to the King, were neutralised. As we have said, they were gathered in Athens to confer with the legal government, and the putschists had only to round them up. The original 'Prometheus plan' had been modified in this important respect: not only the leaders of the left and centre, but the leaders of the right, who formed the legal government, and most of the leaders of the armed forces, including the air force and navy, were simultaneously arrested. One of the first acts of the Kollias government was to retire five generals and one admiral, and this was only the beginning of the massive purges which were to follow, and which we will examine in detail later. Spandidakis became Deputy Prime Minister and Minister of Defence, perhaps at the King's insistence, for Constantine strangely continued to trust him.

Despite all these measures and despite the purges, a large part of the army and the entire air force and navy eight months later backed the King's attempt to overthrow the colonels. Although they failed, their stand demonstrated that the putschists could scarcely claim to speak for 'the army', but were rather a handful of clever conspirators among the officers of middle rank.[2]

The interests of 'monopoly capital'. The Marxist litany would be incomplete if these interests were not listed amongst those responsible for the coup. However, it is difficult to see what immediate role they could have played. One can scarcely imagine the leaders of the conspiracy consulting before 21 April with Onassis, Niarchos, Pappas, or with representatives of the great American firms. The putsch needed no financial backing, and its perpetrators would have been mad to share so closely guarded a secret with business circles.

Things would have been different if the King and the traditional right, whose links with large-scale capital were far from secret, had wanted the putsch. We have seen, however, that this was not the case. The support which the regime subsequently received in certain international financial circles is another matter, and should not be confused with any backing at the planning stage. The maxim *is fecit cui prodest* is not always a good guide in politics. Individuals, groups and parties have often been instrumental in bringing about situations which are ultimately disadvantageous to themselves; in Greece, the palace and the right proved incapable, when the crunch came, of containing the forces which they had helped to unleash. The opposite can equally well happen, and in the short term at least capitalist interests have derived interesting benefits from the coup without having given it prior support.

The Americans. The United States' decisive role in the collapse of democratic institutions in various third world countries, and notably in Latin America, is well known. The events in Greece strikingly resemble those in Brazil three years earlier. It is tempting to imagine that the American intelligence services in Athens used the same blueprint that had proved so successful in Rio de Janeiro. Such analogies, however, do not constitute proof. Let us look at the history of the United States' relations with Greece.

From 1947 onwards, the United States took over the role of Greece's 'protector' from Great Britain. It supplied the country with important military and economic aid during and after the civil war. Since then it has always had its say in matters of internal policy. Its 'advice', however, was by no means always reactionary. During the Truman administration, the advice the United States Embassy offered to the King was generally consistent with a moderate policy. Thus the U.S. insisted that the Populist right, which enjoyed a strong parliamentary majority in 1947, should form a coalition with the liberal minority groups, under a liberal Prime Minister. In the same way, in 1950-51, the Americans supported Plastiras' accession to power. Altogether they behaved intelligently, and by enlarging the democratic base of the country, they isolated still further the rebel Communist Party.

But under Eisenhower American policy in Greece hardened. Its objective became the stabilisation of the traditional right as the 'party of power' and support for 'safe' military leaders.

President Kennedy once again gave a more liberal character to American policy. One assumes that it was no mere coincidence that from 1961 onwards there was a distinct cooling off in the Greek court's attitude towards Karamanlis, and a willingness to flirt with the Centre Union, resulting in the 1963-64 détente which led to Papandreou's brief premiership. By 1965, however, the reaction under President Johnson was in full swing. The U.S. Embassy was no stranger to the intrigues which resulted in the crisis of 15 July of that year.

And now a brief digression. The servility of most Greek political leaders towards the Americans is rather shocking. It is this alone which has enabled the United States to treat Greece more as a protectorate than it has any other Western country. This servility, the sad counterpart of the communist satellites' attitude towards the Soviet Union, could be partly explained by the civil war in Greece, which other members of NATO were spared. But only partly, for this obsequious attitude persisted twenty years after the civil war, in a Greece no longer depressed or directly threatened. There are deeper reasons for it. Let us recall what we mentioned earlier, the Greeks' insistence on appealing to one or another of the Great Powers, and on confounding their own interests with theirs ever since the Ottoman period. It is not a pleasing trait, but one which had deep roots. The palace and the Communist Party behaved precisely as the 'anglophile' or 'russophile' Greeks of the nineteenth century did. And they were not necessarily 'bought'; they sincerely believed that the country's salvation lay with their chosen country, which alone was well-disposed towards Greece. It is this naïveté, shared even by educated people, which has so often prevented Greece from pursuing a rational foreign policy. This attitude has also been fostered by the factional disputes which have divided the Greeks, under different labels at different periods, and have resulted in their readiness to ally with foreigners in order to combat their domestic enemies. This also is a trait with very deep roots. It is to be found in classical antiquity, when the Athenians and the Spartans showed no hesitation in allying in turn with the Persians to do each other down. We have scarcely matured in two thousand five hundred years.

To return to American policy. From 1965 onwards, the situation becomes confused. Should one look on the palace's moves towards reconciliation and restoration of normal democratic procedures at the end of 1966 as a response to advice from Washington, where at a late stage the sensible policies of the Truman era were being recalled? It is by no means out of the question. But what is certain is that American official policy did not encourage the putsch of 1967, which took place against the King's will. The United States had great confidence in the King. Had the Americans wanted a *coup d'état* they would have carried it out in co-operation with the King, the right, and the military hierarchy, not with a band of unknown colonels. The official reaction from Washington, which took the form of a suspension of heavy arms deliveries and statements urging a rapid return to the parliamentary system, would appear to confirm such an interpretation.[3] In Brazil, the White House congratulated the putschists openly, almost on the very day of their coup. But this had been carried out, as is only proper, by high-ranking generals.

We have deliberately spoken of 'official' American policy and of 'official reactions'. This is because there were, and there are still, other very different policies. It is no secret to anyone in Greece that the American military establishment are delighted with their Greek colleagues' regime. Nor is there any doubt about the favour which the regime has been shown by the C.I.A. from the very beginning, although this favour is obviously less overt and more difficult to prove than that of the Pentagon. There are certain indications that agents of the C.I.A. and the Pentagon in Greece knew in advance that the coup was in preparation. Did they actively encourage it? If so, what is one to make of the State Department's and the Athens Embassy's reaction, as they appeared to be disagreeably surprised by the event? It may well be a case of sheer hypocrisy: official America protests and then washes its hands of the business, while unofficial America rubs its hands, and gets them dirty. But it could equally be a question of a simple lack of co-ordination between the State Department, the Pentagon and the C.I.A. There have been plenty of instances of this. Each of the services has its own policy, often very different from that of the others. Unless the President is serious and energetic, these contradictory policies can verge on schizophrenia. Thus one must subdivide the question of American responsibility. Which America are we talking about? To what extent is each of its different arms responsible?

The question arises more than once. For question-marks not only hang over 21 April 1967,[4] but also over the American role in the royal counter-coup of 13 December 1967. Did the Americans encourage it? Or did they betray it in advance, as Andreas Papandreou has recently claimed? For the time being there can be no answers to these mysteries.

The search for an American motive does not take us very far, for there are a number of ways of looking at American interests in Greece, as the divergences of opinion within America itself indicate. For every intelligent senator who fears the damage to long-term American interests in Europe there is always a less intelligent, to put it charitably, military man who sees only that his Greek military colleagues have a firm grip on power and that consequently all is for the best. Is it the intelligent Americans or the others who have determined their country's policy in Greece since 1967? The indications up till now are scarcely encouraging, but do not rule out a future change of policy.

To conclude, the *coup d'état* of 1967 was not the direct work of the King, the traditional right, the army, or the 'great monopolies'. It was perhaps encouraged by certain American agencies. But who organised it, who set it in motion? Who are the men who seized power, and how have they exercised it? We will attempt to answer these questions in the ensuing sections.

PART TWO

The Present, or what it is like

'Poor mothers gave birth to four great men.'
(From a popular song in honour of the junta)

1. THE 'SMITH' DICTATORSHIP

WHEN confronted with a catastrophe of extraordinary dimensions, it is comforting to be able to see destiny personified by some powerful figure. Nazi Germany in 1941 was a powerful adversary, and it was not a disgrace for Greece to have been conquered by it. The communist dictatorships in the world have been imposed either by an important section of the people, as in China, Cuba, and Yugoslavia, or by the Red Army, as in Eastern Europe. The Spanish and Portuguese dictatorships, in the beginning at least, were supported by large sections of the middle classes. Only in Africa, the Middle East, and Latin America are regimes of the Greek type to be found; i.e. dictatorships by military junta. For the bitter, humiliating truth is that democracy in Greece has been destroyed and the country enslaved by a small band of perjured officers. What is even more galling is that these officers were completely unknown, with a totally undistinguished professional background.

This is a fact of some importance. Not one of the conspirators was the type of officer of whom the armed forces were justly proud: those heroes of the last war, of the resistance, or of the Korean campaign who had been decorated and promoted for bravery. None of them have had brilliant army careers. Quite the reverse, in fact, for the junta which carried out the *coup d'état* and which governs today is principally distinguished by its professional mediocrity. George Papadopoulos himself is a prime example of the type of officer who prefers intrigue to combat and which forms the hard core of the present regime.

The name Papadopoulos is as common a surname in Greece as Smith is in England. There are more than 1500 Papadopoulos's in the Athens telephone directory alone, and of these more than 150 are called George. The dictator, who was born into a peasant family, is said to have been consumed with a frenzied ambition from an early age. Those near to him laughed openly at his absurd pretensions, which included a conviction that 'one day he was going to rule Greece'. He followed a military career and fought in 1940-41 as a young second lieutenant, newly graduated from the Military Academy. Official propaganda makes a great deal of this. How can Papadopoulos be accused of fascism when he himself fought against Mussolini's legions? The regime's propaganda fails, however, to add that he had no choice in the matter. He and all his classmates were sent to the front as a matter of course. Besides, the whole argument itself is flawed. We currently see socialist countries in conflict, although their ideology in theory excludes national antagonisms; it was even more natural for fascist regimes, whose ideology was impregnated with a fierce chauvinism, to fight each other. Semi-fascist regimes in Poland and Yugoslavia fought against the Nazis, as did the Greece of Metaxas.

It was from 1941 onwards, under the German occupation, that the Greeks had a chance to fight on a voluntary basis for their country and their freedom. With the collapse of the government and the military hierarchy, participation in the resistance was a personal decision. Not only every officer worthy of his rank but also every man of spirit, not to mention women and even children, took part. Whether in the ranks of the left or of the right, in the towns or in the mountains, within Greece or with the Free Greek forces in the Middle East, there were many opportunities to fight. Some members of the junta took a certain part in the resistance: Colonel Karydas in the Middle East, Colonel Ioannidis in the right-wing maquis, Pattakos in a clandestine group which communicated information to the General H.Q. in Cairo.

Papadopoulos himself did nothing at all. This ambitious future dictator, who twenty-five years later was to give lessons in patriotism to his fellow-countrymen, considered it unnecessary to lift a finger to liberate his country. Was this out of a sympathy with the Nazis? If so, he would have shown more courage had he fought on their side, by joining one of the collaborationist government's 'security battalions'. The more likely explanation is that he was taking care of himself. He does not care to take unnecessary risks, as the astounding precautions he now takes for his own security indicate: two or three hundred policemen are mobilised for each of his trips between home and office.

The gap for the years 1941-1944 in his official biography speaks volumes. What could his apologists write? That while the whole of Greece fought, Papadopoulos had sought refuge in the accounts office of the Red Cross? For this is the most charitable account of his activities during the occupation. There are others. For instance, that he was a provincial inspector for the Ministry of Food Supply, under the collaborationist government, with the task of extorting a part of their meagre harvest from the unfortunate peasants in order to supply, among others, the occupation troops. It might seem barely credible that there is no precise information on this aspect of Papadopoulos' past, but the reticence of the official biographers is matched by the prudence of those in a position to know the truth.

Normally, conduct of this sort on the part of a career officer would have led to his being cashiered soon after liberation. But Papadopoulos had, it seems, an influential relative close to a certain minister. However this may be, he continued to follow a military career, and this included a brief tour at the front during the civil war. Afterwards he was mainly in the intelligence services, notably K.Y.P. (Central Intelligence Service), an off-shoot of the American C.I.A. From the 'fifties onwards he began to plot, joining groups of officers who had 'decided to save the country' if the politicians failed in their duty.[1] Marshal Papagos had had to stamp vigorously on a demonstration in his support by these officers on the day he retired as supreme commander in 1951. However, the organisers of this demonstration went virtually unpunished: there were only a few discreet retirements. Those who remained in the army continued to plot. Papadopoulos had the effrontery to try to initiate his immediate superior, Colonel Papaterpos, into his group. Papaterpos reprimanded him severely but did not report him, out of a sense of loyalty to a fellow-officer. This incident lay behind Papadopoulos' profound hatred of him, which reached its culmination in the ASPIDA affair (see p. 52).

We have looked at Papadopoulos' role in the 1961 elections and in the 'sabotage' affair of 1965 (see p. 51). Slowly he learned how to worm his way into the confidence of extreme right-wing groups, who looked on him as a useful and loyal supporter. Of his superiors, General Patilis, who until his retirement in 1965 was the leader of these factious officers, particularly appreciated his services. (During the occupation Patilis had begun by joining E.L.A.S. Later, however, he turned a complete *volte-face* and enlisted in the collaborationist 'security battalions'. Papadopoulos made him a minister in 1967, and then second Deputy Prime Minister.) Being over confident, Papadopoulos moved too quickly. One day, while still a major, he sought an audience with a minister without portfolio in the Karamanlis government, and presented him with a bulky file. He explained that it was a plan for a sweeping reform of all the country's institutions, starting with the Constitution. After leafing through several pages, and stifling a groan, the minister returned the dossier, politely suggesting that in the future to confine himself to strictly professional duties.

Papadopoulos realised that his political genius would go un-recognised so long as the politicians had the last word. So they must be bypassed. He began to construct his own group in the army. Patiently building on the nucleus of former groups that he already knew, he gathered dozens, then hundreds, of young officers who acknowledged him as their leader. Even less educated than he was, they were carried away by his pompous clichés that passed as an original theory of state, government, religion, and in fact of all knowledge. His ambitions and intrigues amused other military men, and he was regarded as a pocket Nasser. Curiously, his military superiors did not seem to have frowned on these extra-curricular activities. They seem to have been taken in by his assurances that he was their docile servant.

The officers in the conspiracy were mainly of humble origin, like their leader, and indeed the great majority of army officers since the inter-war period. Their rudimentary education, scarcely improved by their studies at the Military Academy, had led them to hate Soviet communism, not as an inhuman and illiberal system but as opposed to the traditional peasant and petit bourgeois values of 'religion, fatherland, and family'. This trinity, in which property was also tacitly included, well expressed the fundamentals of Greek conservatism. The fact that these slogans came uncomfortably close to those of Spain or Vichy France was not regarded as anything to worry about. On top of these beliefs was a disgust with 'parliamentary corruption', and an impatience with any kind of dialogue, criticism, persuasion, or compromise—in other words, with everything that smacks of democracy. More-over, they were increasingly consumed by feelings of class resent-ment, of being left out of things, of being treated like faithful watchdogs by the establishment. Why should they not be the equals of those they were supposed to protect? They knew how to command a company, so why not the entire country? They would know how to govern it with the necessary vigour without letting legal niceties stand in the way.

In many parts of the world career officers are given to such daydreams. But in civilised countries they do not act out these fantasies. Democratic traditions are too firmly rooted. Nor does one find right-wing parties in, say, Holland or in Great Britain exhorting the army to be on guard against the 'anti-national' designs of opposition parties, as in fact happened in Greece during this period. In Greece, as elsewhere, officers swore an oath to the Constitution. But not much attention was paid to this at the Military Academy. Their training stressed a loyalty to the King and to 'the Nation', conceived as a metaphysical entity distinct from the people. Who then is to decree what at any particular moment devotion to the 'Nation' entails? Certainly not the despicable politicians who, while engaged in idle talk, tolerate the monstrous activities of atheistic communists and are even prepared to co-operate with them. The King, as the symbol of the 'right thinking' elements in the nation, is the fount of authority. But the sovereign must also inspire respect. This King Paul did, and during his reign a military uprising would have been unthinkable unless on his express orders. He would have personally arrested the first rebel who dared to appear before him, and the others would have submitted in fear and trembling.

King Constantine was far from enjoying a comparable authority. Not only was he too young, but he possessed none of the requisite qualities. Certainly his lack of education, remarkable in a civilian, was not in the least shocking to military men who regarded Papadopoulos as the fount of wisdom. What they could not stomach was that he led the sporting life of a play-boy while wearing stripes and decorations which he had done nothing to earn. At least his father had graduated in the normal way from the Naval College. There were numerous officers whiling away gloomy and, as it seemed to them, ill-paid lives in bleak garrison towns or offices with no hope of rapid promotion, for the top-heavy officer corps suffered from a chronic promotion bottleneck. These people read in right-wing newspapers during 1966-67 that the country was in danger. A few pages later, they would read that the King had flown to Milan for the day, to take part in some 'jet-set' junket.

Papadopoulos was so openly compromised by 1965 that his career would have been in jeopardy if the Centre Union had won, but he knew how to play on all these sources of disaffection. He persuaded enough of his colleagues that the time to move had now come and that elections must be avoided at all costs. It was within their power to save the country and, as an added attraction, themselves become the new ruling class.

Thus a vague and anachronistic chauvinism and a total ignorance of the real nature of contemporary problems, allied with personal ambition, incited these men to rebel on 21 April 1967, and gave birth to the dictatorship of the cunning colonel-politician.

2. THE STRANGLEHOLD ON PUBLIC LIFE

'The Revolution must purge anti-national organisms from the body politic. It must expel those cells which act in an anti-national manner.'

Papadopoulos

On the morning of 21 April, the rebel officers issued a decree, allegedly signed by the King and the 'government', which declared a state of martial law. In fact, the King had refused to sign this decree, and at the time it was issued there was no government of any kind. The legitimate rulers, namely Kanellopoulos and his colleagues, were under arrest and the junta's government was not sworn in until evening. The decree was therefore a forgery pure and simple. But it would have been unconstitutional even if signed by the King and the legitimate government, because it made no provision for recalling the dissolved Parliament to ratify it, as Article 91 of the Constitution expressly required.

A lie and a forgery were mere peccadilloes to the colonels. They needed martial law not only to establish their position but also to maintain themselves in power. Indeed, martial law still remains in force four years after the coup, which must be something of a record.

Under martial law, Articles 5, 6, 8, 10-12, 14, 18, 20, 95, and 97 of the 1952 Constitution, that is to say all the articles guaranteeing human rights, were suspended, and the military authorities were given practically unlimited powers. A decree published on the day of the coup created special courts-martial, with powers to judge whatever cases they saw fit. Any citizen could be arrested without warrant, and detained indefinitely without trial. Any assembly of more than five persons, in public or in private, was forbidden without special authorisation. The right to strike and the right to criticise the government were abolished, under threat of up to five years in prison. Any publication or transmission of news, in whatever media, was subject to preventive censorship.

This was a formidable legal arsenal with which to bind and gag the entire country. Political parties were dissolved. All political activity, all legal opposition became impossible. This, it might be thought, would have been enough to avert the 'danger of anarchy' which the coup was supposed to forestall. But this would be seriously to underestimate the ambitions of the putschists. Not content to exercise absolute and unfettered executive power, they also assumed the legislative powers of Parliament and initiated their own programme of legislation.[1] However, certain provisions of the Constitution which remained in force still imposed some limits on their arbitrary power. After about a fortnight they woke up to this and began to promulgate 'constitutional acts' which modified or suspended the offending articles of the Constitution. We shall see examples of this later on.

Armed with all this power, the junta set in motion a carefully thought out plan to gain control of all the nerve centres of public life. The key ministries were personally taken over by the leaders of the conspiracy. Papadopoulos took charge of the Ministry to the Prime Minister, which controls press and radio. The Ministry of the Interior went to Pattakos, who behind his 'bluff but good-hearted soldier' façade, hides a formidable peasant malice towards those he dislikes and a capacity to lie outrageously without batting an eyelid. The Ministry of Co-ordination, the ministry which directs the country's economic life, was entrusted to Colonel Makarezos, who seems the most mysterious of the three as he is generally the least garrulous. Other members of the junta look on him as an economic expert because, while military attaché in Bonn, he had attended some university courses in economics. There is some doubt, however, as to whether his knowledge of German was adequate for him to have benefited from this. Makarezos had sense enough to keep on his predecessors' experienced advisers, and he has managed to avoid flagrant gaffes in his particular sector, except when powerful interests have entered the arena. His stupidity and intellectual pretensions, his bad faith, and his vulgarity are revealed only in his rare oratorical outbursts, which we shall discuss in the section on the regime's style.

The portfolio of Defence was given, as we have seen, to General Spandidakis, but effective control of the army passed to General Anghelis, who was regarded as 'safe'. Some other ministries were entrusted to civilians personally known to and trusted by the putschists, men such as Matthaiou, Makarezos' brother-in-law, who took over Agriculture. The lesser ministries were left for men trusted by the King and Prime Minister Kollias. However, in all the ministries headed by civilians the junta installed a military 'secretary-general', who wielded effective power. One of these, wishing to make the matter quite clear to even the dimmest of civil servants, issued a circular expressly forbidding the implementation of any order by the civilian minister which was not countersigned by himself.

The part of these arrangements which was intended as a compromise between the junta and the King was of course swept away immediately after the royal coup in December 1967. The puppet Kollias was replaced as Prime Minister by Papadopoulos himself, and the decrepit ex-judges installed in the cabinet on the King's insistence were ousted.[2] Apart from this there was no change in the system. Papadopoulos has always refused to give other ministries directly to officers. He does not like his government to be described as 'military', and he even insisted that officers in the government, even the secretaries-general of ministries, resign their commissions, as he himself did. He prefers to decorate his ministries with civilians, who are attracted by the prestige of being called 'minister', no less than by its material rewards, raised by the junta to a monthly total of 45,000 drachmas.[3] This is quite a lot for a country which is scarcely rich, especially when one adds the displacement allowance which is on the order of £16 per day. And the junta's ministers travel indefatigably on speech-making tours in the provinces, just as the 'corrupt politicians' did in the past. But then the displacement allowances were smaller.[4] It is well known that for the less scrupulous ministers there are other means of augmenting earnings under a system where there is no public accountability. Despite these lures, it is to the country's honour that the junta has had difficulty in recruiting ministers who are even remotely presentable. Cases are known of ministries being offered to as many as five or six people before finding a taker.

Needless to say, the civilian ministers have no real power. Questions of general policy which are beyond the competence of the military secretaries-general are the responsibility of the ruling 'troika'. There exists in addition an unofficial 'Revolutionary Council', composed of several dozen officers who were, with Papadopoulos, the leaders of the conspiracy. This is the junta proper. It is in this Council that the important decisions are taken, and these are later transmitted to the ministers for execution. The Revolutionary Council's role is essentially that of the old cabinet, which now has only formal functions.

The junta has not been content to control the activities of the government in the narrow sense of the word. It has nominated trusted supporters to direct all the major state or semi-state enterprises. These new directors are almost all serving or retired officers. Officers have been appointed to Telecommunications, Electric Power, Tourism, the Opera, Youth and Sport, and Civil Aviation. This last post was initially given to the former Air Force Colonel, Skarmaliorakis.[5] They have also been placed in charge of the National Theatre, the Agricultural Bank, students' clubs and several other institutions, while four of them have taken over key posts in the Ministry of Foreign Affairs. Officers were also appointed as government commissars, placed by the junta in all the universities and principal centres of higher education in Greece.

In 1969 another officer was appointed 'Commissar of Administration', a newly created post corresponding to the 'Ombudsman' who, in the Scandinavian countries, exercises the functions which formerly belonged to the Council of State in Greece, as in France. Apart from the apparent duplication of effort involved, which is basically aimed at lowering the Council of State's prestige, the choice of the person appointed to protect citizens' rights has a certain irony. He is, in fact, General Vellianitis, a former director-general of the National Security Police, whose task it is to track down, arrest, and frequently torture dissidents.

It would be tedious to list all the important posts given to military men. The examples cited, plus the fact that most of the provincial governorships and two major embassies have been entrusted to military men, illustrate the general trend well enough. But even worse, the junta has destroyed the entire tradition of local self-government by dismissing the elected mayors and municipal councils throughout Greece. It has replaced them with those it considers worthy of favour, that is to say those quick to demonstrate an appropriate servility, and here again it has shown its clear preference for the military. In the villages it is often an ex-sergeant who becomes mayor. Elsewhere, ex-officers of appropriate rank are appointed: an elegant suburb of Athens has had a former brigadier-general foisted on it, although he does not even live there.

In a number of cases, however, the junta, or rather Papadopoulos in person, has overcome this fixation with the military. Thus an important and confidential post at the Ministry to the Prime Minister has been given to a civilian, Charalambos Papadopoulos. True, he is the brother of the dictator. Formerly a petty clerk in the Ministry of Commerce, he was promoted by the junta four times in a few weeks until he ended up as director-general of a ministry.

The practice of infiltrating regime supporters everywhere knows no bounds. The junta disbanded the elected council of the Athens bar and deported its chairman. Afterwards it nominated a new loyal council. The same has happened with most professional and private associations. Those which inclined to the left, such as the Writer's Society, were simply dissolved, along with several hundred other similar bodies. In other cases, the authorities have exercised irresistible pressure to get rid of any unwelcome members on the governing bodies. It has been the same with student organisations. Even when a professional association is still allowed to elect its own secretariat, no one dares to oppose candidates known to enjoy the favour of the police. Even if an opposition were to stand for election the majority would swallow its true feelings and vote against it. For everyone knows that a secretariat disliked by the authorities has no hope of efficiently promoting the interests of its association.

Nor was the Church spared by the junta. Contrary to canon law, one of the first acts of the regime was to force the Archbishop of Athens (primate of the Orthodox Church in Greece) to resign, and to nominate in his place Ieronymos Kotsonis, the royal chaplain. This clerical *coup d'état* was followed by a more thorough purge, in which several bishops suspected of hostile opinions were ousted, often to the accompaniment of sordid accusations of immorality, as in the case of the Metropolitan Panteleimon of Thessaloniki.

The scandalous elevation of Ieronymos to the archiepiscopal throne was at first considered to be a favour to the King. If this were the case, the sovereign was able to measure his protégé's gratitude on the evening of 13 December 1967. As soon as the royal coup was known to have failed, but while the King was still in Greece, the new Archbishop swore in General Zoitakis as regent. His devotion to the dictatorship has never since been in question.

In the beginning the putschists had no need to tamper with the leadership of the Greek General Federation of Labour, the country's central trade union organisation. For the independence of this organisation had for long been purely notional. It had never played the social and political role that would normally have fallen to it. This fact is closely linked with the lack of a serious socialist movement in Greece. Both result from the fact that industrialisation and the beginnings of trade unionism coincided with the foundation of the Third International; the Second had passed by unnoticed. To prevent the Federation from falling under communist control, or on the pretext of preventing it, the right when in power had managed to install leaders whose corruption was as proverbial as their attachment to 'national ideals'. These conservative leaders, vigorously supported by the police and the Americans, had succeeded by intimidation and fraud in remaining in the saddle for decades, save for a brief interlude under the Papandreou government. They were reinstated by the 'apostates', and were the first to welcome the coup of 21 April and the imposition of martial law, which incidentally removed the right to strike. It was almost two years later when they protested against this unparalleled onslaught on the workers' liberties—and that was only when the junta promulgated a law which removed them from office.

There were two sides to the junta's attempt to control public life. The first involved packing the key posts. Then, for the stranglehold to become complete, there was another, negative side: removing the real or imagined opponents of the dictatorship throughout the machinery of state and public utilities. This was the object of the great purges which began in 1967 and reached a peak in 1968.

We shall not deal for the moment with the fields of justice, education, and the armed forces, which we shall treat in special sections. There remain the purges in the civil service and important sectors such as electricity, supply, telecommunications, banking, etc.

A series of 'constitutional acts' was necessary to initiate the witch hunt, for the Constitution contained some awkward guarantees of tenure for civil servants. The regime's legal experts had trouble inventing formulae which were sufficiently plausible and yet flexible enough to permit the dismissal of all undesirables. The initial ground for the purge was, of course, to flush out all those holding 'anti-national opinions'. The term was already in existence. But whereas before it applied only to communists, now it was widened to include a very broad spectrum of democratic, liberal, and even royalist opinion. The need for additional grounds was quickly felt. A first attempt, by means of Constitutional Act No. 9 of 18 July 1967, had proved unfruitful. Civil servants 'imbued with communist ideas' or 'carrying out anti-national propaganda' were difficult to come by; for public life had been minutely controlled for the past thirty years to ensure that such types were kept out of government. The only result had been an enormous mass of paperwork. All civil servants had to complete a long questionnaire on the associations to which they had ever belonged (some jokers wrote 'tennis club *x*', or 'boy scouts'), on their possible personal contacts with communists, on any participation in 'peace marches', on their family's place of residence, and on numerous other details of their private lives.

Constitutional Act No. 10 in August of the same year remedied these inadequacies. It lifted the tenure of civil servants for four months, later extended to six, and permitted the dismissal of any civil servant in the following cases: if his conduct was incompatible with his functions, if he was not up to his job, if he did not fulfil his duty in a satisfactory manner, if he lacked the necessary good reputation, or if he had openly been a supporter of a political party. This time the formula was comprehensive enough to satisfy the most exacting. Those in charge of the purge were no longer under an obligation to prove their case. As a final precaution, the

same law forbade the victims any recourse to appeal tribunals or
to the Council of State.

The purges began. During the winter of 1967-68 the newspapers
almost every day carried long lists of civil servants and officials
who had been dismissed. Several thousand people lost their sole
means of livelihood. The majority of these were scarcely opponents
of the regime, at least not active ones. They were frequently
wholly apolitical, but fell victim to private feuds and vendettas.
The matter reached such scandalous proportions that even newspapers unquestionably loyal to the regime protested. The junta
was obliged to back down. Papadopoulos publicly complained of
calumnious denunciations which had misled the authorities,
ordered that the victims should be informed of the reasons
for their dismissal, and reinstated a certain number. The
resulting administrative and fiscal disorder was such that at the
end of 1969 it was still not clear who exactly had been reinstated
and who not.

The charges given to the victims revealed things which would
be laughable if their consequences were less serious, for the individuals concerned as well as for the state. For example, a senior
civil servant, a family man of irreproachable morals, was stupefied
to read that he 'appeared to be homosexual', a very grave accusation under the military regime, as we shall see. A bank
employee learned that he had professed 'anti-national opinions'
fifteen years earlier. This was when, learning that a Greek-
American convention prevented his bringing a complaint against
an American whose dog had bitten him, he had exclaimed: 'So,
even American dogs now enjoy extra-territorial privileges?' Another civil servant, who had fought against the communists, saw
himself described in an official report as 'of extreme left-wing
views', without the slightest proof or explanation. A secretary in
the archaeological service found out that she had been fired
because, according to the police, 'her fiancé consorted with left-
wingers in cafés'.

There is no need to multiply these examples. Despite errors
committed at the junta's expense, for in an excess of zeal it
dismissed certain of its faithful civil servants, the real object of the
purge was achieved. Those civil servants fortunate enough to be
spared were terrified and tried to appear as humble and docile as
possible. A large number of families were made miserable, the
state was deprived of many of its most able servants, and those
who remained lost their initiative and any desire to speak openly.
Nevertheless, the junta considered it worth the price. For its
stranglehold on public life had now become complete.

press published a number of slanderous accusations against them, while the censorship prevented any kind of reply.

But they were to be hit even harder. The regime was not satisfied with destroying these judges' careers, and with smearing them because they had shown too great an attachment to legal procedures and an irritating tendency to base their decisions on the law and their own consciences. It was bent on making an example of them, by subjecting them to hardship and even to hunger, for such was the case with those who had not yet established pension rights. Thus they were not allowed to practise at the bar, the only profession for which they were qualified. The victims appealed against this ban to the Council of State. This body was in the process of considering the matter in May 1969 when the junta, rightly fearing that it would annul the measure which was as illegal as it was inhumane, rapidly promulgated a special law, to be applied retrospectively, forbidding any dismissed judge to practise at the bar.[4] The Council of State had no option but to yield before this retrospective legalisation of the ban.

This purge and the persecutions which accompanied it were not without the desired psychological effect. The remaining judges were terrified and submitted, as had the civil servants. It is quite obvious that there is no longer even the shadow of independent justice in Greece. It is hopeless to bring proceedings against anyone well regarded by the junta. Two examples will suffice.

An Athenian lawyer was called to defend someone in the provinces who, having obtained a concession from the state, was suddenly charged with embezzlement. The lawyer rapidly realised that the charge was a tissue of lies, and that his client was innocent. He told a local colleague who was to help with the defence that he was confident of obtaining a straightforward acquittal. 'O, Lord no!' exclaimed the colleague, obviously worried. 'It is obvious that someone in high places wants to see him convicted and deprived of his concession. We can do nothing. We're here only as a formality. Above all, don't tangle with the police witnesses. They would as soon as not arrest and deport you without the slightest explanation.' Incredulous, the Athenian lawyer carried on as usual and began to put embarrassing questions to the police witnesses. The moment of truth was obviously near. The president was visibly irritated and adjourned the court. Outside the prosecutor approached the Athenian lawyer and said to him with ɐ sigh, 'What are you after? We have precise instructions from K.Y.P. Don't make life any more difficult for us than it already is.' It was only after his client had been convicted that the lawyer got to the bottom of the business.

A firm in which two junta colonels had interests wanted to ruin the accused so as to get the concession itself.

The second example is similar. In the spring of 1969, wishing to show that it encouraged popular culture, the junta ordered all newspapers in the country to publish extracts from the works of a different modern Greek author each week. A list of writers had been drawn up by the cabinet, with the help of the writer Renos Apostolidis who, despite the fact that he calls himself an anarchist, collaborates with the regime. Permission from the writers included in this 'State Anthology' who were still living was not sought. Several of them protested. Lawyers representing the family of the famous novelist, Myrivilis, brought an action against one of the papers, which had announced the publication of extracts from his writings. As the law clearly forbids publication of material without the consent of its author, the case appeared to be a foregone conclusion; especially so as the newspaper's lawyers did not contest the validity of the plaintiff's arguments, but only pleaded as *force majeure* the instructions issued by the regime. The judge, terrified, said that he would give a suspended judgment. Some time later, apparently having consulted the authorities, he handed down the most shameful judgment known to Greek jurisprudence. Flatly ignoring the law, the judge declared that since the publication of a text was always advantageous to an author's reputation there was no need to gain his prior approval.

The Council of State. The Council of State is modelled on the French pattern and has existed in Greece for forty years, enjoying universal and well-deserved respect. It has included among its members a number of the country's most distinguished lawyers, and has always acted with impeccable objectivity. No government, not even the dictatorship of Metaxas, had dared to touch it. The junta, in its early days, spared it. It was not included in the purge, and it studiously continued its work, seemingly oblivious to politics. Its president, Stassinopoulos, known for his conservatism and devotion to constitutional order, had conceded along with his colleagues, that a regime established by a *coup d'état* could create its own law. What was required was to see that it was scrupulously applied.

All went well until the dismissed judges appealed to the Council of State, arguing that their dismissal was illegal. The matter was complex. Constitutional Act No. 24 forbade all recourse to the Council. The Council deliberated with due consideration and on 24 June 1969 delivered an historic judgment. This held that the Constitutional Act could prevent any challenge of the reasons for the government's dismissal of any particular judge. What it could not prevent, however, was recourse to the Council of State on the grounds that the Act was erroneously applied. The Council claimed that there was a technical flaw in the procedure, for those concerned had no chance to defend and clear themselves. Although this right was not expressly allowed by the Act, the right to defend oneself is a general unwritten principle of the law and the legislative power was bound to respect it. The dismissal of the judges was therefore declared illegal, and as such was annulled by the Council of State. The judges were automatically reinstated in their posts.

This decision had the effect of a bomb. The junta was beside itself. Disregarding his own 1968 Constitution which, like previous ones, guaranteed the independence of the Council of State, Papadopoulos on 26 June declared the judgment illegal, null and void, and publicly demanded the resignation of the President of Council, Stassinopoulos. This was refused. According to the Constitution he could not be removed from office. The junta went further. It published a decree accepting his resignation and nominated a new President. This was yet another fraudulent decree, for Stassinopoulos had never resigned. A dozen members of the Council of State resigned in protest. Since then the Council of State, the last refuge of the rule of law in Greece, has for practical purposes ceased to exist.

Lawyers. The junta's judicial policies would have been incomplete if they had not included interference in the legal profession. In fact, it employed several kinds of intimidation against those who tried to plead cases regarded unfavourably by the regime. The president of the Athens Bar Council was, as we have seen, stripped of office and deported in the very early days of the regime. All possible steps were taken to place 'sound' lawyers at the head of legal associations. Furthermore, all lawyers were subjected to an indirect pressure on their professional interests. Those who were regarded as unfriendly to the regime saw a rapid decline in their clients, who realised that with a lawyer unpopular with the authorities they would have less chance of winning their cases.

These pressures were much more direct in the military courts. The president of one of these courts was heard to remark to an over-zealous defence lawyer: 'Shut up if you don't want to find yourself in the dock.' These were not always idle threats, as will be shown later.

The most flagrant measures of oppression were taken at the time of the Council of State appeal. The three lawyers who had successfully pleaded the dismissed judges' case were arrested a few days later, and deported to mountain villages where they were kept for several months. The reason? 'They had led the Council of State astray....' At the same time, one of the men dismissed, Prosecutor Floros, was exiled for having pleaded his own case too well.

One of the exiled lawyers was George Mangakis. He is a conservative lawyer who has been the courageous defender of many political detainees of all shades of opinion, and he has taken part in most of the important political trials under the dictatorship. The regime feels a bitterness towards him that has not lessened since his deportation. Soon after his release, in November 1969, he acted once again as a defence lawyer in a political trial. He twice asked permission to reply to the crown prosecutor, and each time was refused. He then got up to leave, muttering to a colleague: 'I have no intention of playing a merely decorative role.' The presiding judge overheard him and accused him of having insulted the tribunal. He was fined on the spot. During the next trial the accused renounced their defence lawyers, 'for their own protection'. It is rare that an insult of this severity, and so well deserved, is administered to an entire judicial system.

The leaders of the junta are less stupid than one might think from their speeches. Papadopoulos, at least, does not lack political insight. He was well aware of the enormity of the Council of State affair and the arbitrary arrest of the defence lawyers, and knew that inevitably he would have to face an indignant reaction abroad. The fact that he nevertheless acted so brutally, in a manner which in itself justifies everything that has been said and written about his regime, shows that he thought it would be worth while—in order to terrorise all the judges and lawyers in Greece. He needed a judicial system like those of Hitler and Stalin, where defence lawyers outdid the prosecution in heaping abuse on their clients. He could not tolerate the residual guarantee of human rights which an even partly independent judicial system might have allowed. His policy has borne fruit. Fewer and fewer judges have the courage of their convictions, and increasingly few lawyers are prepared to risk the defence of clients accused of having 'anti-national' opinions.[5]

4. EDUCATION

' The revolution does not look to the past, but seeks to snatch the future of youth from the sins of the past and to lead it towards a future that is positive and full of hope.'

Papadopoulos

The junta often claims that it attaches the greatest importance to education. For once it is telling the truth. For it counts on education and the regimentation of the young to create a solid foundation for its future power.

The colonels instinctively distrust intellectuals, who often display an inconvenient attitude of scepticism. 'We don't have all that much need of educated people', Papadopoulos is said to have declared privately. The dictatorship's educational policies are in keeping with this view. The period of compulsory schooling, for instance, has been lowered from nine to six years, while the number of students entering higher education fell from 19,000 to about 11,000 between 1967 and 1969.

Apart from these general measures, the regime has taken specific steps to exclude the politically undesirable from higher education, to condition young people, at all educational levels, to support the extreme right, and to apply political pressure on parents through the schools.

Exclusion from higher education. In 1967 the junta decreed that in future a certificate of 'civic reliability' would be required for admission to the universities and other institutions of higher education. This was a simple and undisguised device for excluding young people whom the police thought might be tainted with subversive ideas.

This system of selection, however, generated ill-will without being sufficiently effective, and was abandoned the following year. For the police rarely had time to keep tabs on the opinions of schoolchildren of 18. They began to employ more subtle methods. For instance, according to reliable reports, entrance exam results are scrutinised and when necessary fixed by the police before being made public. Undesirable candidates can be made out to have failed, while a boost can be given to 'right-thinking' candidates with low marks, be they police spies or simply the children of officers. This is aimed at raising 'the moral and patriotic tone of the student body'. The same type of thinking lay behind Law No. 40 of 1967, which was to be put into force by decree.[1] This laid down that, in future, 10 per cent of admissions to higher education would be made on the strength of school testimonials as to the candidate's 'morality and character' with no competitive examination. Considering the competition for university places (in 1969 there were five times more candidates than places), to be spared a competitive examination would be a considerable lure, and one which would encourage school pupils to demonstrate their enthusiasm for the regime.

But most of the effort to get rid of undesirables took place at the universities themselves rather than by controlling entry. For a start, the most important student body, the centrist National

Union of Greek Students, was dissolved and then reconstituted under the supervision of the police, who nominated its new officers. This was followed by a number of preventive as well as repressive measures to ensure that students conform.

Prevention is in part assured by the extraordinary degree of police surveillance in the universities. The police have a university branch on each campus which is concerned only with security. These branches each have a number of young policemen who dress in plain clothes like ordinary students, and share as much as possible in the studies and leisure activities of their fellow-students —and then go away and report on them. This also used to happen before the junta seized power, with the difference that police spies then could only observe and report, and had no power over students as long as they did not break the law. The police also expend a great deal of effort in recruiting bona-fide students as informers through various kinds of blackmail. Holders of state scholarships from poor families, for example, are faced with the choice of spying or losing their grants. Obviously the police try to attract as little attention to themselves as possible. But they do not hesitate to show themselves when necessary, for example to stifle an incipient demonstration against the dictatorship, however harmless it may be. Two typical instances occurred in the University of Athens' Faculty of Law during the winter of 1968-69. The first took place on the day that George Papandreou's death was announced. Then, at the suggestion of two students, the entire lecture theatre stood up and observed a minute's silence, and there were then shouts of 'Everyone to the funeral'. The second took place when Professor George Mangakis spoke of the relationship between the law and freedom at his farewell lecture. His students applauded him and after he left noisily protested against his dismissal. In both these instances about ten 'police-students' hurried to silence the speakers, to disconnect the loud-speakers, and to note the names of the ringleaders, who were later arrested by the ordinary police.

The purge of university teachers can also be considered a preventive measure. For teachers often have a considerable influence on their pupils, a phenomenon not unknown even at the Army Cadet College. If students are to become docile citizens, with a proper respect for military rank, they must be kept away from any contact with teachers who might put other ideas into their heads. And older teachers are in general less malleable than the young, for they fear less for their careers, which in any case are often nearly over. Again, it could be awkward if faculties were to elect their own professors freely, basing their decision on purely academic grounds, for a candidate might easily be well qualified without holding 'healthy social opinions', which under the new order are so much more important than competence.

The junta's policy with regard to university appointments seems to be based on such considerations. About sixty university teachers were dismissed in a single stroke by means of Constitutional Acts 9 and 10 (the same that were used against civil servants). For the most part the victims were well-known scholars, men of integrity who had made the mistake of being considered liberals. There was no question of their being communists or even fellow-travellers, for a certificate of 'civic reliability' had for decades been mandatory for any university post. The police granted these certificates only after a minute examination of the candidate's past and of all his possible political activities and affiliations. The best indication of the quality of those teachers dismissed in this way is that many of them promptly received offers of jobs in French, English, and German universities. The junta in many cases refused them passports (although some were granted passports in 1970). Nor was there any way in which they could reply to the slanderous accusations made against them, which included 'unacceptable political activities', 'a domèstic situation inconsistent with good morals', etc. Needless to say there was no right of appeal to the Council of State. And in order to prevent spontaneous demonstrations of sympathy by students towards their dismissed teachers, some of these were even forbidden to set foot in their university or to work in the university library. A dozen or so of the victims were reinstated after participating in a humiliating appeals procedure; an almost equal number of teachers were dismissed later, or resigned in sympathy with their colleagues.

The upper age-limit for professors was lowered from 70 to 65. This led to the immediate retirement of several dozen. It is true that among these were a number of regime supporters as well as its opponents and some who were politically uncommitted. But it was to the overall advantage of the junta, which was able to ensure that all new appointees were their supporters. Constitutional Act No. 28 of September 1968 gave the government the right to intervene in the selection of professors, either by refusing to confirm the faculty's choice, or in certain cases by itself directly appointing to a chair.

In all, the universities lost about a third of their teaching staff. It is not difficult to picture the harm this did to the efficiency of higher education in Greece.

To ensure that its policies in higher education are carried out the junta has created the post of 'government commissar', with powers as wide as they are menacing to what remains of academic freedom. The commissar takes part in all meetings of the University Senate, and of the faculties, and has access to all documents including university correspondence. All these commissars are military men. They play the same role, in effect, as Soviet commissars—with the important difference that in the U.S.S.R. they are civilians who watch over, among other things, the army, while in Greece the reverse is the case.

We now come to the repression of student agitation. As it apparently considered that martial law and Law No. 509 were inadequate to deal with student opposition, the junta issued Decree Law 93, called the 'Student Code' in January 1969. This provides that any student convicted in the courts for a political offence is not only to be sent down from his university but may also be permanently excluded from any further chance of higher education. The same penalties apply to any student deported by administrative order. Furthermore, a student can be expelled if 'his conduct and his ideas are incompatible with "national ideals"'. Given that the regime identifies itself with the nation and with national ideals, it necessarily follows that any student who expresses opposition to the junta is liable to be unable to continue his studies. These sanctions have already been imposed on several dozen imprisoned or exiled students. This has led to a virtual reign of terror in the universities, the more oppressive as the disciplinary boards charged with enforcing these sanctions are no longer composed, as was the case before the coup, of professors nominated by the faculties. They are now manned by professors chosen by the government for their pliability, plus the government commissar. It is difficult to imagine these boards refusing to obey a police request to expel a student for having 'anti-national ideas'. In some cases students have been expelled under this law without being heard by the disciplinary board, in contravention of the regime's own law.

University studies were already dependent to a considerable degree on police good-will even before this law was passed. The police, for example, from time to time sadistically arrested opposition students on the eve of their exams, only to release them just afterwards. But from now on, the police will have much more power, and will be able to decide the futures and the careers of all young Greeks aspiring to higher education.

Indoctrination. The indoctrination of young people is actively pursued in the universities. It is carried on by the more obsequious professors, who agree to the authorities' request to give lectures on the ideals of the 'National Revolution'. They also preach the gospel of the 'National Revolution' in the countryside, accompanied by groups of pro-regime students. However, most of the indoctrination effort is aimed at primary and secondary education.

Here, too, the teaching personnel underwent a brutal purge. More than 250 teachers were dismissed from state schools, together with some fifty officials from the Ministry of Education. As was the case with other civil servants, a number of these were later reinstated. Nor were teachers in private schools spared. There could be no official purge in their case for they were not state employees. The authorities contented themselves with requiring these schools to dismiss those regarded as undesirable by the security police. There was no way of refusing such demands, for private schools could operate only with a licence from the ministry, and were thus subject to its strict control. The number of victims of this 'unofficial' purge is not known.

For the first time since 1930, the purist language, which is closely bound up with reactionary attitudes, was introduced into primary education. Children of 6 to 9 are taught in the demotic language, which is described by Law No. 129 of 1967 as the 'mother tongue', while the purist language is described as 'Greek'. This amounts to saying that the mother tongue of the Greeks is not Greek! From the age of 9, schoolchildren must set about learning a different grammar and a different syntax, in fact a language which no one speaks, not even the colonels among themselves. The confusion which this creates is indescribable, and, of course, greatly impairs the children's capacity to absorb more useful knowledge. Not only will new school textbooks be written in the purist language, but it must be used for all classroom teaching. Headmasters and school inspectors are instructed to see that this is done. Since almost all the classics of modern Greek literature, including the national anthem, Solomos' *Hymn to Liberty*, are written in the demotic, one result of the regime's linguistic policy is that some of these writings have had to be 'purified' for inclusion in school anthologies.

School textbooks have been rewritten, not only to change their language but also their content. There is now even more emphasis than in the past on the very narrowest sort of nationalism and the most bigoted piety. Compulsory religious instruction has also been increased. The new textbooks on history and civics lay considerable emphasis on the cult of the army, which 'saved the country on 21 April 1967': children of 11 or 12 years are told how the political parties had led the country to the brink of the abyss and how, at the very moment the wicked communists were preparing themselves to destroy it, the good officers seized the initiative. All schoolbooks are adorned with a splendid portrait of Papadopoulos.

The teaching of civics bears no relation to what was taught before, when the stress was on the basic rights of the citizen in a democracy. Now the stress is on patriotic duties, and among these loyalty to the 'National Revolution' figures prominently. The 'thoughts' of Papadopoulos also form a part of the civics curriculum. His published words (six volumes so far) are distributed to schools, and teachers are instructed to expound on choice morsels from them and to set extracts as essay subjects. (An order of the Ministry of Education, in 1971, expressly forbids teachers to give essay subjects other than those recommended by it.)

The regime is well aware that in the villages and small towns teachers are held in particular esteem because of their education. For this reason they are required to make speeches in favour of the regime—and woe betide anyone who refuses. A grammar-school teacher in the provinces retorted, almost weeping with shame, to those who reproached him for lending himself to these indignities: 'What could I do? I received precise orders, and a prepared speech, as my last one was considered too lukewarm. The gendarmerie sent a man to spy on me, to see that I left nothing out. . . . They had their eye on me. If I were to be sacked I would have no other means of earning a living.'

Informing is also encouraged among schoolchildren. A typical incident took place in Thessaloniki in 1969. A 14-year-old girl told her classmates the latest anti-regime joke. Another girl repeated it to her father, an officer. This resulted in the first girl's being expelled, and it was only with great difficulty that the punishment was limited to this, instead of entailing a ban from every school in the country, as was originally intended.

This regimentation of young people reaches a peak when the dictator is to make a speech. In the spring of 1969 the pupils in the top three classes of Athenian grammar schools were assembled in the Stadium, where Papadopoulos was to speak to them. Teachers were held responsible for the compulsory presence of all their pupils, except those excused on the basis of a medical certificate signed by *two* doctors. The children were shepherded by hundreds of plain-clothes police, who saw that they applauded at the appropriate times. This, however, did not prevent whistling and booing. The following day the press described in glowing terms the spontaneous enthusiasm which had greeted Papadopoulos.

It is scarcely necessary to add that all critical and rational thought is debarred from all levels of education. The police maintain a close watch on all university seminars where discussion takes place. Students who have a tendency to express personal opinions are 'recommended' by the police 'for their own good' to avoid drawing too much attention to themselves. University professors have been ordered to publish all their lectures. For the regime does not consider the university to be an institution where one learns to learn, but rather as a somewhat advanced school, where a fixed sum of knowledge, contained in one book, is dictated by the teacher to the student. The same kind of thinking lies behind the authorities' disapproval of book lists which contain foreign titles. For subversive works may lurk in these, despite the instructions issued to those in charge of departmental libraries to purge all 'leftist' books.

The regime's conception of the role of the universities does not stop there, however. The junta does not like thinking citizens, or even thinking scholars. What it does want is gullible technocrats. A quotation of Papadopoulos' neatly illustrates this. Speaking at the University of Thessaloniki on 5 January 1968, he invited the academic staff to 'mobilise itself in the service of the rebirth of the Greek spirit'. What he meant by this piece of bombast became clear in the sentences that followed: 'The university must become the church of the spiritual development of the nation. Teachers must abandon their role as researchers, as instructors who pass on specialised knowledge. They must guide the nation . . . the moral order must become once again the guiding thought, the framework of human life. We must return to the mentality which preceded the violation of the moral and social order.' From this verbiage, which is reminiscent of that of the fascist dictators of the 'thirties, the essential message stands out: 'teachers must abandon their role as researchers . . .'. The picture is clear. The university should no longer cultivate the sciences and humanities, but should put itself at the head of a politico-religious crusade for a new kind of uniformed noble savage.

Education as a means of pressure. We have seen (p. 48) that in 1964-65 the government had initiated a programme aimed at improving the nutritional level of schoolchildren. These free school meals were abolished by the junta and replaced by an allowance given only to *poor* families with school-age children.

The disadvantages of this new system are obvious. To start with, parents who are poor but too proud to submit to a means test are excluded from benefit. Moreover, there is no guarantee that those parents who do get the allowance will use it to improve their children's diet, not necessarily out of ill-will, but for practical reasons. When parents leave at dawn for the fields and the child leaves for school, possibly several kilometres away, how can they feed the child during the day?

At first one is tempted to think that the only reason the junta abolished school meals is that they were the work of the Centre Union. But perhaps there is another motive. The allowance system could serve as a means of political blackmail as it is the local gendarmerie which certifies poverty. This puts them in a position to reward 'right thinkers' and to punish the rest.

Another aspect of education which is exploited by the police is higher education abroad. The authorities refuse passports, or foreign exchange, or both, to any student who incurs their displeasure for political reasons. Even worse, young people who have begun their studies abroad and return to Greece for the vacations can have their passports confiscated, either permanently or temporarily, because they have spoken out against the regime abroad in the presence of one of the numerous spies which the Greek police maintain in other countries. In some cases they are told that their passports will be given back, and they will be given pocket money as well, if they will report on anti-regime Greeks in their respective universities. It is for this reason that a number of opposition Greeks, who have been able to send their children to study abroad, dare not allow them to return for the vacations and prefer not to see them for years on end rather than risk police blackmail.

There are a few further facts, chosen at random, which help to round off this portrait of Greek education. Dismissed teachers are not authorised to teach, even privately. They must seek other work. Many university teachers are not allowed to travel abroad, even to attend conferences. Headmasters of state schools have been ordered to spy on the activities of their staff both within and outside school. A candidate for a university chair was refused the necessary certificate of 'civic reliability' by the police. When he surprisedly pointed out that he had never been a leftist he received the reply: 'Today it is no longer enough not to be against us. You must be actively for us. Will you make speeches for us in the villages when told to? No? Ah well, that's why you are not going to get the certificate.'

5. THE CONTROL OF INFORMATION

'Our newspapers are free to write the truth.'
Pattakos

Radio and television in Greece had always been strictly controlled by the government and could scarcely lay claim to an objectivity of the B.B.C. type. Nevertheless this state control, even if partisan, never entailed the suppression of all dissident voices, of all embarrassing truth, of all untrammelled discussion on intellectual subjects. After the coup, however, radio and television came under the immediate control of army officers placed in the broadcasting services, which have simply become instruments of a propaganda machine as intolerant, and as intolerable, as those of other totalitarian countries. Not content with singing their own praises from morning till night, the colonels have imposed their own opinions and standards in intellectual and artistic matters. The result has to be seen to be believed. As far as the intellectual level goes, one example among many will suffice. In 1967 an official of the broadcasting service was dismissed for having proposed a broadcast on Claudel, containing passages from his work which were judged 'obscene' by the officer in charge. In contrast programmes glorifying the armed forces, the police and the gendarmerie are legion, the intervals between them being filled with the most stupefying kind of light music. Not the songs of the Greek *nouvelle vague*, many of which are of high quality and thought provoking, but cliché-ridden so-called 'popular' songs.

Gramophone records are also subject to censorship. Any song considered subversive is forbidden. In the case of the celebrated left-wing composer Theodorakis, the junta went even further in banning every single one of his works, even those innocent of any political or social connotations. His records cannot be played in public, written about in the press, or bought. Realising that a black market could grow up, the authorities excelled themselves in arbitrariness, and ordered the destruction of the entire existing stock of 70,000 records held by the manufacturer.

The theatre is also subject to preventive censorship. Nothing can be performed which is remotely 'left wing', or which 'undermines the healthy morals and customs of the Greek people', in the words of a circular issued by the Ministry to the Prime Minister, dated 30 May 1967. This was based on a law first passed under the Nazi occupation and which had subsequently fallen into disuse. The censors have the right to suppress or to modify passages in any proposed play, as well as to ban entire plays if these, as the same circular puts it, 'propagate subversive theories', 'are defamatory of our country as a nation and are harmful to tourism', 'cast a slur on the Christian religion', 'insult the King, the royal family or the government', 'exercise a bad influence on youth', or 'are capable of warping the aesthetic development of the people'. This circular was sent to all the theatres in the country, signed by Papadopoulos in person.

Classical authors are not exempted from these controls. Plays of Sophocles and Aristophanes were deleted from the repertoire of the National Theatre in 1967, either because they contained passages which could be considered subversive, which was the view of certain opposition circles, or because the accompanying music was by Theodorakis, the official and more plausible view.

The cinema is subject to equally rigorous surveillance. Films which dwell on revolutions or popular uprisings, of whatever period, are not looked upon kindly. A revival of 'Juarez', set during the Mexican revolution against Maximilian, was banned. The censor, Colonel Papapoulos (whose notorious solecisms have delighted newspaper readers ever since, as public prosecutor in the ASPIDA trial, he tried his best to express himself in purist Greek), has ordered Greek film producers to keep to innocent, sentimental subjects, preferably chaste love-stories ending in a church marriage. 'You know the sort of thing, a poor young man who loves a rich young woman, who ends up by loving him too. . . . I like this sort of film', he added with a tender sigh, 'because I myself was once poor.' The country's two best film directors, Kakoyannis and Koundouros, unable to follow the Greek cinema towards these dizzy heights, have preferred to go into voluntary exile.

Lectures on literary and other topics had to be submitted in advance to the censorship authorities. A poet who intended to read his works in public was invited to find substitutes for two shocking words: the adjective 'red' (referring to lips), and the noun 'dawn' (which was the name of the E.D.A. newspaper *Avghi*). Having reworked the two suspect poems so as to avoid these dangerous expressions, the poet could then read his works in perfect freedom. Two plain-clothes policemen, however, attended the reading with the agreed text in hand to ensure that it was adhered to.

In 1967 an index of banned books was issued by the censors. Works included in it could not be displayed, sold or even talked about. This list included individual works considered to be 'left-wing', the complete works of certain 'subversive' authors, regardless of content (as for example Ritsos' poetry and Vassilikos' novels), and a number of works included for reasons that are not immediately apparent. Among these were a Greek-Bulgarian dictionary, a Russian grammar, and a translation of Tolstoy's life of Peter the Great. (The index as such was rescinded in 1970. Booksellers are now free to sell the books formerly listed *at their own risk*, for some may still contravene the Press Law. Addendum 1971.) New books were also subject to preventive censorship by the police, who showed great vigilance. For example, the somewhat anti-papal sentiments expressed in a translation of Stendhal's *Cenci* gave offence. These irreverent passages were excised. The editor of a world goegraphy thought he had acted prudently in listing as the 'dominant religions' of China the traditional ones: Taoism, Buddhism, and Confucianism. To his utter amazement the entire paragraph was struck out by the censor, a gendarmerie lieutenant, who proceeded to explain: 'Taoism, philosophies . . . all this kind of thing leads to anarchy'. A critical study of modern Greek literature was approved only on condition that its author, a very conservative academician, cut out the chapter devoted to George Theotokas, one of the most important Greek writers of recent times, who died in 1966. This was because Theotokas, who did not even figure in the colonels' index, was known for his liberal opinions.

All this applies only to books in Greek. For reasons which we shall examine, the sale of non-Greek books was absolutely unrestricted. The complete works of Marx, Lenin, or Guevara in English, French, or German have always been freely available in any good bookshop in Athens.

Periodicals did not find the going easy. The censors began by intervening in questions of language. They insisted, for instance, that a school magazine tone down its 'demotic' style. One of the most respected law journals had serious trouble over printing the Council of State decree concerning the expropriation of land required for military use. 'You cannot publish secrets concerning national security,' muttered a suspicious censor. 'How did you find out about it?' The editor, already imagining himself in prison, needed all his eloquence to persuade his questioner that judicial decisions were in the public domain. The editor of an economic journal was less successful. Anxious to flatter the junta on its self-proclaimed anti-inflationary policies (see p. 106), he had prepared an article on the decline of currency in circulation, but the censor forbade it: 'Under the National Government nothing decreases—everything increases.'

The daily press suffered most heavily from censorship. The Greek press had a long tradition of freedom, coupled with a reputation for trenchant criticism, partisanship, and biting cartoons. All this disappeared overnight. The left-wing *Avghi* was banned. Three important dailies, two of the right and one of the centre, closed down rather than submit to censorship. Only two of those that did publish actually supported the dictatorship: *Estia*, a straightforwardly fascist newspaper with a very limited circulation, and *Eleftheros Kosmos*, founded several months previously, in apparent anticipation of the putsch, by a personal friend of

Papadopoulos, the former Communist Savvas Konstantopoulos. Later a third, *Nea Politeia*, was started by supporters of the regime. These three dailies supported the regime unconditionally and were occasionally allowed to indulge in muted criticism of minor administrative details, of the kind even *Pravda* is allowed to make. Other papers were uniformly drab and boring. There was not the slightest difference between *Vima*, formerly of pronounced centrist views, and *Akropolis*, a monarchist daily of pronounced right-wing views. All published exactly the same controlled information, the same government communiqués. All were subject to the same taboos, and employed the same adjectives to describe the 'delirious enthusiasm' of any meeting where one of the colonels had shown himself. The total circulation of the daily press fell considerably.

The censorship often had comic results. Newspapers could not so much as mention the names of pre-coup politicians, even if it was only to say that they had attended an embassy reception. From time to time they were forbidden to publish certain laws, for example those which authorised salary increases for ministers and officers, although they had in fact already been published in the Official Gazette. For a long time no mention of political trials was allowed. Officially the regime did not recognise the existence of a resistance. Even bombings, at a time when Athens shook almost daily with explosions, were taboo, except when the censors insisted on a statement vilifying the 'cowardly terrorists' whose previous misdeeds had been ignored. Newspapers frequently published, on instructions, the government reply to an attack by some opponent of the regime. But the newspapers did not have the right to publish the original attack so that the form this had taken had to be deduced from the reply, much as early anti-Christian polemics are known to us only in so far as they are referred to by the Fathers of the Church. The censors by no means concerned themselves only with the political and economic sections of newspapers. They scrutinised everything, including advertisements and the literary pages. A critic was forbidden to mention the name of Sikelianos, one of the greatest poets of modern Greece, who had died fifteen years before. 'He was a man of the left,' said the censor. The critic got around this by writing about the 'poet of *Alafroiskiotos*; the title of one of Sikelianos' major poems—thus making clear to any reader of even average education, though not to the censors, whom he was talking about. In the pages and advertisements devoted to the cinema, it was forbidden for a time to mention foreign cinema directors or actors, such as Alain Resnais and Rex Harrison who had signed appeals on behalf of the victims of the Greek dictatorship.

The censorship extended to world news. Events in Vietnam could never be presented in a way that showed the United States in an unfavourable light. In September 1969, for instance, newspapers were forbidden to dwell on the murders committed by the Green Berets. When the U.S. Ambassador to Greece left at the beginning of 1969, a cartoon depicted two Greeks who were saying to him 'Remember us to the Statue of Liberty'. The cartoon was forbidden by the censor. News of demonstrations for freedom were not always treated in the same way. They were played up if they had taken place in Prague, but played down if they had taken place in Madrid.

However, the censors did not interpret their role in a wholly negative way. Government services forced newspapers to publish at length pre-written articles. These were sometimes signed by some paid hack of the junta, sometimes they arrived with instructions that they should appear as an editorial. Not so much as a comma could be changed in these texts, which either praised the activities of the government or attacked 'anti-national' elements. Even the make-up of the paper was controlled by the propaganda services. The censors insisted that large chunks of the colonels' speeches, together with their photographs be published. Much publicity was, of course, given to the few compliments paid the regime abroad; but unflattering remarks, which were much more common, could not, needless to say, be printed. The official propagandists had no scruples about taking a single flattering phrase out of a clearly hostile context and displaying it prominently. If a British provincial newspaper, for instance, were to criticise the colonels' regime vigorously but claim that the Greek economy was improving, the Greek newspapers would trumpet that 'the British press admires the progress made by the national government'.

After two and a half years preventive censorship was abolished and in November 1969 the junta announced, with appropriate publicity, the restoration of press freedom. True, this freedom was hedged about with a number of ominous restrictions concerning public order and national security. Nothing could be published which might 'undermine the economy' or 'revive partisan passions'. Offences of this sort continued to be within the jurisdiction of military courts. Despite all this, for a week or two there was a true press renaissance, an 'Athens spring' for newspapers and their readers. Once free of the need to submit their copy in advance, newspapers showed considerable ingenuity in criticising the junta while apparently staying within the bounds of the new laws. For an amused and excited public the word of the day was 'Did you see the cartoon in *Nea* today! Sensational! Did you notice that headline in yesterday's *Ethnos*?' This might have been a headline reading 'We are fighting for democracy!', with a much smaller subtitle, 'says Chancellor Brandt'. Without some knowledge of the existing situation it is impossible to appreciate what this very modest freedom meant to readers. Foreign news benefited most from the new law. For the first time liberal dailies could publish details of the massacres in Vietnam, and of the American peace marches. One of them was able to serialise J. K. Galbraith's satire, *The Triumph*, which had previously been banned. The circulation of liberal newspapers, which began to take on some of their former individuality, shot up.

The colonels did not find all this to their taste. Pro-regime newspapers railed against journalists 'who had learnt nothing and who had reverted to their bad old ways'. Pattakos in a press conference thundered that he regretted the abolition of censorship. The authorities were particularly nettled by the publication in the press of protests by bishops against the illegality of Ieronymos Kotsonis' elevation to the archiepiscopal throne two years before. For the first time the true extent of this ecclesiastical scandal became apparent, through the courage of dissident prelates. It was obvious that the junta had underestimated the degree to which its opponents would dare to exploit this quasi-freedom of the press. The regime was even more furious because none of the barbed criticism could be punished in the courts, even under their own legal code. They eventually discovered a way, almost brilliant in its simplicity, of ridding themselves of embarrassing newspapers without at the same time having to arrest journalists, which would have been bad for their image abroad. They unofficially banned their sale throughout the country, except in the centre of the capital and in Thessaloniki. The police and gendarmerie passed on the order, by word of mouth, to all newspaper sellers, and made sure that it was carried out. The system was simple. The police ascertained that a particular newspaper seller received, say, forty copies of *Vima* and thirty of *Ethnos* every morning. He was ordered to tell anyone asking for a copy that there were none left, and in the evening the copies were carefully counted to make sure that he still had the same number as he received. No newspaper seller, of course, dared to infringe such an order. If he did the very least that would happen was that he would lose his licence. But most vendors let those customers they knew in on the secret, and the news immediately got around.

Pattakos denied that this policy of intimidation had the government's blessing, and had the effrontery to declare that if liberal papers failed to sell it was because they did not attract readers. With greater frankness, another minister told a Western diplomat: 'What would you have us do, when the papers publish inflammatory material of this kind? Wouldn't your own government do the same in a similar situation—try to limit their circulation?' This tactic enabled the junta to kill two birds with one stone: it gradually weakened opposition papers while helping pro-regime ones.[1] Pro-regime papers had suffered a serious decline in circulation during the short 'spring' and complained bitterly that their loyalty was so poorly rewarded. Now things got better for them, for the principal newspapers which were actually on sale in the provinces were, inevitably, *Eleftheros Kosmos* and *Nea Politeia*.

The armed forces also played their part in this campaign. In each unit, orders were given to officers and soldiers that in future they were not to touch 'wrong-thinking' papers. They were also recommended to advise their relatives and friends similarly.

(This coercive system was abandoned after March 1970, the heavy sentences passed on the owners and writers of *Ethnos* having proved a sufficient deterrent. See introduction, pp. 2-3.)

In a further move to limit foreign news coverage, the government-controlled Athens News Agency has signed agreements with most of the large foreign news agencies. These guarantee it the exclusive right to distribute their news despatches in Greece. This means that Greek newspapers no longer have direct access to news from Reuters or the Agence France Presse, but must draw on them via the Athens News Agency, which is free to suppress anything displeasing to the authorities. Only a large American agency has, to date, refused to sign a similar exclusive contract.

We have seen that foreign books sell freely. The same is true of the foreign newspapers even when they contain material critical of the regime, with the exception of the communist papers. This apparently liberal approach, which contrasts with the practice in Eastern Europe, can favourably impress the casual visitor.

In fact, it is less a matter of liberalism than one of astute calculation. The regime realises that to ban foreign books and papers would be a deterrent to the tourists which the country so badly needs. But by allowing them in, the regime is able to present a façade of liberalism at no great cost to itself, and this for two reasons.

In the first place the number of Greeks who have access to foreign publications, who can both buy them and read them, is limited in practice to a few thousand people in the large towns. These people form an intellectual and social group which, almost by definition, is wholly opposed to the regime. It is not these people that the junta hopes to win over, but the peasants and semi-educated petty bourgeoisie. This is borne out by the fact that there is one category of foreign newspaper whose import into Greece is strictly embargoed: the Cypriot papers. These, being in Greek, could contain material damaging to the junta which would be widely accessible.

The second and perhaps more important reason is that, with or without foreign newspapers, the great mass of Greeks can find out what is happening by tuning in to the Greek-language programmes of a number of foreign radio stations. The fervour with which these broadcasts are listened to can only be appreciated by those who have been similarly deprived of free information. Even in the smallest villages, people rely on transistor radios to listen to London, Moscow, Paris, and especially *Deutsche Welle* in Cologne, whose Greek transmissions are by far the most outspoken and critical of the dictatorship. At the times of these broadcasts the streets and coffee houses of villages empty. The following morning one of the main subjects of conversation is 'Cologne said yesterday that . . .' and 'London confirms . . .'. In this way the statements of those in opposition, those in exile, and of the resistance organisations are made widely known. It is also thanks to these broadcasts that the arrests of Greeks who are held incommunicado by the authorities are publicised.

The contribution that these broadcasts make to the maintenance of morale should not be underestimated. For thanks to them, not only do the Greek people learn what is kept from them by their present rulers, but they also feel less isolated morally, less betrayed by the outside world. In the present struggle in Greece for freedom and human dignity, these broadcasts play a role comparable to that of the B.B.C. during the Nazi occupation.

A word in conclusion on the transmission of information from Greece. Foreign correspondents are not subject to censorship, but their freedom of action is no less seriously inhibited by the threat of expulsion which constantly hangs over them. It is not an idle threat. Several foreign journalists have already been expelled, beginning with Leslie Finer, for many years correspondent for the B.B.C. and the *Observer*, who had the courage to report what he saw and what he thought. Not all of his colleagues are equally courageous. Even if they do not allow themselves to be bought (which is not in fact unknown, and the whole of Athens could name certain individuals always ready to sign anything the regime's propaganda services dictate to them), they measure their words. This is a weakness quite understandable among men who are not anxious to be thrown out of a country to which they have become acclimatised, or where they sometimes have family ties. It is only special correspondents, those who come for a few days or weeks and are immune to sanctions, who are in a position to write the whole truth, provided they are not suborned by the princely hospitality that the colonels are always ready to offer them at the taxpayer's expense.

6. GOVERNMENT AND THE NEW RULING CASTE

'Beware of an excessive lust for goods.'
Papadopoulos

A classic argument for dictatorships is that they are more efficient than parliamentary democracies. Hitler for instance solved the unemployment problem in Germany, through re-armament, while Mussolini made the trains run on time. How does the Greek dictatorship fare in this respect?

As early as 1967, Prime Minister Kollias pronounced that 'Bureaucracy is henceforth abolished'. By this he meant bureaucratic delay. Powerful memos were circularised enjoining civil servants to answer all queries from private citizens within a fortnight, under pain of the most terrible sanctions. The naïve were delighted. It took some time to realise that the bureaucratic structure, not being designed for speed, was nearly collapsing. Panic-stricken civil servants answered queries with any kind of absurdity rather than be accused of delay. The administration would have ended up turning somersaults in the air if its old instinct for inertia, or to put it another way, for survival, had not gradually gained the upper hand. By the end of the second month things were more or less back to where they had been before.

But not exactly to where they were before. The purges, the denunciations, the fear of taking responsibility had taken their toll. Political matters, now called 'security questions', cropped up in the most unlikely quarters. An engineer who had submitted a technical study to a ministry waited several months for a commission to carry out the project, for which he was the most highly qualified Greek specialist. Finally he learned that a rival firm, enjoying the protection of a colonel, had denounced him as a communist, which of course meant that he could not work for the state. Fortunately for him, the engineer in question was such an obvious conservative that the accusation could not be made to stick, but seven months had been lost meanwhile.

Apart from its dilatoriness, Greek bureaucracy had always

suffered from two evils: favouritism and, to a lesser degree, corruption. The junta has tried to put the blame for both on the parliamentary system and the old political world, although it has not yet been able to uncover a serious scandal that can be pinned on the latter. The fact is that a free press and a Parliament in themselves constituted useful checks, and if they did not always prevent dubious transactions they did at least limit their extent.

Now that there is no control whatsoever, favouritism knows no bounds. True, it is no longer exercised on behalf of deputies, but for officers and their protégés. It is difficult to see, however, how the taxpayer benefits from the change. As for corruption, its present level astonished even a big shipowner living abroad who came to Greece for business reasons, a man who was used to this sort of thing since he also does business with the Congo and Santo Domingo. 'I have never seen anything like it,' he confided to a Greek friend in November 1969. To appreciate the new business climate, it is sufficient to note that major contracts concerning public works and industrial investments are no longer put out to tender. Now it is ministers, or rather the colonels' secretaries-general in the ministries, who make the decision in 'the light of the national interest'.[1] At the end of 1969, a group of three unknown businessmen with virtually no capital obtained the exclusive concession for a car factory to the value of 110 million dollars; they were then free to resell this privilege to the highest foreign bidder. Even the newspaper *Estia*, although a devoted supporter of the regime, on this occasion protested that 'similar things could not have happened even under the corrupt regime of the past, because there would have been questions in Parliament'.

Greece has become a happy hunting-ground for dubious speculators of every nationality. Even the Cosa Nostra has managed to open a casino in Athens. This will be closed down shortly, but only because another group, patronised by one of the most influential members of the junta, wants the concession for itself. Large foreign firms battle to obtain fabulous concessions, staking their hopes on one or another of the 'in' figures of the day. The giants Onassis and Niarchos, formerly brothers-in-law and now arch rivals, fill the pages of foreign financial newspapers with their duel to acquire a petrol refinery. Twice ministers have been appointed or fired through involvement in this fight, which at the moment is still going on.[2]

In other fields, the junta has tried to promote a progressive image. It greatly publicised an increase in workers' wages which in no way differed from those regularly granted in the past, every two or three years, as the gross national product has risen. It has also given a great deal of publicity to the abolition of agricultural debts, which in fact has mainly benefited those with large holdings who were behind in their loan repayments. The seven and a half billion drachmas which this cost would have been better employed in improving roads, irrigation, etc., which would have benefited *all* farmers.

However, we must be objective. There are matters which the dictatorship has dealt with effectively. One of these is to increase the number of taxis in Athens and also the number of bus stops. It has also regulated the status of a number of temporary civil servants. It is in these areas that the colonels' government has achieved its most imposing successes.

The Roman Empire was supposed to have kept its subjects happy with bread and circuses. We have seen what the Greek censorship has been able to offer in the way of entertainment. As for bread, in other words the economy, the junta seems well pleased with itself. 'We have revived the economy, which was suffering from a morbid depression,' declared Papadopoulos in 1967. Let us look more closely at this miraculous cure.

During the years 1962-1966 (years of morbid depression, democratic chaos, anarchy, etc.) the real national income per head of the population had grown by an average of 7·1 per cent, one of the highest rates in the world. In 1967-68 this percentage fell to 3·6.[3] At the same time, the rate of increase of industrial production fell from 10·3 to 5 per cent, that of consumption from 6·2 to 5 per cent, and that of investment from 17·2 to 5·3 per cent. Expansion was slowed down by the fear and uncertainty created by the very military coup that was supposed to reassure the country about its future. Trying to stimulate demand to get the economy moving again, and at the same time to pander to the consumer, the government was prodigal with advances, mortgage facilities, wage and salary increases, and budgetary expenditure of all kinds. The total supply of money, currency, and current account deposits, has risen very rapidly. It represented 34·6 per cent of the national income in 1966, and rose to 42·1 per cent in 1969. The result of this policy has been an extreme monetary liquidity, which makes the present apparent stability highly precarious.[4] The least doubt as to the future of the drachma could unleash a galloping inflation.[5]

It was only thanks to this dangerously inflationary policy that the economy finally began in 1969, to expand at a rate approaching that of the years preceding the putsch.

The balance of payments situation, for long the weak point of the Greek economy, has become much worse under the present regime. It is true that the rate of increase in imports slowed during the relative depression in the years 1967-68. But the advantage to the balance of payments from this slow-down was more than cancelled out by other factors.

The annual rate of increase in exports, which attained an average of 13·7 per cent between 1962 and 1966, fell to 6·8 per cent in 1967-68. Receipts from tourism, which were formerly increasing at the rate of 25-30 per cent per annum, fell from 143 million dollars in 1966 to 120 million in 1968.[6] Migrant remittances, which had doubled between 1961 and 1965, remained static after 1967. State expenditure in foreign currency, including payments to the numerous spies maintained abroad and enormous propaganda expenses, has more than doubled: from 24 million dollars in 1966, it rose to 28 million dollars for the first half of 1969 alone. Again it should be remembered that of the 24 million spent in 1966, about 10 million was for the expeditionary force in Cyprus (see p. 113), an expense which ceased in 1968. This means that present expenditure is effectively four times the normal expenditure of 1966. The cost of servicing debts and remitting foreign company profits abroad doubled between 1966 and 1969.

The result of all this is that the current account deficit, which reached 145 and 151 million dollars during the first half of 1965 and 1966 respectively, has risen to 185, then 212 million for the corresponding periods in 1968 and 1969. Short-term commercial credits, which were running at the level of 293 million dollars in April 1967 (that is to say, slightly less than the total foreign currency reserves of the Bank of Greece), in June 1969 reached 428 million. At the same time the reserves, officially almost stable,[7] have in fact been considerably depleted because a substantial portion of them has been handed over as security for foreign loans.[8] In any case, even taking the reserve figures at their face value, they now represent the value of current imports for only two months, instead of three and a half months as in the past.

While the balance of payments deficit increases, means of filling the gap become increasingly expensive. In the past, one could count on the import of private investment capital, or loans, on reasonable terms. Now these sources are visibly drying up, again for political reasons. Between 1965 and 1968 the import of capital fell from 155·5 million dollars to 129 million. Major foreign firms are less and less inclined to invest in Greece. Or if they do, they demand and obtain terms which make their investments highly unfavourable to the Greek economy. The junta made much of the agreement with Litton International which was to bring in investments of 800 million dollars within a few years. Two years later it was clear that the deal was an almost complete fiasco: Litton had scarcely managed to raise 10 million dollars.[9] And firms which undertake to finance large-scale public works do so on crippling terms, with interest rates of 7-8 per cent[10] repayable over five to seven years. Greece has also forfeited, because of the political situation, the credit of some 100 million dollars which would normally have been available from the European Investment Bank. This is lent at an effective interest rate of only 3 per cent, and is repayable over twenty or twenty-five years.

To bridge the gap, the junta is feverishly negotiating short-term loans in foreign currency from private banks, at interest rates of up to 10 per cent, and is also trying to obtain loans from Onassis and Niarchos in return for oil refinery concessions, without showing the slightest concern about mortgaging the future of the country. These loans are immediately spent to cover the current deficit, and do not necessarily represent investments in real capital.

The effects of this irresponsible policy will become increasingly obvious in years to come. The well-being and economic independence of future generations are being jeopardised. The servicing of all these debts will consume an increasing part of the country's meagre foreign currency resources. It has been calculated that, within a few years, these repayments will absorb a sum equal to the entire income from tourism.

It should be added that the links between Greece and the E.E.C., far from being strengthened as was originally envisaged, and as would have been to Greece's advantage, have virtually collapsed. The agreement of association has been frozen. For the Community, a co-operative venture of democratic countries, shows signs of rejecting the Greek dictatorship, as the Council of Europe already has done.

The budget of a country is a good guide to the objectives of its government. The detailed analysis of current Greek budgets has become very difficult. First, there is no means of obtaining information, and where the official figures are available they are deliberately couched in a manner to confound serious analysis. It is impossible, for instance, to know if the construction of new prisons is paid for out of the normal credits of the Ministry of Justice or out of those earmarked for 'investments'. Second, important modifications to the budget are made during the course of the year and these become apparent only much later. (The final accounts for 1968, for example, had not yet been published by early 1970, and for good reason.) With these reservations, it is possible to make some observations on the junta's financial policy,[11] based exclusively on the official figures.

Firstly, the receipts from taxation and duties have greatly increased between 1966 and 1969, not only in absolute terms but also as a percentage of the gross national product.[12] The junta's claim that this increase has been achieved without any new taxation is not wholly accurate, for there was a considerable increase in stamp duties which affected all commercial transactions. None the less much of the increase in revenue did come from the existing backlog of unpaid taxes, payment of which was prompted by severe measures to limit fraud. But this severity was exercised mainly at the expense of the middle-income groups, particularly small shopkeepers, artisans, and the free professions.[13] On the other hand, certain categories of wealthier taxpayers received favourable treatment. For example, those living off unearned dividend income are no longer liable to normal taxation of up to 60 per cent, but are taxed at a rate varying between 30 and 38 per cent. The most obvious scandal, however, concerns the shipowners. Under Law No. 465 of 1968, guaranteed by Article 23 of the Constitution of 1968—a provision which it is theoretically impossible to abrogate—shipowners are exempted from all taxes on purchases, sales, gifts, legacies, inheritances, and dowries provided that these take the form of ships over 3000 tons gross, or shares in a shipping company possessing such boats. By this same law, the tax on income deriving from shipping has been lowered. Under another measure, the total exemption from taxation of revenue deriving from a boat newly registered in Greece, which was formerly granted for only a limited number of years, has now been indefinitely extended.

Secondly, forecasts of public expenditure have increased by 66 per cent between 1966 and 1970, but this increase is distributed in a very unequal way between different sectors. The increases accorded to education and to the social services, for example, are proportionately very much lower than the average: 39·6 and 28·9 per cent respectively. The total sum of the credits that have been provided for these two sectors represented 20·3 per cent of the budget in 1966 but is now only 16·5 per cent. On the other hand, the credits allowed for defence expenditure have increased by 120·3 per cent, and those for the security forces by 83·2 per cent. Together they now represent 23·8 per cent of the budget as opposed to 21 per cent in 1966. The cost of servicing the public debt has risen by 122 per cent. The Ministry to the Prime Minister, whose basic task is propaganda, has had its annual budget more than doubled. But the record is held by the Directorate of Youth and Sport, whose share has quadrupled. Colonel Aslanidis, who is its head, sees a potential source of popular support for the regime in the financing of football and political youth organisations in favour of the junta.[14]

Thirdly, between 1963 and 1966 a budget surplus corresponding on average to 6 per cent of current expenditure was transferred to a special investment account, of which it constitutes on average 26·8 per cent (the rest consisting mainly of loans). Between 1967 and 1970, the predicted surplus corresponded to only 4·2 per cent of current expenditure and constituted only 17 per cent of the investment account.

This brief sketch will suffice to show that the junta's financial policy is very much consumption oriented. Its principal features are, firstly, favourable treatment for large-scale capital; secondly, certain purely demagogic expenditures; and thirdly, the growth of non-productive expenses necessitated by the militarist and police nature of the regime.[15] Such policies accentuate the short term dangers of inflation and an increased deficit in the balance of payments.[16]

We have seen how defence expenditure has increased at a dramatic rate under the present regime. It is understandable that this sector should receive preferential treatment by a government of colonels who pride themselves on having 'reorganised the armed forces'. In fact, the dictatorship has had disastrous consequences for the discipline, morale, and efficiency of these same armed forces.

From the point of view of discipline, the very fact that the rebel officers perjured themselves by overthrowing the legitimate government and by arresting their own superior officers has created a thoroughly disastrous precedent. (We would remind those who persist in thinking that Greece has always had putsches of this sort, that the last successful one was in 1926.) Once the idea of legitimacy is thrown to the winds, once it is accepted that the power of tanks is greater than that of law, what is to prevent younger officers from satisfying their ambitions, not within the traditional hierarchical structure but by plotting against their superiors? Since 21 April 1967 this new atmosphere has been felt especially in the army. Senior officers who have remained, but who do not belong to the junta, have in fact had to submit to the control of subalterns, who belong to the new politicised élite. Generals tremble before majors, colonels take orders from captains. Mutual distrust and denunciations for 'lack of loyalty' towards the ruling clique are ruining the old *esprit de corps* and regard for seniority. It is not an exaggeration to speak of the 'sovietisation' of the army, the role of 'commissar' or 'soviet' being held in each unit by that officer or officers trusted by the junta.

As for morale, one might argue that the whole of the military profession initially received a boost from the influence and artificial prestige conferred on it by the regime. We have seen military men placed at the head of all important branches of public life, and all effective power placed in their hands. They take precedence over civilians in everything, even in the petty details of daily life; a recent decree, for example, entitles them to jump the queue at bus stops. Officers of some seniority can even allow themselves to break the law in a way which would cost lesser mortals dearly.[17] Their insolent contempt for civilians is unbounded. The doorkeeper of the Academy tried one day to stop an officer's wife from parking her car in the place reserved for the President of the Academy. The woman immediately complained to the Military Police. The unfortunate porter was seized by a patrol, and hauled off to a barracks for three days where he was so mistreated for showing 'lack of respect towards the army' that he was in bed for a week when freed.[18]

Officers have also received very substantial material benefits under the junta. The putsch could almost be defined as a move by the officers' 'trade union'. On top of an official increase in salary averaging 20 per cent, they are entitled to all sorts of perks: free travel, mortgage loans which are virtually gifts, discounts on cars. According to car salesmen, who eagerly compete for their custom, officers have become their best clients. A recent decree has granted, retrospectively, a significant increase in the special allowance payable to members of the Cyprus expeditionary force between 1964 and 1967. Other laws and decrees have raised the pension of officers, as well as the 'golden handshakes' to which they are entitled on retirement. There are also other financial perks which are difficult to verify because they are virtually state secrets. One hears, for instance, of a system by which a certain number of officers particularly favoured by the regime regularly receive travel allowances for non-existent journeys. What is beyond doubt is that the majority of officers have a standard of living very much higher than is justified by their official salary. It is impossible, to take only one example, to fathom the mystery of the personal budget of a particular colonel whose nominal salary is about 10,000 drachmas a month when his wife insists that he in fact gets around 24,000.[19]

Despite these advantages accorded to the military class,[20] or rather because of them, the morale of army officers is dangerously low. In so far, that is, that officers believe in the old and noble concept of 'service and honour', and are not carried away by the insolence that political power, material wealth, and contempt for civilians tend to breed. There still exist decent officers, faithful to their oaths, who are ashamed of what is happening and aware of the hatred which they inspire in most of their fellow-citizens, who look on them as a kind of army of occupation. Some have confided to their friends that they are ashamed to be seen in uniform. For no officer with any kind of conscience could feel at ease knowing how many of his comrades have been dismissed, not to mention arrested and deported, to make way for his own promotion.

As for the present state of efficiency in the Greek armed forces, an efficiency that was once proverbial in NATO circles, it is enough to cite some facts. Firstly, their essential task is now that of a police force, enforcing obedience. The crack army units are no longer stationed on the frontiers, but near Athens and Thessaloniki and in Crete, an island with too liberal a tradition for the colonels' liking. Secondly, the purges which were intended to remove all those potentially hostile to the junta have turned into veritable massacres. In 1967 and 1968 about 1500 officers, almost a sixth of the entire officer corps, left the armed forces, when the annual average of retirements between 1963 and 1966 had been about 330. The picture is even grimmer when one looks at the percentage of senior officers and generals included in the purge. In the army, for example, 40 per cent of the officers removed between April 1967 and June 1969 belonged to the four highest ranks, colonel and above, against only 27 per cent in 1963-1966. In the navy and air force, the corresponding percentages are even more striking. During 1967-68, 20 and 54 per cent respectively of retired officers belonged to the four highest ranks, against 10·4 and 22 per cent respectively in 1963-1966.[21] It is no exaggeration to say that the armed forces have been decapitated. They have been deprived of all the senior officers who had distinguished themselves in war, and who, because of their professional qualities, had enjoyed the absolute respect and confidence of their allied colleagues. It is precisely these distinguished men that the junta wanted to get rid of, partly because their records contrasted so pointedly with those of the present rulers, and partly because the junta feared the influence they had over their comrades. And the United States, which had for long honoured these men, several of whom had formerly been trained at considerable expense in American military colleges, calmly allowed the junta to get away with it. It seems that the Pentagon's reasoning was that 'provided the military are in power, it is just too bad if they are not the best men available'.

Secondly, pre-coup governments in Greece sent and maintained, in and after 1964, an expeditionary force to Cyprus to help the island to defend itself against a possible Turkish attack. Seven months after the coup the regime gave in to the first threat from Ankara and evacuated the contingent. For the junta could not face the crisis which mobilisation would have brought about, and was unable to trust armed reservists.

Thirdly, the junta distrusts the navy so much that, despite the purges, a special corps of marine commandos, praetorians selected for their loyalty to the regime and under the command of the dictator's brother, has been created to keep watch on the fleet. As an additional precaution, fearing that some ships might 'choose freedom', they are supplied with only small quantities of fuel. It is the same with the air force, and this has been put forward as the reason for the absence of an air force contingent in the 1969 Independence Day celebrations. Another, and more plausible, explanation of this very noticeable absence is linked to the air force's technical deterioration, due to the inexperience of the newly promoted officers. There were so many fatal accidents, never of course mentioned in the press, during the winter of 1968-1969 that the authorities dared not allow the planes to fly on that day, because of an overcast sky which in normal times would have presented no problem.

7. STYLE AND IDEOLOGY [1]

'Devote yourselves to philosophy like Greeks for the benefit of man and develop your intellectual activity in the area which the world wide effort of mankind must follow.'
Papadopoulos, addressing students
9 February 1968

The officers who rule Greece do not belong to the 'strong and silent' strain of the species *homo militaris*,[2] those who are content to bark curt orders. Our colonels are certainly strong but they are also incredibly verbose. The speeches made by Papadopoulos alone in the course of two years fills four volumes totalling some eight hundred pages. Published at the taxpayers' expense under the title *Our Creed*, they are distributed free to these same grateful taxpayers. They contain reflections on every conceivable subject. A glance at the index to the volumes shows that among the topics discussed are 'anguish', 'the sporting spirit', 'puns', 'mini-skirts', 'panslavism', 'divine providence', 'Marx', 'rifle ranges', 'whispering', 'mosaics', 'Aristotle', 'the jungle', 'the Russian fleet', and 'the moon'.

Lesser lights such as Pattakos and Makarezos, are not honoured by such publications. But this does not inhibit them from printing their own views at great length. Sometimes the press is obliged to publish these, and sometimes the treasury pays, at the normal advertising rates for the necessary space. The latter was the case in the autumn of 1969 when Makarezos published a series of articles affirming that all was for the best in the best of all possible Greek economies.

This mass of verbiage is a delight to connoisseurs of humbug. We will necessarily have to examine some specimens while trying to extract, in so far as possible, a coherent ideology for the dictatorship. Let us begin with the 'National Revolution' of 21 April 1967. Who carried it out? In the beginning, the official answer was 'the Army'. Later this was changed to 'the People and the Army', which sounds more democratic. As the malicious might ask what role the people has been able to play in a purely military putsch, it is sometimes suggested that 'the Army acted on the mandate of the People'. How was this remarkable process achieved? 'The people', explains Papadopoulos with his customary lucidity,[3] 'lived in an anguish of uncertainty about its future security in all sectors, awaiting like an inert explosive material, the spark which would lead it to the revolution for its liberation.' There are, however, more prosaic explanations. For example, as the journalist Konstantopoulos, a personal friend of the dictator, has explained to his readers,[4] Papadopoulos had begun to plan the country's salvation by the Army (in other words, began to plot) from 1958 onwards, if not earlier, and it was the inertia of the King and the leaders of the armed forces that forced him to take the initiative.[5]

Why this 'national revolution'? The initial reply was, as we have seen, to 'ward off the imminent danger of a communist seizure of power'. The junta, however, realised that such a claim was becoming increasingly less tenable, and that in any case it did not in itself provide a sufficient justification for the indefinite prolongation of the dictatorship. Better reasons had to be sought. 'Communism has never been widespread in our country', Papadopoulos explained on 7 March 1969. 'And this has been so, because it is incompatible with the Greco-Christian spirit. But the soil was fertile for the serious spread of communism, with injustice and the lack of fraternal affection. These are the things in our society which nurture the existence of anarchistic individuals, of split personalities, of individuals in revolt against themselves.'[6] Elections had to be prevented at all costs, for these same 'split personalities' were quite capable of voting for anarchy and corruption, while in their hearts not really wanting it. The regime's psychological doctrine is based on this schizoid quality: 'We have revolted against our own selves.'[7] 'The greatest enemy of man has always been himself.'[8] As one can see, the 'split within the individual' can be advantageous when it is the better half which takes the lead and binds the other hand and foot.

The task of the 'revolution' is to undertake thorough-going reforms, which will make a return to the past impossible. This is a monumental task, since it is not only a question of reforming all public institutions, the constitution, legislation, the civil service, the economy, trade unionism, education, the church, justice, etc., but above all of reforming the very temperament of the Greeks: 'We must change our habits of thought and rid ourselves of individualism.' This period of change, it must be understood, could last a very long time—decades, perhaps generations. For the Greek people, although 'the elect of God',[9] none the less perversely clings to its evil habits, thus justifying the wrathful cry of its leader: 'no one intends to give up even the least of their weaknesses of the past'.[10] The positive ideal proposed by the regime is not, however, difficult to grasp and achieve: 'Individuals must cease to be anarchic, materialistic individuals, and must become social individuals.'[11] And Papadopoulos adds, driving the point home to those of mediocre intelligence: 'We are now at the stage of trying to combine the two systems of rule by society and rule by the individual with their harmonic division, where individual interest and individual iniative, while not being limited in an oppressive manner by the influences and by the interests of collectivity, are none the less made to move always within a predetermined framework.'[12]

What about liberty and democracy? The junta believes in these concepts with all its heart. It is precisely the salvation of them that impelled it to impose the dictatorship, it endlessly claims. 'We are all democrats', the notorious Lambrou, foremost torturer of the political police, loves to repeat to resisters whom he is interrogating. On the question of whether democracy and liberty now actually exist in Greece, or whether they are rather being incubated, the regime's spokesmen behave rather like the schizophrenics mentioned above. Sometimes they maintain that democratic freedoms have never known such a flowering. 'Our government is human, liberal and democratic,' Pattakos said on 11 December 1969. 'It is true that we arrest those who agitate too much, but we do not interfere with their liberty,' he added on another occasion during the same month. If we are to believe Papadopoulos, we live in a democracy, albeit without realising it: 'The true meaning of liberty and democracy is our guide, quite independent of all external appearance and form.'[13] More often, however, it is suggested that the present regime (never referred to as a 'dictatorship', but rather by some euphemism such as 'concentrated government') is only preparing the way for the good, true, and healthy democracy of the future, which will be in fact a model for the whole world. According to this theory, the regime will play the same transitional role as the dictatorship of the proletariat (which is also no longer openly called a dictatorship) does in the marxist scheme.

It is interesting to note the numerous analogies which the curious enquirer can find between the ideology of the Greek junta and that of certain marxists. Both contain a kind of crude determinism. 'The Revolution was an historical necessity' one can read on the roadside hoardings of Greece. This profound thought is attributed to Papadopoulos.[14] There is their shared contempt for liberalism. In a speech before fifteen or so Greek ambassadors on 26 August 1969, the Foreign Affairs Minister, Pipinelis, explained that in the 'self-styled Western democracies', real power is exercised by the owners of a few large daily newspapers, who use them to manipulate public opinion. Only a reference to the 'monopolistic interest' that shelters behind these newspaper-owners is lacking for this view to match the marxist analysis of the Western democracies.[15] Finally, the colonels also parrot the arguments put forward by marxists concerning the development of the third world. 'The great leap forward on the economic front cannot be achieved with a Parliament,' Papadopoulos declared in a speech of 6 September 1969. And Konstantopoulos, the editor of *Eleftheros Kosmos*, went even further. 'Democracy', ran the substance of his article on the 19th of the same month, 'is a luxury for highly developed countries.' The junta, however, fails to specify at what exact stage of economic development the Greeks will be able to afford the luxury of an elected government and of individual liberties. When the annual *per capita* income, now on the order of seven hundred dollars, will have reached that of the French? The Swedes? The Americans? This is the only uncertainty that remains. (Papadopoulos has since decreed that the Greeks will begin to be mature enough for freedom when the annual *per capita* income rises to 1100 dollars, which should be achieved by the mid-seventies—Addendum, 1971.)

It would be a mistake, however, to imagine that economic development is the only precondition for the new Greek democracy. The Greek people must also become politically mature. They must not be rushed. To set in motion this process of maturing the regime is showing great concern for the civic education of its citizens. A manual of civic education, filling six hundred pages, has been announced by Papadopoulos as being in the press.[16] When it appears it must be read by all, and afterwards each citizen will be expected to conform to 'the rules of the moral order', and to see that his neighbours do so also—that is to say, to denounce them if they still show signs of 'weakness in outlook'.[17]

Every self-respecting revolution has a motto. The first deputy Prime Minister, Pattakos, has suggested one which could scarcely be more appropriate. Evoking the historic words which have marked Greek history, such as the famous 'Come and get them' with which the Spartans at Thermopylae answered the Persians when they demanded that their weapons be handed over, he has added the 'Halt or I shoot' of 21 April 1967.[18]

Some suspect Pattakos of secretly working for the resistance, and trying deliberately to ridicule the regime with his gaffes. And indeed if Pattakos did not exist he would have had to be invented by the dictatorship's opponents. His speeches—clearer than those of Papadopoulos,[19] and at the same time more candid—allow the true thinking of the junta to show through.

The regime had begun by claiming that it is free of all the political attitudes of the past. 'From today there is no right, no centre and no left—there are only Greeks,' Prime Minister Kollias, an unconscious master of black humour, proclaimed on 21 April 1967. Slowly, however, the true ideological orientation of the junta has become apparent, partly thanks to Pattakos. The other colonels covertly revered the dictatorship of Metaxas; Pattakos himself reveres it openly. The great mistake of the military revolutions of 1909 and 1922, he explained during his speech of 25 April 1968 in Crete, was to hand over to the 'politicians' soon afterwards (that is to say, to re-establish democratic institutions). But Metaxas kept power for himself, and, he added, 'we are inspired by his example'.[20] We note in this connection, that an overtly fascist periodical, called *4th August* after the date of Metaxas' takeover, not only circulates freely but has on occasion published articles by regime members such as Colonel Ladas. One of its issues, for instance, carried an article by Colonel Ladas entitled 'Rise up, O youth of Greece!'

There also exists a link, although it is not of course officially admitted, between junta circles and certain war-time collaborators of the Nazis. This explains why former officers in the 'security battalions' created during the occupation (see p. 29) have obtained important posts under the regime. Besides Patilis, who has already been mentioned, the retired General Kourkoulakos, who was commandant of the 'security battalions' of the Patras region was appointed Governor of the Agricultural Bank. A law on the 'National Resistance', published in 1969, places all the communist resistance organisations in the 'enemy' category. On the other hand, to have fought one of the battalions, even if one was at the same time a collaborator, entitles one to be designated 'a national resister', and therefore to be eligible for a pension.

The regime does not hide its preference for the right during the post-war period, and has for long tried to cultivate E.R.E. and Karamanlis personally, though not Kanellopoulos, who is considered to be the representative of his party's liberal wing. 'I always voted for him,' complained Papadopoulos, when Karamanlis expressed his unyielding opposition to the dictatorship. Anarchy, the disorder which the 'National Revolution' intended to end, was expressly stated to have existed only during the period 1963-1967, which followed the downfall of the right. The great bogy which dominated the regime's propaganda was Andreas Papandreou, the *bête noire* of the conservatives. *Eleftheros Kosmos* unflaggingly tried to convince supporters of the traditional right that the present regime was in some way its logical continuation, inspired by the same 'national ideals' and, even more important, working for the same interests. It is the junta's persevering effort to attract to it traditional conservative circles which dictated its moderate policy towards the King, even after the latter's failed counter-coup. It was only two years later that the 'Royal Navy' became discreetly the 'War Navy', while portraits of the sovereign still decorate government offices.

The regime's sympathy is more sincere towards the right-wing underworld, towards the terrorist elements who do not shrink from assassination, as the Lambrakis case proved. (This affair was, of course, the subject of the novel, *Z*, by the émigré writer Vassilikos. It was also made into a film of the same name.) Gotzamanis, the assassin condemned to eleven years in prison, was released in 1969 after serving only six and a half years. The authorities gave him the greatest possible remission for 'good conduct', and also granted him a generous period in which to pay the costs of the trial which were awarded against him. He has even managed to get back the motor-cycle combination with which he killed Lambrakis, while typewriters, cars, etc., used by the resistance nowadays are immediately confiscated. The gendarmerie General Mitsou, who had been prematurely retired for his 'negligence' in the same affair,[21] was recalled to active service, promoted, and once again retired, with a correspondingly higher pension and an honourable citation.

In foreign policy matters, the regime displays an unquestioning loyalty towards the United States, NATO and the 'defence of Western civilisation'. It is not amused, however, if the preamble to the Atlantic Treaty, with its talk of democracy and liberty, is taken literally.[22] The colonels make no bones about wanting to see the West follow their own example. 'By the Revolution of 21 April, Greece was the first to enter upon the correct route by which mankind will overcome the crisis.'[23] The government press has, on a number of occasions, warned Italian neo-fascists to 'act like the Greeks before it is too late'. The same advice was offered to France in May 1968. Existing dictatorships, provided they are of the right, are highly regarded. In a recent school textbook, Portugal is defined as a 'corporate democracy'. American liberals such as Senator Fulbright are described as 'agents of Moscow' by *Estia*, the pro-government daily which least minces its words.

Western Europe, it is true, let the colonels down by showing them the door at the Council of Europe in December 1969. The junta took the whole matter with great pride, decking out Athens with flags, and broadcasting slogans such as 'No to Europe, yes to eternal Greece' to the accompaniment of loud military marches. Pattakos, lecturing foreign pressmen on the Council's attitude towards the regime, spoke of the 'decadence of Europe'.

But what will become of a Greece cut off from Europe? The regime has its answer ready: it will become African. In his New Year's message for 1970, Papadopoulos took care to emphasise Greek-African links. This is not surprising. The African countries are not peopled with 'hypocritical pharisees' like the Western democracies, as Pipinelis put it in his speech to the Ambassadors.

Such self-confidence in the face of universal opposition can only be based on a system of thought which resolves all problems. And, in fact, the colonels have a passionate interest in metaphysical speculation. On 12 May 1967, for example, Makarezos defined the 'philosophy of the revolution' for the benefit of a group of Turkish journalists, who were evidently interested in metaphysics:

'The most important thing at this time is to set aside the tragic consequences of a poor linguistic heritage and to pose the problems

ad ovo [sic] on a Cartesian basis. Myth, a matter of prime importance in the soul of the Greek—we know that even the Greek of the
classical period was profoundly interested in the wounds of the
Centaurs, while the historical dimension of Lycurgus left him
rather indifferent—the myth, as an element in the temperament
of this people, must rapidly return to its own domain, driven out
from the domain of the objective evaluation of criteria into which
the unthinking corruption of a political world, which has clearly
failed, has dragged it . . .'.[24]

Discussions must, at times, have been lively in the philosophical
debating groups in which the colonels prepared their seizure of
power. For the Cartesianism of Makarezos scarcely harmonises
with the mystic relativism of Pattakos, as expressed in a speech at
the School of Political Sciences on 27 May 1969. Here are two
particularly edifying extracts:

'Science is knowledge, it confirms experience. A certain knowledge, but not permanent. The law of probabilities confirms the
mutability of knowledge. . . . What was the 21 April 1967? The
hour when the God of armies and of wills gave the strength to
some to raise up the Nation from the mud in which it was stuck
fast, led by guides who ran or staggered about, who sang or who
lamented, pursuing will-o'-the-wisps, but never playing with
death, thriftless but lacking in pride, demons, yes, but never
different and always the same.'[25]

Papadopoulos himself seems to hover between a neo-Bergsonian
vitalism ('Nothing is born in nature solely to live; but to create,
that is the great problem of life')[26] and an Orthodox Christianity
pure and simple—with the stress on 'simple'. The great slogan
which he has launched, and which is in danger of detracting from
Pattakos' 'Halt or I shoot', is his 'Greece of the Christian Greeks',
which is now blazoned on walls, in neon signs at the airports and
along the motorways. The dictator's piety is exemplary. When he
escaped the attempt on his life in August 1968, he quickly had
himself photographed lighting a candle before an icon, and
modestly declaring 'God has saved me because the country has
need of me'. His great dream is to build a new cathedral in Athens
which will eclipse even the basilica of Santa Sophia in Istanbul,
and which will imortalise the regime. A gigantic fund-raising
drive has been launched. The major banks and municipalities
have been ordered to subscribe large sums. Few private firms have
dared to refuse their contribution. The cost of the edifice, which
will include rich gold decorations—nothing is too luxurious for
the God of the Christian Greeks—has been estimated at some 700
million drachmas (rather less than £10 million). This is not bad

going for a country which, as we have seen, is too poor to allow itself the least democratic freedoms.

The regime encourages Sunday schools. It teaches 10-year-olds that if ice is lighter than water and rises to the surface, it is because the Good Lord has arranged things out of consideration for the fish.[27] It protects youth groups sponsored by the Church and organisations of bigots such as the famous *Zoi* ('Life') to which Pattakos belongs, and which has become so influential that it virtually exercises a veto over university appointments. Speaking on 5 January 1968 at the University of Thessaloniki, Papadopoulos told the students that they should consider the Rector's sending a letter to the student's home village, where the priest would read it to the assembled faithful, as a punishment far more serious than expulsion from the university.[28]

This compulsory piety does not only concern young people. Besides schoolchildren who are to be taken to church every Sunday by their teachers, civil servants are exhorted to attend church, and they are in fact obliged to obey, at least in the provinces where there is little hope of escaping detection. In a similar vein the Court of First Instance in Athens ruled on 9 January 1970 that Freemasonry was to be forbidden as being a 'religion' incompatible with public order, good morals, and official religion. And this although it has a long and untroubled history in Greece, and includes good Christians within its ranks. (Freemasonry is also attacked in one of a series of booklets written by a priest and distributed by the army. Other targets of these pamphlets include the Jehovah's Witnesses and 'zoolatry', i.e. love of pets. Violent attacks, partly based on the Protocols of the Elders of Zion, are also made on 'international Jewry'.)

The colonels' piety goes hand in hand with an obsession with sexual morality. Unquestionably the most zealous in this respect is Colonel Ladas. Fired by an implacable hatred for homosexuals, he personally led police raids on homosexual haunts when he was the effective power in the Ministry of Public Order. His other great passion is for Greek antiquity. 'No other people', he explained on 6 December 1969 to the students of Jannina, 'have any philosophers. The Greeks have exhausted the subject. You may tell me that certain peoples have produced philosophers. I concede this, but what good has it done them? The Greeks have said everything. . . . Foreigners can only imitate them.' One day, however, Colonel Ladas' two passions came into conflict, and it became apparent that his knowledge of antiquity did not match his admiration for it. A weekly magazine published an article on homosexuality through the ages, which pointed out that most of the worthies of classical Greece had been homosexual. Ladas issued a furious denunciation, had the offending journalists arrested on the spot, and brutally beat them up in his own office. Later, taking exception to the way in which the B.B.C. Greek service had dealt with the matter, he issued a second statement: 'The B.B.C.'s commentator has taken it upon himself to defend the culprits . . . and has repeated, with an ironic emphasis, my statement about the insult done to the memory of our nation's great men. Given that, according to this pornographic article, homosexuals support each other, the untimely action of the B.B.C. becomes intelligible.'

When the matter came before the courts, however, the journalists were acquitted after they had offered documentary proof that the contents of the article were true, and that they had drawn on the substance of an old article by Theophylaktos Papakonstantinou, who at the time of the trial was the Minister of Education. Ladas was flabbergasted to learn that not only Plato and Aristotle had deviant tastes, for after all they were intellectuals from whom that sort of thing might be expected, but also Alexander the Great—a soldier, and a kind of prototype colonel. Papadopoulos was irritated by the episode, which made the junta a laughing stock. He transferred Ladas to the Ministry of the Interior where, closely watched by Pattakos, he had fewer chances to make a fool of himself.

It would be wrong to conclude from all this that the whole of Greece has been transformed into a monastery inhabited by pious and asexual ascetics. It may well be inhabited by Christian Greeks, but there is no less vice than before. In 1969 an English visitor published travel notes in which he commented on the licence prevailing in the islands, such as Mykonos and Hydra: drugs, promiscuity, nudity, it was all there. Early in 1970, at a private gambling club near Athens, much frequented by junta officers, a drunken businessman was lured to a baccarat table where he lost some two million drachmas (about £28,000), for which he was made to sign I.O.U.s. When, later, his lawyer tried to challenge the legality of the debt thus incurred, the manager of the club threatened him—the lawyer—with deportation or worse: It turned out that two of the most prominent junta colonels were not only customers but actual owners of the place. The businessman had little option but to pay up.

The explanation that the tastes of all tourists must be satisfied to gain foreign exchange is not enough. All unpopular and authoritarian regimes know that it is wise to allow a politically oppressed people to distract itself in its private life, provided that appearances are maintained. Two incidents illustrate that this type of reasoning lies behind the regime's attitudes in these matters. On the eve of the referendum on the new Constitution a group of young people were arrested for having chalked 'No' on walls. In the police car in which they were taken away, they received their first beating. Stopping to regain his breath, an angry policeman lectured one of the youths whom he had just been hitting.

'Aren't you ashamed to have done such a thing? If you had stolen, or molested a girl, I could have understood. But to say "no" to progress!'

At the trial of another resistance group, the president of the military court asked a young defendant, 'Why did you do this?'

'For freedom.'

'Come on now! Does anyone try to stop you going to bars, or riding motor bikes, or seeing girls? No. So you are perfectly free. Why get mixed up in matters which don't concern you?'

It is precisely because there are so many Greeks who persist in getting mixed up in matters which don't concern them that Papadopoulos so often employs his famous medical metaphor. In the first variant of this, Greece is an invalid who needs an operation, but is hesitant about it. So, in his own interest, he must be strapped to the operating table. In the second variant, the operation has already taken place, but the invalid must still remain in plaster for an indefinite length of time.[29]

It is time to see what the 'sick man' himself thinks about all this.

8. THE GREAT FEAR

At the beginning of this work we described the formation of the Greek character during the long Ottoman domination with three principal types developing: the *raya*, the *Phanariot* and the *klepht*. This was intentional, for these three archetypes to a greater or lesser degree survive in every modern Greek. In normal times these attitudes are scarcely apparent. But at times of national crisis they surface in the shape of unexpected, ancestral reflexes—primitive or cunning, heroic or despicable. (We have seen, for example, how the raya attitude was stimulated by the Metaxas dictatorship between 1936 and 1940, but was displaced by that of the klepht during the war and occupation.)

Between 1961 and 1967 the majority of the Greek people were nearer than they had ever been to experiencing the rights and self-respect of free citizens. This majority would have expressed itself in the 1967 elections by a massive vote for the Centre Union which, despite all its shortcomings, reflected this growing awareness. During this period there had been no need to take refuge in resignation, in collaboration with the powerful, or in revolt against them.

The coup of 21 April changed all this. The Greeks found themselves abruptly deprived of all their rights, and subjected to a military occupation. They could no longer vote, nor could they even express themselves in the simplest ways. They had to choose between the submission of the raya, the collaboration of the Phanariot, or the resistance of the klepht. We will examine the choices which they have made in this and the following section.

Let us begin with the phenomenon of the Phanariot. We have seen how the junta's propaganda, except for a few demogogic slogans which were quickly contradicted by its actions, was directed from the very beginning at the conservative right-wing mentality, emphasising the sacrosanct 'individual initiative' in economic policy. If this propaganda had borne fruit, and if the military regime had managed to win over the traditional right— a good third of the electorate at the last elections—it would have found itself considerably strengthened. Fortunately for the prestige of the right, and even more for the future of the country, the attempt failed. Only a minority of conservatives approved of the putsch when it happened and this number has since dropped. Those who in good faith had believed in the 'communist danger', and in the need for a temporary army intervention to forestall it, withdrew their support when the myth was exposed and the regime showed its true colours. Today the regime's only supporters consist of a few convinced fascists and of unscrupulous adventurers. There are also certain groups of businessmen, such as the shipowners, always ready to trim their sails to the prevailing wind, together with some timid ultra-conservatives who fear 'anarchy' above everything. It does not add up to a very impressive total. Even the most generous estimate gives the junta only the support of 10 per cent of the population.

The dictatorship has recruited its collaborators from these circles. On the ministerial level, the only recruit of any stature from the old political world was Panayotis Pipinelis, who became Minister of Foreign Affairs in October 1967.[1] He had been a diplomat, then one of the leaders of E.R.E., where he was one of the 'hard liners' opposed to Kanellopoulos. Pipinelis had long been a believer in absolute monarchy, and was thought to be devoted to the palace, as indeed was the Archbishop Ieronymos. Like Ieronymos, however, Pipinelis opted for the junta at the time of the King's coup. His hatred for democracy overcame his Metternichian obsession with legitimacy; he placed his undoubted talents at the colonels' disposal, for he could be certain that they were unlikely to favour elections or other liberal abominations.

Pipinelis aside, the level of ministers was, and is, scarcely brilliant. The junta's next best catch was Triandafyllopoulos, who joined them around the middle of 1968. Triandafyllopoulos was an academic lawyer, vain enough to believe that by accepting office he could exercise a moderating influence on the regime. His career in government lasted precisely ten days, when he resigned disillusioned, showing incidentally how impossible it is to play the well-intentioned Phanariot in such a dictatorship. His successor, Kyriakopoulos, was also an academic, but one more apt to become the colonels' lackey; he had previously been indicted, following a financial scandal, and had benefited from an indefinite adjournment after repaying the sums which he had illegally appropriated. This type of man found himself in suitable company in a cabinet including, for instance, Makarezos' brother-in-law, Matthaiou, who had had six convictions; Sioris, who after the war was refused membership of Kanellopoulos' party on the grounds of alleged collaboration with the Nazis; the economist Evlampios who was successively an enthusiastic supporter of the Centre Union, of the 'apostates', and of the junta—steadily progressing from a simple bank employee to under-secretary of the Ministry of Co-ordination[2]; the journalist Theofylaktos Papakonstantinou, a marxist intellectual before the war, a passionate liberal soon after it, and later a pronounced conservative, denouncing both the permissive society and liberal intellectuals, whom he regarded as communists or imbeciles. Once the junta was firmly established, he appeared to enjoy the confidence of Papadopoulos, who marvelled at his knowledge[3] and offered him the Ministry of Education, where Papakonstantinou was responsible for the purges described earlier.

Others agreed to collaborate at more modest levels. One of these was Stamatopoulos, a former socialist, who had previously provoked a split in his group because he felt that the majority were deviating from marxist orthodoxy. He became the junta's official spokesman and in that capacity exhibited a remarkable degree of impudence. For example, when questioned by foreign journalists about the arrest of some royalist officers, he coolly replied, 'The communists are not the only enemies of our democracy. There are also fascists, like those you have just mentioned.' In 1970 he was replaced by George Georgalas, a former communist who had spent many years behind the Iron Curtain actively engaged in propaganda against the Greek state, notably during the period of the Civil War. He has gradually assumed the role of official theoretician of the junta, to the indignation of many of the colonels' more conservative supporters. Several hundred others agreed to accept appointments as mayors or in administrative posts. Some academicians and academics of fascist leanings have lauded the 'National Revolution' in public speeches.[4]

Falling between these willing and zealous supporters of the dictatorship and the mass of resigned citizens are a significant number of men in responsible positions—civil servants, academics, and others—who, without feeling enthusiastic about the regime, and even while cursing it in private have agreed to support it in public. Their defence is that of the collaborators throughout the ages: 'I cannot afford to lose my job. Besides, by remaining, I can render some small services and help to soften the impact of the dictatorship. If I leave, someone worse than me will follow.' One hears this kind of talk from senior officials in ministries, provincial governors, university professors, and ambassadors. It is difficult, as in the case of the Phanariots during the Ottoman period, to decide where necessary compromise ends and where treason begins. The slope is certainly a slippery one. A number of people have stayed on, firmly resolved to remain 'neutral', only to realise later that the regime will not admit neutrality. Papadopoulos and Pipinelis have both made this clear: it was possible, and even proper, for civil servants to keep out of politics as long as governments represented a mere party; today, when the government represents 'the totality of the Nation', it is unacceptable to remain aloof. Government employees great and small are forced to compromise more and more with the regime. Otherwise they may lose the very post which they had hoped to hold on to without too great a sacrifice of their self-respect and their convictions.

Among these collaborators are those that play a double game. There are many who privately claim a loyalty to democratic institutions, and let it be understood that they carry on resistance secretly. Sometimes they are sincere, and are the source of useful information. Sometimes they are simply hedging their bets. A typical case is that of the senior civil servant who is trusted by his minister but quietly boasts of recommending the most disastrous policies to him, so as to damage the regime. Or that of the tax inspector who leans hard on taxpayers to increase their resentment against the dictatorship.

One thing is certain. The moment the dictatorship is seriously threatened, its civilian collaborators not only will not defend it but, with a few rare exceptions, will be the first to denounce it.

But, one might ask, how is it that the colonels' public appearances are sometimes greeted by crowds of thousands? How is it that numerous resolutions lauding the regime are passed by trade unions and other associations? Why does the Academy of Athens celebrate the anniversary of 21 April with great pomp? Why have there been so few resignations of civil servants, of teachers, and of other groups? Martial law can account for the absence of hostile demonstrations, but not for the pro-regime ones.

This leads us to the attitudes of the raya, of the frightened subject, submitting to all sultans and pashas, whether Ottoman or native. The reaction of the great mass of the Greeks to the putsch was a combination of confusion, indignation, shame, anger, and fear. In most cases confusion and fear were preponderant.

For four hundred years, the realities of life under alien rule encouraged prudence, submission, servility, and deception. These were the pre-conditions for a subject people's survival, rather as they were for the Jews of the ghettoes. A century and a half of independence has not destroyed these reflexes. It is true that the Greeks behaved quite differently under the Nazis. But then the circumstances were completely different. At that time Greece was fighting foreign invaders, and she had the whole world at her side; Greeks were in such a miserable condition that they had little to lose.

None of these conditions are present today. The Greek people feel abandoned by the Great Powers, who appear to be in collusion in allowing the junta to govern as it pleases. Virtually no help can be expected from abroad. Nor is it like a war with ultimate victory within sight. On the contrary, there are the depressing examples of Spain and Portugal where fascism has existed untroubled for several decades. Unlike the Nazis, the occupying force today is not comprised of foreigners with manners, a language, and a uniform marking them out as such. They are the same as we are, as are their spies, and we are surrounded and overrun by them. Friend can no longer with certainty be distinguished from foe. They know us much better than a foreign army ever could. Moreover, the Greeks have for several years enjoyed a standard of living which is higher than ever before, and noticeably higher than fifteen or twenty years ago. The consumer society softens the will, blunts resistance, and renders horror more tolerable. Men who cavalierly risked their lives during the occupation now hesitate to risk their liberty or comfort, because of the relative well-being to which they have grown accustomed.

There is also another factor which must not be underestimated, namely the increased power which modern technology gives to any contemporary government. The perfection of electronic techniques, and the ever-increasing use of computers, gives the executive an unprecedented control over citizens' lives and over communications if it so wishes. Moreover, the public, by having an exaggerated opinion of these powers, becomes even more afraid. Thus even educated Greeks were convinced that during the referendum on the Constitution the authorities had special equipment to discover the way people voted, even in the Athens polling stations, the only ones where the vote was truly secret.

The state, omnipotent from the technical point of view, also possesses greater means of applying economic pressures, for it continually intervenes in all branches of the economy. There is scarcely a profession or business, even in private hands, which is free from government pressure or blackmail. All this discourages any tendency to oppose a merciless and efficient state mechanism which can hound citizens daily in innumerable small ways. Their very banality makes them even more terrifying, while they are difficult to establish and to prove.

Greece today is a Kafkaesque world. For a start, no citizen, of whatever background, can be sure that he is not watched by the secret police. Telephone conversations must be made with care, for no one can be certain that his is not one of the thousands of lines that are tapped. The most innocent remark, if it could incidentally have a political interpretation, can lead to difficulties. People have been imprisoned for a year or more for a single sentence critical of the junta, and no one knows whether his neighbour, in the café or in the bus, is an informer. To live night and day in such an atmosphere creates a true psychosis of fear in many people and this is reflected even in their least remarks and gestures.

Private correspondence is scrutinised, especially that going to or coming from abroad, despite official denials. Many citizens have been summoned by the police and asked to explain remarks contained in a letter they have sent or received. Many people, innocent of any political activity but known to have previously professed democratic opinions, have been questioned by the police about their life and the company they keep. They are usually asked to sign a statement denouncing communism and 'all those who assist it', notably Andreas Papandreou, and to pledge their loyalty to the 'national government'. The police know that such forced declarations have no bearing on the real opinions of those signing, but they also know that they help to sap their morale and to wound their self-respect.

A particularly tragic case was that of Theophilos Frangopoulos, an assistant professor at the School of Agricultural Science in Athens, a kind of hermit who lived only for his work. A man of liberal and humanitarian opinions, he detested the communists, for E.L.A.S. had taken him as a 'hostage' in 1944 (see p. 31). He had, however, innocently taken part in a 'peace march' organised by E.D.A. in 1964 or 1965. One day, at the beginning of 1969, he was summoned to the headquarters of the security police. Exactly what happened is not known, but that afternoon, deeply upset, he confided to a colleague that he had been asked to do 'improper things'. That evening he shut himself in his laboratory, where he was found dead the following morning. He had taken potassium cyanide, leaving the note: 'I prefer to die standing than to live on my knees.' The note was later confiscated by the police.

This was clearly an extreme case. More often those summoned for questioning are allowed to go, either immediately or after several days of detention. The following is a typical example. The police arrested a girl student who attended a weekly gathering of a small group of friends, including a former professor of literature. They interrogated her for ten days, refusing to believe her story, for the simple truth was that the group read and discussed the poetry of Seferis. 'Come on,' mocked her interrogator, 'who do you think you're kidding? If you were not plotting, then you were having an orgy. Come on, speak up. Who was sleeping with whom?' Finally they had to accept the evidence: that there exist people warped enough to spend their evenings talking about literature. The psychological condition of the young girl on her release is not hard to picture. Sometimes people are arrested, detained for days or weeks, and later released without ever learning why, with no interrogation, no word of explanation. This forms part of the war of nerves against those suspected of being anti-regime.

Most of the declarations of loyalty are obtained under the direct or veiled threat of loss of work. These are not idle threats, for innumerable people have lost their jobs in the private sector, after police suggestions which no employer can resist.[5] Similarly, employers are reluctant to offend the police by taking on those who have been dismissed elsewhere for political reasons.

The employers themselves, merchants or small shopkeepers, industrialists or craftsmen, also depend, in varying degrees, on the authorities' good-will. Sometimes they need a licence or a loan from the banks (which themselves are under strict government control); sometimes they have to face a public health or tax inspection. It requires a great deal of courage on the part of a café proprietor or a taxi-driver to refuse to display pro-government slogans in his window or on his windscreen when asked to by the police. The farmer who is not in favour with the local gendarmerie may be refused an agricultural loan. This explains why, in the countryside where everyone knows everyone else, it is almost impossible for people to avoid attendance at meetings organised by the local authorities to hail a passing colonel.

The professions enjoy no greater protection from such pressures. We have seen the difficulties facing lawyers. A doctor risks being refused employment in hospitals. The architects and engineer will not receive any official commissions. The painter and man of letters will not have their works bought by the Ministry of Education, which in Greece has responsibility for all cultural matters. A chemist needs a certificate of 'civic reliability' in order to run a pharmacy. A similar certificate is required to get an ordinary driving licence, or a hunting licence. And as the certificate becomes increasingly essential, so it becomes correspondingly difficult to obtain. Before the dictatorship it was refused only to communists. Now anyone opposed to the junta can be charged with 'anti-national' views, and thus be refused a certificate. The following case is typical. A candidate for a government job, known to be a conservative royalist, explained his views to the security policeman on duty, who refused him the certificate. The policeman, pointing to a portrait of the King in his office, added 'These days I would even refuse *him* one'.

The issuing of a passport has become a political favour.[6] Whether the trip is for business or pleasure, for health or for study, the formidable General Directorate of National Security, which supervises all the country's police forces, has the absolute discretion to grant or refuse authorisation. To be in possession of a valid passport means nothing. A simple administrative order can place a passport holder on the black list, without notification. He will only find out at the airport or at the frontier, bags in hand and ticket in pocket. Professor Zolotas, ex-governor of the Bank of Greece, is one of those who have got as far as the plane only to be called back by loudspeaker. The black list includes most of the former politicians, dismissed academics, and civil servants, as well as a large number of intellectuals, artists and, in short, anyone liable to tell the truth about the regime abroad.

We should add to this that under martial law the junta has absolute power, and that it does not hesitate to use this to deport or imprison its adversaries. The public's awareness of this adds to the atmosphere of fear, even among those who have not themselves been victimised. The fact that the colonels have their clownish side, as we have seen in previous sections, matters little, for they are dangerous clowns. To return to Papadopoulos' own favourite metaphor—a schizophrenic surgeon is scarcely likely to be of much comfort to a patient strapped to the operating table.

The organisation of this police state depends on a 'chain of terror'. The citizen is frightened of the civil servant, the civil servant of the policeman, the policeman of his boss, and so on. The impression is thereby created that any sign of disapproval of the dictatorship, or even a failure to praise and serve it, could be disastrous for the individual concerned.

This by itself would not be enough to stifle the hatred that the overwhelming majority of Greeks feel for the dictatorship, if they felt that the sacrifices and risks inherent in any resistance would not be fruitless. But the average Greek does not at the moment feel that he can hasten his country's liberation. For a start, practically all Greeks are convinced that the regime is backed by the United States. 'Could we fight against the Americans?' is one of the most frequently met reactions. It is accompanied by a resentment which if muted is no less profound. 'Who would support such a fight?' For the majority there is no question of turning to the Eastern bloc, as the memory of 1947-1949 is still too much alive. Few Greeks would countenance a new civil war, even supposing that one could be started. For if it succeeded it would result only in exchanging the present dictatorship for another, of the 'people's democracy' variety. The left itself is profoundly disillusioned with the Soviet Union, whose policy towards the junta has been invariably 'correct'. It realises that the Russians have no more intention of infringing upon the American sphere of influence in Europe than of tolerating American interference in Czechoslovakia. It is difficult to say which was the greater setback for the Greek communists: the events in Prague, or the Soviet Ambassador's warm handshake with Pattakos before tens of thousands of spectators at a football match between Greece and the U.S.S.R. The latter was the prelude to a progressive strengthening of ties between the two countries, including an increase in barter deals, the installation of a power plant in Greece with Russian aid.

The lack of a common faith, or a plan, or a positive ideology, greatly contributes to the passivity of the Greeks. For each enlightened democrat who says 'Let us get rid of the dictatorship, and let the people elect their leaders', one finds ten average Greeks who personalise their political attitudes, and say 'By all means let us get rid of these bastards, but who will follow them?'

'Me fight for the King, for X, or for Y? No thank you.' According to who is speaking, X or Y is Karamanlis, Andreas Papandreou, or Mitsotakis. This is a consequence of the disrepute into which the political parties had fallen following the manœuvrings of 1965.

This portrait of the present-day Greek raya is scarcely cheerful, but we can plead in mitigation the failure of most public figures to give a lead. This has constituted a *'trahison des clercs'* on an unexpected and distressing scale. We do not refer to the few open collaborators of the regime but to an entire élite which, while detesting the regime, had done nothing to express its disapproval openly. One can count on the fingers of one hand the senior civil servants who have resigned, the academics who have resigned their chairs, the academicians who have dared to absent themselves from ceremonies fêting the dictatorship. The example of submission, of wretched servility, has come from the top, and the people have simply followed this lead. Let us recall here what we have said about the example set by the King on 21 April 1967. Eight months later, when he tried to oust the junta, it was too late to reverse the consequences of his initial submission.

In these circumstances we should not wonder at the number of those who acclaim the colonels, but we should rather be astonished that it is not in fact larger. The same applies to the pro-regime resolutions voted by various associations. The techniques of totalitarianism in these matters are well known. These resolutions are about as spontaneous as those of Stalin's trade unions, their text being dictated through government channels. It is none the less regrettable that the Senate of the University of Athens agreed to pass a resolution condemning Professor Karayorgas, who was accused of terrorist activities, even before he had been convicted in court.[7]

9. THE RESISTANCE

As we have seen, the junta has organised a reign of terror to reward the submission of the raya and to penalise the least attempt at opposition. Despite this, the klephtic spirit is far from dead in Greece: the many demonstrations against the dictatorship are proof of this. What should one think of these demonstrations? When does a simple refusal to acquiesce become 'opposition'? Where does this latter end and 'resistance' proper begin? These distinctions are not always easily made. But considering that under such a regime there can be no legal opposition, and that even refusing to co-operate carries a risk, all these degrees of opposition, passive or active, open or secret, may justifiably be described as resistance in the wider sense of the term.

With few exceptions, the old political world has behaved with dignity and courage, beginning with the right, from which the least was expected. The majority of E.R.E. deputies have refused to collaborate with the colonels, and several dozens of them have publicly demonstrated their opposition through statements to the foreign press, and through appeals to the Council of Europe and to the United States administration. A number of party leaders have personally suffered the consequences of this intransigence, as we will see in the following chapter. But the best example of all has been set by Kanellopoulos, who has fought with indomitable courage against the junta, by word and by pen, and has won the respect and even the admiration of all Greek democrats, including his former political opponents. He has had to pay the price for this, having twice been placed under house arrest for several months.

The Centre Union was hit even harder in the beginning. The octogenarian George Papandreou was placed under house arrest, in absolute isolation, only seeing his younger son once or twice a month, for most of the period until his death in November 1968. Despite this, and despite his declining health, he continued to fight. Some months before his death a resistance group succeeded in smuggling abroad a tape with his recorded appeal to world opinion, and the whole of Greece was moved when it was broadcast by foreign radio stations. Andreas Papandreou himself was imprisoned for eight months, in total isolation. Finally, apparently in response to American pressure, the junta freed him and allowed him to go abroad, where he has kept up the fight against the dictatorship.

Several Centre Union deputies, arrested at the beginning or in 1968, are still in prison or in exile in remote villages.[1] Others, arrested at various times, have spent long periods in prison. Nevertheless, almost all of them have continued to demonstrate their total opposition to the dictatorship. George Mylonas, the former Centre Union minister, exiled for more than a year on a small island, succeeded in making a spectacular escape in September 1969 and has since continued the fight abroad.

A number of 'apostates', notably Dimitrios Papaspyrou, former speaker of Parliament, feel the same way as their colleagues of the right and centre. One of the best known among them, Constantine Mitsotakis, who was arrested at the beginning and later released has also managed to escape and join the fight abroad. The only political leader to have shown a benevolent neutrality towards the dictatorship is Markezinis, leader of a small extreme right-wing party. It seems that he hopes one day to be summoned by the colonels, either to join the government or to help in the transition between the dictatorship and some form of parliamentary government within the framework of the 1968 Constitution, which he alone among the politicians has recognised.

E.D.A. was the most badly hit of the parties. Almost all its deputies, as well as thousands of its leaders, were arrested on the night of the putsch and deported, with the result that the party was paralysed. Mikis Theodorakis, the well-known composer, was one of the few left-wing deputies who escaped during the first wave of arrests. He immediately organised the 'Patriotic Front' (PAM) resistance organisation, but was arrested soon afterwards, and then amnestied. The junta would have much liked to win him over. Colonel Ladas personally paid him a number of visits to try to convert him. Furious at being rebuffed, the colonels arrested him again in the summer of 1968, without the slightest grounds, and since then he has lived in prison or in exile, forbidden to communicate with anybody. But this has not stopped him, despite shaky health, from smuggling new songs abroad, which are at the same time calls to resistance.[2] Another E.D.A. deputy, Brillakis, has succeeded in escaping from Greece and at present leads the Greek left in Western Europe.

The junta's propaganda machine has replied with gross sarcasm to all these manifestations of open opposition on the part of the old political world. If they complain, it suggests, it is only because they have been deprived of their power, with its attendant honours and privileges. We will now turn to similar manifestations by other opposition elements, who can scarcely be accused of being influenced by their own personal interests.

In the public service there have been honourable exceptions to the behaviour described in the preceding section. Some provincial governors and diplomats have resigned rather than serve an illegal regime. In the universities, certain professors have had the courage to speak of liberty and human dignity to their students. Among these are Professors Manessis and Maronitis at the University of Thessaloniki, and Professors Mangakis and Pesmazoglou at the University of Athens. All, except Professor Pesmazoglou were later arrested. Pesmazoglou is a distinguished economist who resigned his post as deputy governor of the Bank of Greece, at the same time as the Governor, Xenophon Zolotas, and has made numerous public declarations urging a return to democracy and criticising the regime's economic and educational policies. All these men were cheered by their students, and their ovations provoked police reprisals.[3]

Several priests, refusing to conform to the servile line of the official Church under the renegade Ieronymos, have preached according to their convictions. Several have sought, as true Christians, to help the families of political prisoners. The authorities, aided by the official Church, have pursued them, harassed them in various ways, and sometimes imprisoned them.

One of the most striking examples of resistance has been set by Mrs Helen Vlachou, the owner of two major conservative dailies and a weekly periodical. She stopped them from appearing immediately after the coup, and refused to obey the colonels' orders, mocking them with great gusto, and giving interviews to foreign journalists. She was placed under house arrest but managed to escape abroad, where she works unceasingly to enlighten European opinion about the true nature of the Greek situation. Another newspaper proprietor, Panos Kokkas, has also scuttled his daily newspaper and escaped abroad.

Journalists within Greece continued to protest within the limits of the possible, firstly against the censorship, and then against the press law. Christos Lambrakis, proprietor of a group of centre newspapers, was imprisoned and deported for having refused to co-operate with the regime. Even after the lifting of censorship he declared that he would refuse to publish any political commentary as long as martial law forbade free discussion, and he went on sending protests to the International Press Union, particularly at the time of the ban on the sale of his newspapers in the provinces.

From the first day of the regime, almost all Greek writers— save a few fascists, opportunists, and members of the Academy— went, by tacit agreement, on a silent protest strike (see p. 10). They refused to publish a line under censorship. Of the two leading literary periodicals, one, the left-wing *Epitheorissi Technis*, was banned, and the other, the liberal *Epokhes*, closed down of its own accord. Little by little, as in the Soviet Union, uncensored mimeographed poems, plays, and essays began to circulate from hand to hand. One of the authors added to each of his the motto: 'Illegality has become the last refuge of Justice.'[4]

Painters and sculptors followed the example of the authors for more than a year. No artist of any renown or talent exhibited. Later, by common agreement, they agreed to participate in strictly private exhibitions. Only a number of second-rate artists sent their works to the Panhellenic Exhibition of 1969, which was sponsored by the government. In the same year Kaniaris, a sculptor of some repute, caused a sensation by showing, in a private gallery, some compositions clutching red carnations in plaster, the tragi-comic symbol of the regime, with barbed wire and hands held out in supplication. The police were probably the only ones not to grasp the allusion, or perhaps its chiefs had the intelligence not to intervene, for fear of making fools of themselves.

In 1969 the great poet Seferis, a Nobel prize winner, broke his silence to give a powerful warning—pointing to the impasse in which the nation's cultural life found itself thanks to the regime's obscurantist policies. He spoke of the catastrophe which the continuation of the regime would inevitably bring. His declaration produced a profound impression when broadcast by the B.B.C. and *Deutsche Welle*. For weeks after he received letters of congratulation and telephone calls from every corner of Greece. Deputations of young people and schoolchildren brought messages of gratitude and flowers. The junta, enraged, could find no better reply than to accuse him of being senile.

A month later, eighteen younger writers published a protest against the lack of intellectual freedom in which they declared their solidarity with Seferis, as well as with Czech and Soviet liberal intellectuals. Their message was that 'liberty is indivisible'. Almost at the same time, the great Greek actress, Anna Synodinou, who had refused to appear on the stage since the coup, made an individual protest against the dictatorship.

In December 1969, fifty-five public figures signed a manifesto in which 'as Greeks and Europeans' they demanded an end to the dictatorship, and that the people be free to elect 'a government of its own choice'. An additional twenty people signed the manifesto later. Among the signatories were members of the High Court, admirals, diplomats, former ministers, intellectuals and artists.

So far I have dealt with acts, individual or collective, or open verbal resistance. Clandestine and anonymous resistance is another field where volunteers, and even martyrs, have also not been lacking. Immediately after the putsch several underground groups formed, and of this first wave 'Democratic Defence' (*Demokratiki Amyna*) of centre leaning, and the 'Patriotic Front' (*Patriotiko Metopo*), already mentioned, have survived police persecution. Later there were a multitude of other groups, whose existence usually manifested itself through clandestine tracts.[5] Among these are the 'Free Greeks', who seem to be linked with right-wing and royalist circles, and the 'Panhellenic Liberation Movement'

(P.A.K.), directed by Andreas Papandreou, whose activity seems mainly centred abroad.

'Democratic Defence' distinguished itself both by the scope of its clandestine publications, for it published a substantial printed newspaper for a long time, and by the calibre of its arrested leaders and the gripping trials which followed. Among the distinguished defendants accused of belonging to this group were the sociologist Notaras, the jurist Filias, Plaskovitis, a writer[6] and assessor to the Council of State, General Iordanidis, one of the Greek Army's rare intellectuals, Zannas, a cinema critic and translator of Proust into Greek, and Protopapas, President of the Union of Social Democrats. Most of the defendants in the 'Trial of the Thirty-Four' (see Introduction) belonged to it.

The 'Patriotic Front', for its part, has attracted some of the best elements of the left, men such as Theodorakis, Filinis, a veteran communist intellectual, and the archaeologist Leloudas.[7] These men, disgusted by the expatriate communist leaders' servility towards Moscow, have assumed the leadership of a new left, which is marxist but independent of foreign influence and responsive to the national interest. The Moscow oriented wing of the left is distinguished largely by its non-participation in the resistance, for reasons which we will analyse later. A student offshoot of the Patriotic Front, called 'Rigas Feraios' after a hero of the movement for national independence, carries out important work in the universities.

Obviously, not much can openly be said on the subject of resistance organisations, but it must be admitted that despite the sacrifices of their members, they have not yet become truly mass movements. Their activities are limited by their small membership, they have come up against immense technical difficulties, and they do not seem to have spread much beyond the great urban centres. All of them have suffered serious setbacks, many of their principal leaders having been discovered and arrested by the police fairly rapidly.

The only mass demonstration which has taken place in the four years of dictatorship was totally spontaneous. This was the funeral of George Papandreou on 2 November 1968. It happened only once, but on a massive scale. On that day, half a million Athenians[8] of all ages and backgrounds marched for two hours crying 'freedom', 'free elections', and 'the army back to the barracks'. This huge and peaceful crowd broke the shackles of terror for half a day. It was an unforgettable occasion for those who took part, an absolutely unique experience of solidarity, of loyalty to our maligned free institutions, and to our self-respect as citizens.

When it was not tearfully singing the national anthem which is dedicated to liberty, the crowd cried out over the wreath-strewn coffin of the democratic leader 'Rise up, old man, to see us!', and 'You are the Prime Minister and this is our referendum'.[9] Kanellopoulos was wildly applauded when he gave a moving funeral oration before the coffin of his old opponent. All party feeling and all class antagonism had disappeared during these brief hours of freedom. Elderly retired conservatives fraternised with left-wing students, society women with concierges.

The police were caught unawares by the size of this unexpected explosion. A number of policemen gave smiles of complicity behind their officers' backs. If the crowd had been organised and led, the dictatorship could have been toppled that same day. It is difficult to imagine troops agreeing to fire on such a mass of people.

This extraordinary event, which occurred under martial law and despite the dire warnings of the authorities, was by far the most important event of 1968 if not of the past four years. It showed everyone, Greeks no less than foreign observers, the extent to which the Greek people is united against the dictatorship, and the extent to which the regime's power rests on armed force alone. It boosted the morale of everyone in opposition, who for the first time realised their scattered strength. It terrified the junta which, it is said, had thought itself firmly enough established to risk a number of superficial measures of liberalisation. But it decided after the funeral to postpone them indefinitely and never to allow similar occurrences. When Bakopoulos, an elderly Centre Union deputy, died a short while later, the authorities refused to allow his funeral to take place in Athens.

Apart from the junta's propaganda machine, one other source tried to minimise the significance of the funeral demonstration. This was Radio Moscow, which scarcely mentioned it in its bulletins and estimated the number of demonstrators at a derisory 50,000. This is less surprising when one realises that the only segment of the population absent from the demonstration were the workers from the 'red' suburbs, loyal to the Moscow wing of the Communist Party. Similarly, the only diplomats who did not attend the funeral ceremony were those of the Eastern bloc countries.

Violent action is a legitimate response to any tyranny. To quote from a clandestine tract that circulated in May 1969,[10] 'If you can't say it with votes, say it with bombs'. The organisation of such activity, however, is always fraught with difficulties. In addition to the technical problems posed in the making of explosive devices and the need for absolute secrecy, etc., there are also psychological inhibitions to be overcome in the average democrat: a lack of familiarity with the use and means of violence, and a repugnance against anything which might cost the lives of innocent people, or even those of secondary supporters of the regime.

Little by little, resolute men were able to surmount these difficulties. A group, probably inspired and helped abroad by the Panhellenic Liberation Movement, organised in August 1968 the famous attempt against Papadopoulos' life, which narrowly failed. The main person behind this attempt was Alexander Panagoulis, then aged thirty.

After several isolated attempts, a wave of plastic bomb explosions took place in May 1969 and continued for several months, mainly in Athens but also in Thessaloniki. The targets of the attacks differed: cars belonging to American agencies, cars and homes of collaborators and police torturers, places frequented by large numbers of tourists, electricity pylons, night spots frequented by the ruling clique. It is clear that some of these attacks were intended as warning: to the Americans that they stop supporting the junta, and to tourists that they adhere to the resistance's boycott on tourism. Others were intended to punish collaborators. Still others, such as those aimed at electricity pylons, were intended to disrupt everyday life.

Most Greeks were deeply stirred. The explosions became the main topic of conversation. There were a few frightened reservations: 'Where will all this lead?', and 'What if my child were there?' But most comment was enthusiastic. Each explosion was felt to be a blow against the dictatorship. People, greatly encouraged, went to sleep and woke up with the hope of hearing of further attempts; their morale shot upwards. The authorities' reaction was extremely nervous, and newspapers were forbidden to mention the explosions. Collaborators of the regime began to panic, and hesitated to speak out. One of them had given an appointment to a foreign correspondent who wished to cover the full range of opinion for a television programme. On the day of the appointment the frightened apologist for the dictatorship excused himself. 'I would rather not speak to you before the camera, one never knows what might happen. . . .' Fear had changed sides, and all this was achieved without a single victim. The attacks had all been carefully planned so as to spare innocent lives. The amount of explosive in those bombs detonated in public places had clearly been calculated to produce only a fairly harmless noise.

This moderation, this humanity even, in employing violent means may perhaps have done a disservice to the cause. Questioned about an explosion which took place two hours previously, a foreign correspondent shrugged his shoulders. 'I telephoned my newspaper,' he said. 'They wanted to know if there were any deaths. Otherwise they are just not interested.' The readers of the international press are too blasé these days, accustomed to massacres in Vietnam or in Indonesia, or famine in India. They must be served with very spicy tidbits to obtain any kind of reaction. Explosions of a purely symbolic character, for the freedom of an oppressed people, no longer have any impact on them. An American observer said to some opposition Greeks: 'If you really want to create an impression, to stop the flow of tourists, and to give my government something to think about, you must kill two or three of my countrymen. Then you will hit the headlines, and there will be questions in Congress. . . .'

Even when fighting against gangsters, however, it is not easy for basically decent people to adopt their methods. And the quality of the people arrested in connection with explosions to date fully explains their moral dilemma. It is with astonishment, mixed with admiration and pity, that the Greeks have learned that a group accused of bomb offences included, among others, two university professors, Mangakis and Karayorgas, as well as distinguished lawyers and economists.[11] Another group, already tried and condemned, was made up of very young people, mainly students. All showed great courage before the military tribunal, as have almost all Greek resisters tried since the beginning of the dictatorship.[12]

Judging by the people arrested and by the tenor of the leaflets accompanying the explosions, the groups responsible for them are almost all centre or right wing in outlook. Tracts signed 'General Akritas', and claiming the responsibility for a number of explosions, express loyalty to the King and Karamanlis. The section of the left engaged in active resistance has taken little part in the violent activity up till now.

However, this action ceased in October 1969. It is too soon to say if all the groups have been broken up by the massive arrests made during the course of the summer and autumn of 1969, or if the present calm[13] is only the prelude to a new wave of activity which is being quietly prepared.

Besides those who have raised their voices against the dictatorship, and those who have fought it with clandestine tracts or bombs, there is an army of people who work secretly at less conspicuous, but equally necessary, tasks.

There are those who run considerable risks making collections for the families of political prisoners, for deportees and for those who have lost their jobs because of their opinions. It is strictly forbidden for private citizens to aid these thousands of families who sometimes suffer quite literally from terrible hunger. If they receive cheques or money from abroad and the police find out, they are submitted to a terrifying interrogation to disclose where the money is coming from. (The International Red Cross has the right to help only those families whose breadwinner has been in prison or deported *for more than two years*.)

There are those who do their utmost to get hold of secret information—cases of torture or incidents in the armed forces, and what is going on in the ministries or the prisons—and transmit this information to the right quarters. It is largely due to these anonymous resistance workers that the Council of Europe's Sub-Commission on Human Rights gathered the material necessary to compile its famous report. It is thanks to them that correspondents, newspapers, and foreign broadcasting stations learn what is going on in Greece—concerning economic development as well as police arrests, resistance declarations as well as government lies. There are some groups that concern themselves with escapes, thanks to whom many victims of the junta, among them a number of those who have been tortured, have been able to reach Western Europe and testify at Strasbourg. There are loyal military men who study maps and prepare contingency plans.

There are many more such people than one would suspect, to judge from the more or less calm appearance that Greece presents to the unwary visitor. It is this apparent normality, in the broad light of day, that forces resisters to live in such a strange ambiance. The present dictatorship is not apocalyptically visible to the naked eye, as was the Nazi occupation. There is no hunger, no immediately obvious misery, no guerilla force in the mountains, no shooting in the suburbs. One goes to the café, or for a walk, or meets with friends and continues to work at one's job. Telephone conversations are of a uniform banality: 'Will you come for a drink?', 'Yes, I have found the record you were looking for', 'The children are well, thank you', 'Aunt Katherine was in a good mood last night', 'It seems that Theodore arrived a bit late, but in good form.' This could mean, *en clair*: 'I must see you', 'I have the information you want', 'The group is well', 'Cologne Radio had some good news for us last night', 'P. arrived in Cyprus rather later but in good health.' Precautions of this kind have become such second nature to us that we shall probably have difficulty in ridding ourselves of them even after liberation. Other precautions are necessary for certain contacts and visits. Meetings of a mundane or social appearance often have but one aim, to facilitate talk without looking conspiratorial, and the subject for discussion is resistance. A car which contains a happy group of boys and girls, apparently *en route* to a bouzouki spot, could also contain a clandestine duplicating machine, pamphlets, or even explosives. The police realise this, and car searches are frequent. The tourist himself only notices outward appearances, and concludes that everything must be normal and peaceful in a Greece where everyone seems carefree and without fear.

The devotion and the spirit of sacrifice shown by these latter-day klephts cannot disguise the fundamental weaknesses of the Greek resistance. Frankness in these matters seems preferable to the optimistic clichés found in various pamphlets and pompous proclamations which appear occasionally, in Greece as well as abroad.

For, as we have said, the resistance has not succeeded in establishing itself on a large scale. It still remains essentially the concern of a small élite. The raya admire this resistance from afar, but do not participate in it. It is not an act of resistance merely to curse the regime, to spread the latest jokes against it, or to deface its hated badge (the soldier in the midst of a phoenix being reborn from its ashes) on a matchbox. No organised demonstration of passive resistance, even a short strike, has yet been successful.

This is partly explained by the lack of coherence, unity and direction in the resistance. Despite certain agreements made between 'Democratic Defence', the 'Patriotic Front', and the 'Panhellenic Liberation Movement', the different organisations most frequently act on their own and without any co-ordination. This dispersal of effort has major advantages from the security point of view, as the police cannot trace one group through another. But it also has very grave disadvantages from the point of efficiency. The unification of resistance groups, which would greatly increase their total strength, is prevented by the ideological differences and the mutual distrust that still exists between, for example, royalist and left-wing resisters; by the excessive individualism of the Greeks, and the petty jealousies and vanities which prevents one from taking orders from another, and vice-versa; by the lack of agreement between the émigré opposition leaders who would have the necessary authority to impose a programme of unified action on their supporters in Greece.[14] The left, which is the most experienced in clandestine activities, is weakened by internal divisions, which absorb much of its energy. (Certain indications lead one to suspect, but without any degree of certainty, that these feuds within the far left have even led to mutual denunciations to the police.) Bourgeois political groups are by definition less suited to waging non-parliamentary battles. Besides, the Centre Union also suffers from a lack of united leadership. All its leaders are far from accepting Andreas Papandreou as George Papandreou's successor. The right, too, is some way from political unity. Although its official leader is Kanellopoulos, the prestige of his predecessor Karamanlis is much greater among an important section of E.R.E.

One may argue that the resistance should produce its own leaders, and free itself from the old political groupings. This has happened to a certain extent and has produced the élite groups who have carried out the resistance. But how could the new leaders, in the present situation, make themselves known, reach the masses, and get them to accept their orders? There could be only one way to achieve this: if the leaders were to throw themselves into clandestine activity, leaving their homes, their families, and their work to become full-time revolutionaries, under their own names, they would soon acquire an authority proportionate to their actions. But all this is not easy, either to decide upon or to carry off successfully. The rare attempts made up to now, namely by Filias, Theodorakis, etc., have resulted in as many failures.

One final word on the struggle being carried on by the Greeks abroad. Almost all the Greeks living in Western Europe at the time of the putsch—intellectuals, artists, students, and especially workers (there are almost two hundred thousand workers abroad, mainly in West Germany)—were immediately and openly hostile to the junta. Only a few businessmen, led by the rich shipowners, have supported it. Later there was a wave of refugees fleeing the dictatorship—politicians, journalists, intellectuals, and other victims. These included, besides those already mentioned, Professors Vegleris, Despotopoulos, and Tenekidis, well-known actors and actresses, such as Diamantopoulos and Melina Mercouri, Irene Papas and Aspasia Papathanassiou, economists and sociologists such as Krimpas and Tsoukalas, journalists such as Lampsas and Lambrias.

All these people fight against the junta, either by helping the internal resistance in different ways or by helping to enlighten foreign opinion as to the situation in present day Greece by means of books, periodicals, brochures, meetings, and personal contacts. In this last area, given the particular nature of the Greek problem, which can only find a solution in a larger European, if not Atlantic framework, the resistance abroad is of the greatest importance. We are grateful to those of our émigré comrades who have devoted themselves to this sometimes thankless task. We will discuss this topic at greater length in the last part of this work.

10. REPRESSION

A foreign observer has described the present regime as a 'despotism tempered by inefficiency'. There is some truth in this. One hears, for instance, that the military governor of a certain district forbids the sale of opposition newspapers A and B, while a colleague in his own particular fief allows the sale of A, but not of B and C, and a third bans not only A, B, and C, but even the government newspaper *Nea Politeia*, because its literary pages are in the demotic. This lack of logic and co-ordination does not, however, make the repression any more tolerable. It only increases uncertainty as to exactly what is permitted and what not. Besides, in matters concerning the junta's security, repression does not depend on the idiosyncrasies of military governors, but on the security forces, which are highly centralised.

Yet the security services, police and gendarmerie, are far from being as politically homogeneous as one might imagine. Despite the purge which they have undergone like the other state services, they still include a large body of men who are scarcely enamoured of the regime.[1] Most of them, however, do not dare to show their sympathies openly. They feel that they are under observation, are worried about their careers, and those whose reliability is in doubt are usually in provincial or unimportant posts, where they have no effective power. The functions of a political police are carried out by a handpicked number of officers, assisted by the Military Police—a new occurrence in Greece. (The Military Police are actively involved in hunting down civilian opponents and in interrogating them. A number of its officers have acquired a certain notoriety as torturers: Major Theofiloyannakos who had played an important part in the ASPIDA trial is an example. To be detained in a Military Police station is even more frightening than to be in the hands of the ordinary police or the gendarmerie.)

Even with this revamped organisation, the security forces are far from being infallible. The plastic bomb explosions had them baffled for a long time. At the beginning of summer 1969, the junta, disappointed with their performance, simultaneously sacked the chiefs of the police and gendarmerie, although they had been appointed only a short time before. It needed an unforeseeable accident, the explosion of a small bomb in the hands of Professor Karayorgas, to put the police on the track of the group subsequently accused of a number of attacks. But in general it is true that while the state machine is becoming increasingly decrepit, the security forces remain the most efficient branch of the government. They excel in tracking down opponents once they are known, in extracting their secrets once they have been arrested, and in making life unbearable for those whom, for one reason or another, the junta cannot or does not want to bring to trial.

For this last group there is firstly the whole range of petty administrative persecutions already described in earlier sections, which can have a repressive as well as a preventive character. Those in disfavour can be prevented from working, for example, or from having a telephone, or from driving a car, or from travelling abroad, either because their opinions displease the security police or because they have openly opposed the regime. These persecutions, of course, escape the investigations of organisations such as the Council of Europe or the International Red Cross.

Next comes the suppression of individual freedom by administrative means. There exist several variants. The first is house arrest which George Papandreou, Panayotis Kanellopoulos, and several other major personalities, such as the former minister George Mavros and Helen Vlachou, have been subjected to. The person under house arrest is locked up in his own home and cannot receive any visitors. Policemen watch his home night and day, and search members of the family and domestic staff as they arrive and depart. Sometimes there are policemen in the house itself, following the occupant from room to room and not allowing him even to close the door of his bedroom or bathroom. Those who have experienced this treatment say that it is calculated to break the strongest of nerves, worse in certain respect than deportation to a remote village.

And yet there is nothing pleasant about deportation. It is sometimes applied as a preventive measure, sometimes against people who have incurred the wrath of the junta. This treatment is decided on by the security services alone without any sort of trial. No concrete accusation is necessary. A simple administrative decision is all that is needed: 'X is a danger to public security', and X is off, under a heavy escort, to an island or a mountain village where he will stay for as long as it pleases the colonel in charge of his case. Seventeen drachmas per day (about 25 pence) is allowed to the deportee for all his needs, including food, lodging, and subsistence for his family. In other words, if he does not have other means available, he is liable to starve. And it should be remembered that the International Red Cross has the right to help a family only after two years in detention.

The bulk of those in detention consists of former left-wing militants arrested during the first few hours of the putsch and dispersed in a number of concentration camps in the islands. These amounted to several thousand in the beginning and include a high percentage of the elderly and sick, as well as women.[2] Conditions in these camps were essentially the same as those in the prisons, and were particularly bad from the point of view of hygiene, space, food, and permission to correspond and receive visitors.[3] It should be stressed that there was not the least accusation against the victims save the offence of adhering to their beliefs, yet they were in detention for up to four years. Those who have been freed are generally those who have signed declarations repudiating their convictions. Those who remained are those who had too much pride and self-respect to sign. It should be noted that some of these men and women were undergoing their second or third internment in twenty-five years, and having spent the prime of their lives in prisons are such human wrecks that no sane person could consider them a danger.

These prisoners were the subject of a memorable dialogue, shortly after the putsch, between Pattakos and a delegation of European socialist deputies who were enquiring about the fate of political prisoners. 'There are no political prisoners', Pattakos told them. Questioned about 'these people who all the same are on Yaros', he replied that they were not political prisoners, but communists. 'Aren't communists political prisoners, too?' asked the mystified visitors. 'No, they are brutes', came the reply. Asked if it were right for a Christian such as he to discriminate between human beings, Pattakos replied with the rude soldierly frankness for which he is known: 'I distinguish between men and brutes.'[4] It was also Pattakos who replied 'no' to the wife of a left-wing deputy who was seriously ill, when she asked for a passport to go abroad for an operation. 'But the doctors say that if I do not go, I shall die.' 'Very well then, die', retorted this exemplary Christian.

Apart from the detainees rounded up at the beginning, more than a hundred people underwent 'individual' deportation. Here the system was different, at least until the autumn of 1969.[5] Each deportee was sent to a different place, an island or mountain village. Sometimes if there were two of them on the same island, they were not allowed to speak to each other. For the idea was to break their morale by isolation. In return, anyone was free to rent, on his seventeen drachmas per day, a house or a hotel room. Very often, the village was so poor and backward, without electricity or any modern conveniences, that the deportee was lucky to find any kind of roof to shelter under. The deputies Alevras and Angheloussis were thus obliged to live for several months in the ruins of a house destroyed by an earthquake and declared 'uninhabitable', on the small isolated island of Aghios Efstratios.

These deportees could take their families with them and receive visits from friends if they wished. They were, however, forbidden to see politicians, army officers, journalists, or generally any 'opponents'. They had to report twice a day at the gendarmerie station of the village to sign an 'attendance register', and walks in the surrounding countryside were strictly forbidden. For Theodorakis, the composer and former left-wing deputy, the routine was even stricter. Deported for more than a year to a mountain village, he was additionally put under house arrest, and could not leave his house or see anyone. At the village school, his children were sat on one side, so as not to 'contaminate' the others.[6]

In some villages, the local gendarmerie go so far as to forbid the residents any contact with the deportees, who sometimes have had to order their food from Athens, and even send their laundry there. In those villages where contact with the local population is allowed, the inhabitants continually demonstrate their warm sympathy. 'We are all with you', one of them was told, the day after his arrival, by the mayor of a village, who went to welcome him with the local council. 'But be careful', he added in a lower voice, 'of the butcher and the priest, who are pro-government.'[7]

Who are these dangerous people who have been deported? Dozens of E.R.E. and Centre Union supporters, among them a number of former ministers such as Rallis, Mavros, Zighdis, and Papaspyrou. University teachers such as Professors Evrighenis and Manessis. Lawyers such as those mentioned on pp. 86-7. Former senior civil servants such as George Kavounidis, the former director-general of the Ministry to the Prime Minister, and Peponis, the former director-general of Television and Radio. Distinguished journalists, such as Christos Lambrakis and George Drossos. Distinguished retired military men, some of whom have occupied the highest command posts in the Armed Forces, such as Generals Peridis, Kollias, Erselmann, Lengheris, Koumanakos,

Tsepapadakis; colonels Opropoulos, Papaterpos, Zervoyannis; Admiral Rozakis, navy Captain Konofagos; air force Generals Deros, Koniotakis and Antonakos; air force Colonel Diakoumakos —to name just a few. The majority of these men are of the right, particularly loyal to the King.[8]

In the Dantesque world of the junta's victims, the non-communist deportees, such as those we have just mentioned, belong to those whom one could call, after Solzhenitsyn, 'the first circle'. Their condition is infinitely better than that of the communist internees of Leros, Oropos, and Halikarnassos. These, for their part, live better than the non-communist detainees arrested in the spring of 1969 and kept hidden since then in two hotels near Athens. They are held in complete isolation, each in a room with hermetically sealed windows, and with no contact with their fellow-prisoners. They can scarcely move, let alone exercise. By day and night they have only artificial light, and they can read and eat only what their families bring them, for they are not even fed by the authorities. They know neither why they are there nor how long they will remain. 'We will leave only as corpses', one of them desperately said to his wife during the course of the weekly ten-minute visit which they are allowed. In this they are more fortunate than the communist internees, who are entitled to a visit from their families only once every three months.

They are for the most part conservatives, especially military men, whose lives have largely been spent in working for NATO. They include Generals Tzannetis, Vardoulakis, Panourghias, Tsikhlis, and Kehagias and a large number of senior officers of the three services.[9] Others arrested at the same time were exiled, including General Ghennimatas, former joint Chief of Staff.

At the time of the massive arrests of prominent personalities from the right and centre, Papadopoulos declared, at a press conference on 7 June 1969, that a plot to overthrow the government had been discovered which implicated conspirators ranging from royalists to Communist Party members. He seemed unaware of the extraordinary confession he was making—namely, that Greeks of all opinions are against the regime. In fact, no communist was arrested in this round up, nor were the detainees charged. The promised revelations are still awaited.

The most plausible explanation for this wave of arrests is fear, the fear which the junta feels quite as much as it inspires. Its members know how weak the dictatorship's foundations are, and are conscious that only a spark is needed to set fire to the powder legal training. It should not be imagined, however, that their presence constitutes any kind of guarantee of even rudimentary justice. They are too fearful of the four other members of the tribunal, before whom they feel inferior, and whom they often seek to equal in severity. These four other members are regular officers, belonging to any branch of the army and appointed *ad hoc* for each occasion by the military authorities. The authorities are evidently afraid that if these men attend too many trials they may acquire some legal notions, and being less terrified than the civilians could get it into their heads to apply them. This fear seems to have little foundation. These officers are carefully selected from among the hard liners, those whose blind and unconditional attachment to the dictatorship is softened by no humanitarian scruples, and whose decisions are dictated in advance by the military authorities.

These tribunals apply the summary procedure intended for courts-martial at the front line during wartime. The conduct of the trial varies in relation to the number and importance of the foreign observers attending it, and also in relation to the individual temperament of the judges and the instructions they have received. There were cases, especially at the beginning, when there was, if not courtesy and objectivity, for that would be too much to expect, at least a certain order and a willingness to respect convention, for example, in allowing the defence to speak freely. These cases became increasingly rare. The judges now do not always trouble to control themselves even in the presence of distinguished observers. At the trial of the Thessaloniki 'Democratic Defence' group, which took place in November 1968, President Karapanos, formerly a civilian judge removed for dereliction of duty, made no attempt to conceal his venomous hostility towards the accused, who were all well-known intellectuals. He continually interrupted them and their lawyers, and was insolent and insulting. This caused a foreign observer to remark, 'Why do they need a public prosecutor when the president acts as one?'[13] A year later, at the trial of a group belonging to the 'Patriotic Front', two young girl students were convicted without ever speaking one complete sentence in their own defence, the president silencing them each time. Very often, as in Nazi and Soviet courts, the president and the members of the tribunal launch into political speeches supporting the dictatorship.

The courts-martial refuse to hear defence witnesses who might prove embarrassing. Thus at the trial of Mrs Mangakis, accused of slander for having publicly expressed fear that her husband was being tortured,[14] the court would not allow him to appear as a witness. Had the rule of law prevailed this would have resulted in the whole procedure being declared void. In the same way, at the trial of Major Pnevmatikos, the tribunal refused to allow his officer brother, serving a prison sentence for similar political reasons, to appear, on the grounds that 'there was a danger that he might escape'.

Under preventive censorship, in force until October 1969, the newspapers could publish only the expurgated versions of political trials given them by the propaganda services. Thus, at his trial, Alexander Panagoulis (see p. 139) complained of having been tortured, showing his feet and hands which still bore the marks. The court not only refused to take note of his complaint, but condemned him on the spot to two years in prison for contempt of court. The papers mentioned this interim sentence, without giving the full reason, for the word 'torture' was taboo. This same punctilious censorship, however, does not stop newspapers loyal to the regime from treating the accused as guilty before the trial. Thus a group to be tried for bomb explosions was described in headlines in *Eleftheros Kosmos* as 'the guilty ten'.

In theory the public has free access to the trial proceedings, but in practice it is restricted. The policemen on duty do everything possible to discourage visitors. They interrogate them, noting their names and addresses and ask what interest they have in the trial. To those who are not intimidated by these methods, they generally finish up by saying 'there's no more room'. This is often true, the small court-rooms being completely filled with the accused, their lawyers, their guards, their relatives, some journalists, and a hoard of plain-clothes policemen. Moreover, when the authorities fear the revelations which a trial might bring, they conduct it *in camera*. This was the case with Major Pnevmatikos, who recounted how he had been tortured. The trial took place *in camera* under the pretext that one of the items of prosecution evidence was a defamatory letter written by this officer to Papadopoulos, and it would be sacrilegious to reveal it to the public.

Given the composition and procedure of the military tribunals, the worst might have been expected. And it happened. The severity of the sentences, against which, of course, there exists not the slightest redress, is frightening. A few examples will suffice: four and a half years in prison for having shouted 'long live freedom' at the funeral of George Papandreou; three years for 'the dissemination of false news'; the same for 'having lent a work on biology, translated from the Russian, to a minor'; ten and a half years to Zannas (see p. 137); on several occasions sentences of over *twenty* years to left-wing students for distributing clandestine are made to adjourn his trial indefinitely, and at the same time he is kept from appearing as a witness in any other trial where he might, from the witness box, recount what happened to him.

If the accused proves to be particularly stubborn, his trial takes place *in camera*. Such was the case, as we have seen, with Major Pnevmatikos, to prevent his telling of the 'Mexican torture' to which, among others, he had been subjected by the military police. This involved his being buried up to the neck in mud and being hit on the head by masked men who circled around him. Any member of the detainee's family who dares to denounce the tortures inflicted on his relative is punished. Thus Mrs Mangakis (see p. 150) was sentenced to four years in prison, later reduced on appeal to eleven months. Delegates of international organisations such as the Red Cross were, under an agreement of November 1969, allowed to visit 'all prisons, detention camps, etc.'. But the places where torture is actually being carried out do not come into these categories, and are not officially known. A 'negative' certificate by the organisation in question, is then produced, to the effect that they have 'established nothing' in the localities visited. This is then used to deny the allegations of the 'enemies of the nation'. (In any case the agreement with the Red Cross was not renewed in November 1970. Addendum 1971.)

The delegates of the European Commission of Human Rights were not allowed to see Gerassimos Notaras and Alexander Panagoulis,[18] who had both loudly denounced the tortures to which they have been subjected. To take the first case, Notaras made his allegations in July 1968. Eight months later, in March 1969, he was not allowed to appear before the delegates of the European Commission of Human Rights on the grounds that an enquiry was being made into his allegations. The delegates left. Another year passed, and no more was heard of this fictitious enquiry; it was only a cheap ruse meant to fool the 'foreign imbeciles'.

In every country where torture takes place there are always some people who falsely claim to have been tortured, in order to attract interest or to excuse a betrayal. Any moderately efficient police knows well how to exploit these false depositions, and if need be to forge them, using *agents provocateurs*. At the strategic moment it releases them to discredit the truthful depositions. Any generalisation on the basis of similar cases in Greece therefore has no foundation.

A medical examination with a negative result is not always meaningful, even if it is carried out by a specialist other than the official forensic doctor, Kapsaskis.[19] There exist terrible tortures which can break a man without leaving discernible physical traces. Such is the torture of prolonged sleeplessness, or blinding light, or of long periods of isolation in a cell where it is impossible either to stand up or sit down. There are also the psychological tortures, a refined specimen of which consists of forcing the detainee to be present at the torture of his comrades, or by forcing him to hear their screams.[20] The police told Professor Karayorgas, scarcely recovered from his wounds following the explosion (see p. 140), that his children had been killed by the blast. This of course was absolutely untrue, but calculated to break him.

The systematic use of torture in our day in Europe is an emotive issue, but should not become an obsession to the exclusion of other aspects of the Greek dictatorship. Torture comprises only one of the means used to break human dignity, the most inhuman certainly, but also the least common. Even if torture were abolished tomorrow, the regime would scarcely become any more tolerable. Such a hypothesis is only academic, however, for the use of torture is a necessary corollary of an unpopular dictatorship. The junta, constantly fearing for its very existence, cannot afford to renounce the most efficient means of fighting its secret enemies, of extracting from an arrested resister the names of other members of his group, their means of printing their tracts, or of obtaining explosives, etc.

Some foreign commentators, knowing little about modern Greece, have patronisingly claimed that there is no need to get unduly excited about torture in Greece, the Greeks having long been accustomed to it, under all regimes. This is as false as it is malevolent. It is true that there was talk of torture during the Metaxas dictatorship, but it has never been proved. It may have been a fabrication propagated by the police at the time to terrify potential opponents.[21] In one hundred years of parliamentary life, torture was unknown in Greece—except, of course, for such beatings-up by police officers as unfortunately happen even in the most civilised of countries. (There were some exceptions to this rule during the civil war, in 1947-1949.) True, there was the 'air force affair' (see p. 41), but even there the existence of a free press and a Parliament permitted public opinion to show its disapproval and forced the government to free the victims.

The junta boasts of having spilt no blood. It is true that, up to now, there have been no official executions. But this is less attributable to the junta's humanity, for other manifestations of which one looks in vain, than to an astute calculation on the part of Papadopoulos, who is conscious of the international uproar that would have followed. Besides, the colonels have no need of executions. Their other repressive measures have, so far, been effective enough to allow them to keep their opponents alive.[22]

This does not mean that resisters have not been murdered. The most prominent case was that of the left-wing deputy, George Tsarouchas, arrested and beaten to death by security policemen in Thessaloniki on 8 May 1968. The police claimed he had suffered a 'heart attack', but would not allow Tsarouchas' family to open the coffin to see him.[23]

PART THREE

The Future, or how to get rid of them

I. THE ILLUSION OF GRADUAL EVOLUTION

THE present regime is destroying not only all the institutions which guarantee the dignity of the citizen and mean a better future for our children, but even that which is best in the character of our people. As the process continues, an increasing number of intellectuals and other leaders, including much of the country's best young talent, are going into exile, in search of the free and civilised life which has disappeared from their own country. Among those who will remain, the most courageous will continue to fight, only in turn to be broken and imprisoned. The cowardly and the cynical will compromise, surviving as bureaucrats and technicians. The ambitious and unscrupulous will go into the army. The rest will retreat into an impotent and bitter silence. Intellectual life, the clash of ideas and criticism will wither. The Greece that we know and love, the Greece for which we have fought, will disappear as a spiritual entity.

Let no one reply that Greece has managed to survive other misfortunes in the course of its long history. These comparisons no longer hold true. Today the rhythm of historical development is completely different. Every year is important in the development of a nation; a single decade could be decisive. The country that will stay out of the race all this time, and even more so the country that will actually retrogress, will be permanently damaged.

Almost everyone is in agreement as to the facts. Opinions differ only on the answer to the question 'How can the dictatorship be brought to an end?'

One answer is that of the 'evolutionists'. 'Certainly', they say, 'we should return to a free and representative form of government as soon as possible. But this cannot be brought about by the violent overthrow of the dictatorship. This regime is too strong, and the people are not determined enough to fight it. Even if they did want to fight it, a bloody confrontation and eventual civil war should be avoided at all costs. Let us be realistic. Let us start by keeping quiet to reassure the colonels. Let us encourage some experienced politicians to enter the government and exercise a moderating influence. Once an atmosphere of calm, of mutual confidence and good-will is established, the colonels will have no reason to delay the implementation of the 1968 Constitution which they themselves promulgated. Even if this Constitution is not ideal, it will surely be better than the present arbitrary rule. Once we have some kind of parliamentary life, things will gradually get better of their own accord.'

The Greeks who hold this view belong mainly to the conservative camp. They were far from numerous at the beginning, and they have grown fewer since. This view, however, is still very widespread in official circles in both the United States and a number of European countries. The soundings, advice, and pressures made by these circles have usually been directed towards such a solution, i.e. accelerating the implementation of the institutions created by the junta itself, principally the 1968 Constitution.

To look briefly at the 1968 Constitution and the legislation relating to it, we will use a deductive process which, we think, will be clearer than a long dissertation. The Western conception of democracy is that of a state where all the citizens are equal before the law and enjoy fundamental individual rights. Where, by means of open debate, every school of thought is free to try to gain a majority, and to elect representatives who will then be empowered to govern. Where everyone can investigate and criticise these rulers, who will be replaced if the majority changes its mind. All this constitutes an 'open' society[1] whose fundamental characteristic is that it can evolve and adapt itself to changing circumstances as these are reflected in the mind and will of its members. The opposite model, that of a 'closed' society, seeks to maintain at all costs the *status quo*, in religious, ideological, racial, social, or economic matters, and to this end thwarts all change and particularly the critical spirit that might engender change. Generally speaking, this latter category consists of primitive societies, traditional aristocracies, and modern totalitarian regimes.

Suppose for the moment that we are a military junta possessing absolute power in a country. We believe that the day may come when we have to go through the motions of restoring democracy. On the other hand, we know that if we really restore it this will be the end of us. Therefore we must prepare institutions which maintain the external appearances of democracy while ensuring the continuation of the substance of our power. We must prepare an officially open society to follow, but this must in fact ensure that the hermetically sealed society which we are in the process of creating will survive.

If we wish to look like a democracy, at least outwardly, we must concede as a minimum the classic individual rights, such as free-dom of expression, of association, of assembly, of industrial action, from arbitrary arrest and detention, and the inviolability of the home, etc. Secondly, a representative system, in which the majority in an elected chamber would designate the government, control its activities and, if need be, overthrow it. (As the presidential system is unknown in Greece we need not discuss it here.)

In order to nullify these apparent concessions, or at least greatly to reduce their impact, we would introduce the following novel measure. We would include all these civil rights in our Constitu-tion, but would effectively limit those that could be dangerous for us. For example: the right to strike would be strictly limited to satisfying economic demands (Art. 19), which would keep our opponents from using them for political ends. Further, we would hedge it about with a number of restrictions and prohibitions such as a very long early warning system, a maximum duration, etc., which would further diminish its effectiveness. Under the old constitution, civil servants were already forbidden to strike. To these we will now add students, the penalty for infringement being expulsion from the university (see the Student Code, cited on p. 91). The right of association in respect of political parties would be limited by a Constitutional Court empowered to dis-solve 'unsuitable' parties (Art. 58).

Freedom of expression in itself is a very dangerous thing. It encourages questioning minds and impertinence towards those in authority. We would, therefore, impose on it new and very strict limits, partly in the Constitution itself, and partly in our press law,[2] or through other appropriate laws. We would forbid the press, under pain of immediate confiscation, to 'provoke a defeatist atmosphere', to propagate the views of political parties which we have outlawed, and to publish information on the armed forces, which are one of our reserved domains (Const. Art. 14, para. 4). We would forbid, and penalise with imprisonment, the publication of anything which 'might reanimate political passions', to avoid any embarrassing criticism through reference to the past (P.L. Art. 52) and forbid, also under threat of imprisonment, the publi-cation of information on our intelligence services, or those of our allies, for example our friends in the C.I.A. (P.L. Art. 50, para. 1d). We would forbid, under threat of at least one year of imprisonment (two years for a second offence) and a substantial fine, the spreading, by word of mouth or in writing, of 'rumours calculated to undermine the public's confidence in the state power [i.e. ourselves] or in the economic or financial policies of the State'.[3] (We have had an example of the application of this law in

February 1970: a man who had suggested, in a village café, that Greece's withdrawal from the Council of Europe would have unfortunate economic consequences was sentenced to a year in prison. Now, this degree of repression will no longer be based on a 'temporary' state of siege, but it will be permanently enshrined in our 'new and healthy democracy'.)

The free publication of parliamentary proceedings, or of the speeches of opposition deputies, if they include items embarrassing to us, will be forbidden (P.L. 53). Moreover, the provisions of the penal code dealing with the accused's right of access to a lawyer, his right to request an adjournment to prepare his defence, to be given a suspended sentence, etc., will not applicable to press offences (P.L. Art. 32 and 35). Nor will suspended sentences be given for contravening Art. 191 of the penal code. In the case of a second offence, substituting a fine for a prison sentence will not be possible (P.L. 36),[4] and if the second offence has occurred within five years of the first, the newspaper could be permanently banned (P.L. Art. 88). Finally, as opposition newspapers will certainly be popular, we will punish them while aiding papers which sacrifice their circulations to help us: exemption from duty on newsprint will be in inverse proportion to a paper's circulation (P.L. Art. 20).

The rights of the individual could still prove a source of embarrassment even when hedged about in this way. We will therefore provide, in our constitution, two provisions for suspending them: for individual opponents, by means of a judgment of the Constitutional Court that they were 'abusing' the Constitution (Art. 24, para. 2); for the entire population, by the proclamation of a 'state of emergency', in case of, among other things, 'a disturbance of, or apparent threat to, public order' (Art. 25). Such a proclamation will not, as previously, need to be ratified by the Parliament, where awkward questions could be asked about the reality of the threat. It will be enough, for the first three months at least, to have it ratified by our 'Council of the Nation', a new and 'reliable' institution, for it will consist of the Prime Minister, the heads of the two largest parliamentary parties, of whom one at least will support us, and may in fact be the Prime Minister himself, the president of the Constitutional Court and the chief of the armed forces, a figure to whom we will return.

Let us pass now to the organisation of the representative system and the relations between Parliament, the King and the government. There are different ways of combining these three arms of government, the extent of each one's effective power varying according to the system chosen. As we have reason to distrust the

King, we will give him a role that is almost purely formal—a reform that will be as popular as he is unpopular. The Prime Minister will be appointed either by an absolute majority in Parliament or by the Council of the Nation. Once appointed, the King will only be able to get rid of him on the advice of the Council (Art. 43). Thus he will not be able to trick us as he did George Papandreou in July 1965.

The government will be considerably strengthened in relation to Parliament, which will not be able to defeat it easily or exercise any control in matters of defence and foreign policy (Art. 77). We will cut the number of deputies and their privileges, which will be a very popular move. We will also curtail their parliamentary immunity, so that they will not be insolent towards the real source of power (Arts. 67 and 68).

It may be objected that however powerful the executive becomes, it will still depend on a parliamentary majority. This is so, but we will be careful to ensure that this majority will be 'right' thinking. First of all, as we have indicated, the political parties will be supervised and, if need be, dissolved by the Constitutional Court. Furthermore, any propagating of ideas contrary to our own will be seriously hampered by the press laws, and the same will apply to any criticism of us which might alienate the electors. Finally, it is not for nothing that we have purged the security forces, the administration, and the legal profession, by eliminating all potentially hostile elements. The whole apparatus of state will be on our side at the elections. And we shall have declared ineligible to stand as candidates all those opponents who have been or will be condemned for resistance activity (Art. 61). If there are still others whom we consider dangerous, we can always disqualify them through the Constitutional Court.

Let us imagine, however, that the inconceivable might one day happen. That the majority in Parliament, and thus the government, might escape from our grasp. Could the enormous power that we have given to the executive possibly fall into the hands of our opponents? Could they in their turn use this double-edged weapon to intimidate us, create difficulties for us, make criticism difficult and change almost unthinkable?

Not at all. Such an occurrence has been foreseen. As you may have perhaps noticed, we have taken care not to invest this omnipotence in the government alone. It will be obliged to share it with the new institutions which we are creating—the Constitutional Court, the Chief of the Armed Forces and the Council of the Nation. As long as the government is supported by them, it will be protected from all annoyance. If, however, a government tries to govern against their interests, they can make life impossible for it. And these institutions will support us come what may. The president of the Constitutional Court as well as all the members, and the Chief of the Armed Forces, once appointed by us, will be immovable, and their participation in the Council of the Nation will ensure a majority for us, unless neither of the two party leaders support us, which is highly improbable. It is especially by manipulating these permanent institutions that our influence on public life will remain entrenched, surviving even a possible electoral reverse.[5]

Let us clarify the role of the Chief of the Armed Forces. By a special law which we will promulgate after the Constitution,[6] we will make the armed forces a totally independent entity, over which the civil power will have no control. This state within a state will have a chief who cannot be removed, and will exercise all the powers of the Minister of Defence, the function of the latter becoming purely decorative (Art. 5, para 11). The Chief of the Armed Forces will be assisted by the three chiefs of the Army, Navy, and Air Force. These in turn will be assisted and watched over by committees of senior officers who will decide on all appointments, promotions, etc.[7] The civil power will have no right to intervene in military affairs, for we have seen that the press is forbidden to discuss them, nor can Parliament involve itself. But this military para-state will be entitled to its say in political matters. Besides his membership in the Council of the Nation, the Chief of the Armed Forces is the permanent pillar of the 'Higher Council of National Defence', the rest of whose membership is composed of ministers (Art. 3). This Council has very considerable powers. It determines the undefined 'special conditions' (Arts. 9 and 27) in which the Chief of the Armed Forces exercises enormous power, including the right to command the security forces directly, and to decide on expenses unforeseen by the budget (Art. 10).

The term 'National Defence' in itself will be given a broad enough definition to embrace practically all sectors of the country's public life in peace as well as in war. The armed forces will have the right to supervise all of these, especially if the potential enemy is defined to include not only hostile enemies, but domestic opponents as well (Const. Art. 129, para. 1). To crown it all, and to avoid any misunderstanding as to the armed forces' real role, the Constitution will say for the first time that the armed forces' duty is not, as in the case of common civil servants, to the 'People', but to the 'Nation'—a metaphysical entity of unfathomable will, which the military alone can comprehend (Art. 129, para. 2).

To recapitulate: our constitutional system will be established so as to satisfy, at first sight, the demands of those naïve champions of democracy throughout the world. But in the words of one of our opponents (now appropriately in prison) it is in essence simply a device to ensure that the first to apply it, namely ourselves,[8] will hold power indefinitely by means of a strengthened executive which will be able to control the parliamentary majority. Even if the latter escapes our control, we will still retain a second line of defence: the administration and the judiciary as we have redesigned them—the new Constitutional Court and, most important of all, the armed forces, created after our own image and entirely loyal to us. If the worst comes to the worst, these forces will be our invincible refuge, from which we can always regain power one way or another. But we hope that such extreme measures will not prove necessary. After several years of dictatorship, with indoctrination of the young and the muzzling of any opposition, we shall be able to count on at least a quarter to a third of the votes, which will suffice for our purposes. The survival of our closed society will thus be assured.

All this is only a logical analysis of the constitutional system elaborated by the Greek junta. Only when one approaches it as an instrument designed expressly to serve the present rulers' future ambitions can its cohesion and astuteness be understood. It is not for nothing that Pipinelis praised the Constitution in his speech of 26 August 1969, saying that the new Constitution, which he had played an important role in drafting, 'contains some interesting provisions, which few people have noticed'. To appreciate this comment fully, we must compare it with another passage from this same speech when, speaking of the situation before 21 April 1967, he said 'it was a period of mob rule, *that is to say, of unlimited sovereignty of the so-called popular will*' (our italics). For Pipinelis, a good constitution was one in which the popular will counts for as little as possible. If he was pleased with it, it is because it approached his ideal. The *Sunday Times* leader writer seriously misunderstood the situation when, on 11 August 1968, he observed that the Constitution's text revealed 'an almost total ignorance of the significance of liberty'. Quite the contrary. The compilers of the text knew well what liberty is, and they have deliberately tried to stifle it.

An example of the colonels' understanding of democratic procedures is found in the referendum on this same Constitution held on 29 September 1968. No critical discussion was permitted in advance. The government's propaganda services organised a gigantic campaign in favour of 'Yes', by means of posters, hoardings, pamphlets, newspaper articles, speeches and illuminated signs. The level of this campaign can be judged from the following extract from a song composed for the occasion, and which was ordered to be played during cinema intervals in the weeks preceding the referendum:

> *YES to progress,*
> *YES to prosperity!*
> *YES, YES, YES!*
> *You will be filled with a YES*
> *O our blue sky!*

At the same time, all opposition propaganda was forbidden under the threat of prosecution, and activity of this sort resulted in prison sentences of up to two years. Not content, however, with this brain washing, the junta made it clear to its opponents that by voting 'No' they would *not* contribute to the downfall of the dictatorship. For Pattakos declared on the eve of the great day that if the Constitution were not approved, the result would not be seen as a vote of no confidence, obliging the junta to resign. Quite the contrary: the regime would prepare a new draft constitution, which would be 'necessarily less liberal, for the present constitution represents the maximum of liberalism'. This did not prevent the junta, after the event, from claiming that the result of the referendum, now conveniently transformed into a plebiscite, was a vote of confidence which had turned the junta into an 'elected government'.

The colonels might as well have saved their breath and, incidentally, the taxpayers' money which financed the whole campaign. For the referendum had been so organised that there was not the slightest doubt as to its outcome. The whole government apparatus had been mobilised for the occasion. Regional military commanders and provincial governors had received clear instructions, and competed with each other to gain a result as near as possible to 100 per cent. They let mayors know that if their villages' vote was not 'correct', that is to say a unanimous 'Yes' they need not bother to apply for credit for public works projects. Throughout Greece, with the exception of the great urban centres where foreign journalists were present, the secrecy of the ballot was openly violated, either by not providing the mandatory curtain behind which the elector seals his envelope, or by issuing electors only with 'Yes' ballot papers. When some determined individual asked for a 'No' slip as well, he would sometimes be given one, while at the same time his name would be ostentatiously noted down. Sometimes he would be told that there were none left; more often the other villagers would beg him not to bring the wrath of the authorities down on their village. Such bold spirits were rare, however, and there are many instances of the opposite type of behaviour. In a few polling stations the judicial representative[9] was up to the job. If he insisted on the secrecy of the ballot, even at the risk of incurring disfavour, frightened electors would refuse to take 'No' slips or to go behind the curtain, insisting that the gendarmerie witness that they voted correctly.

In such circumstances, it is not surprising that there was an overwhelming majority of 'Yes' votes. It is true that the percentage of 'No's' officially admitted for the large towns was very much higher than the national average, for in these one could vote secretly, and the level of education enabled more people to realise the monstrous features of the Constitution. In Athens, for instance, the 'No's' reached almost 25 per cent. And yet there were many opponents of the regime who voted 'Yes', either because they saw no practical purpose in voting 'No' in a rigged election, or because they thought it more sensible to encourage the junta to apply its own constitution rather than have none at all, or, finally, because of their irrational fear of mythical 'electronic devices' which would be able to identify those who voted 'No'. Still others believed in a persistent rumour, seemingly launched by the junta's secret propaganda, that the fingerprints on all 'No' ballot papers were going to be checked. The great terror does not breed only cowardice but also stupidity.

At one moment on the evening of 29 September, the regime's leaders were seriously disturbed as almost all the results from the provinces were running at 100 per cent. The local officials' excess of zeal looked like giving the whole business too Stalinist an air. Frantically, civil servants 'corrected' the results, which had not yet been made public, and boosted the number of 'No's' to arrive at a national percentage of about 92 per cent in favour, which would seem somewhat more plausible than 98 or 99 per cent.

Thus the Constitution of 1968 was 'approved' by the Greeks. However, the junta had prudently added a clause which permitted it to implement it by stages, as it saw fit. To date, only the articles concerning harmless subjects such as the colour of the national flag, the state language and religion, etc., have been implemented.[10] Those articles to do with representative government inevitably still remain a dead letter. The same applies to those relating to civil liberties, with a few exceptions, such as the right of assembly, which have no practical value as long as martial law is in force. As a politician pointed out: 'I certainly have the right to organise a meeting, but then the police have the right to arrest everyone who comes to it.'

These rather lengthy explanations have been necessary to show that the form of government which the regime aims eventually to introduce is democratic only in name. Its implementation will simply be a continuation of the present state of affairs under a transparent camouflage. Why should opponents of the regime support it? The only result will be that much of international opinion will be misled by the camouflage, and will lose their present interest in the fate of our country. Certain governments will understand the truth perfectly well, but they will pretend not to understand, and will undoubtedly welcome this marvellous pretext to resume relations with the Greek government unembarrassed by liberal protest in their own countries.

As for the possibility of politicising the government by including in it a number of politicians, it is difficult to see what advantage there would be in this for the Greek people, given that these recruits would be the simple executors of the colonels' will, as was Pipinelis. For the junta certainly has no intention of sharing even a part of its effective power with this political world which it detests, derides, and humiliates. To an American diplomat who advocated this tactic of collaboration, describing it as that of a 'Trojan horse', a former minister bitterly replied, 'I would gladly enter the government, if they gave me control of the Third Army Corps.' Seeing his interlocutor's astonishment he added: 'But of course, for only then would I be able to play a role, to negotiate on an equal footing. Otherwise I should not be a horse, but more like a stupid ass.'

What makes the 'evolutionist' doctrine seem so unreal is that the junta does not show the least inclination to evolve, either in the constitutional sphere or in the direction of collaboration with the old politicians. All the actions and all the speeches of the ruling clique show that they are firmly resolved to maintain the *status quo* indefinitely. To insist, for example, that prior to the full implementation of the Constitution there must be an unspecified degree of economic development and a 'change of mentality' among the Greeks amounts to saying that it will never be applied.

This leads us to a very important and much discussed question. What is it that keeps the junta from applying the new constitutional framework we have just described? As it would only be a camouflaged prolongation of their dictatorship, why do they not prefer it to an open dictatorship such as they have at present? That Greek democrats should reject the 1968 Constitution is understandable, but why do the colonels reject it, after tailoring it to suit their own political objectives?

A current explanation in diplomatic circles in Athens is that this refusal is due to the pathological loathing the colonels feel towards democracy. Once having got rid of it, they do not want to be plagued even by its shadow. However hypocritical the new 'democratic' regime might be, its application will none the less require manœuvring and energy which they would rather save for more rewarding activities. Accustomed to command, they do not like to have to debate, even with an anaemic and submissive pseudo-opposition.

There is an element of truth in this. Recent episodes involving the press have shown how the colonels cannot bear even the slightest contradiction or criticism, however indirect it may be. Despite the draconian limits imposed on press freedom by the Press Law, which came into force on 1 January 1970, the junta still finds these limits too broad. We have already mentioned the ban on the sale of opposition newspapers in the provinces, a ban which even according to their own Press Law is a criminal offence. In February 1970 the only daily which continued to fight for its independence by invoking the law, the evening paper *Ethnos*, found it difficult to circulate even in Athens.[11] If the colonels were to apply their own Constitution as they have done their Press Law, it would scarcely be worth the effort. No one would be taken in.

Another theory is that within the junta itself a distinction should be made between the 'hard liners', such as Colonels Ioannidis, Roufogalis, etc., and the 'moderates' led by Papadopoulos. If the proponents of this view are to be believed, Papadopoulos wished to move in the direction of increasing liberalisation, of implementing the new Constitution, and of becoming an ordinary party leader. But the 'hard liners' stand in his way and, as he is far from being omnipotent, he has to trim his sails to the wind, and to temporise in order to appease the radicals in the dictatorship.

This explanation has been put forward on a number of occasions to try to reconcile contradictions in the regime's behaviour. Shortly before Christmas 1967, for instance, Papadopoulos announced that all political prisoners would be amnestied in time for the holiday. When it became apparent that nothing of the sort was happening, the rumour began to circulate that it was the 'hard liners' who had vetoed this measure of clemency. The same charade, with variations, has been enacted on a number of occasions since—sometimes in connection with censorship, sometimes with the lifting of martial law, and so on. Each time, Papadopoulos has been featured as the relatively liberal and humane leader who is prevented from acting on his generous impulses by his subordinates. The farce has been so well played that many have been taken in, including a number of foreign diplomats in Athens. It has taken time to recognise that the whole thing was a great bluff to fool the naïve, apparently mounted by Papadopoulos' own propaganda apparatus. The advantages for him in promoting such an image are obvious. All the brutal and unpopular measures are attributed to the hard liners, while the dictator gives the impression of being á decent but misunderstood fellow. And at the same time it affords an impeccable excuse for refusing to yield to foreign pressures. 'I myself certainly want to liberalise,' he puts it to the Americans from time to time, through an intermediary, 'but not the others. Give me time to win them over.' The naïve, or not so naïve, spokesmen for this hoodwinking exercise usually add 'Papadopoulos must be helped, as he means well. If the "hard liners" have their way it will be much worse.' How can a subject people help its dictator against other much worse candidates for the job? The answer is simple—by keeping quiet. The quieter things are, the less cause the hard liners will have to demand even more tyrannical measures, and to oppose a gradual liberalisation. Those who uphold this explanation of why the regime has not yet advanced a step in this direction propound the same policy of keeping quiet as those who maintain the theory that a gradual evolution towards liberalisation is both possible and desirable. That it is generally the same people who propagate the theory of 'Papadopoulos versus the hard liners', and that of a 'gradual evolution' should give pause for reflection.

The junta's deliberations are a closely guarded secret and no one knows exactly what goes on in them. It is reasonable to accept the hypothesis that there exist supporters of more rigid or more flexible policies among the officers who compose it. This occurs in every political organisation, including parliamentary parties. Only there is not the slightest reason to suppose that the differences of opinion within the junta are over anything other than questions of tactics ('Is this concession really necessary to pull the wool over the eyes of those European fools?'), or that they really are of the kind to provoke a split and violent confrontation within the regime. In the absence of evidence to the contrary, it is reasonable to assume that dissident opinions are heard within the junta as in any staff meeting, but that their holders submit ultimately to the leader's decision, the normal sense of hierarchical discipline being replaced in this case by the solidarity of the underworld—and by the awareness that a serious split could place the regime itself in jeopardy. 'If we don't hang together, we'll hang separately', as Benjamin Franklin warned the leaders of the American Revolution. Moreover, it is clear that Papadopoulos is the strong man of the junta, its uncontested and seemingly incontestable leader. No one else who could challenge his authority is anywhere in sight.

We can therefore reject the hypothesis the Papadopoulos' colleagues stand in the way of his implementing the new Constitution. At the same time, he must see the advantage to his international image of applying the Constitution. This advantage is so obvious that he should be able to overcome his rooted antipathy for anything bearing even a remote resemblance to democracy.

The real reason, in my opinion, why the junta does not implement its own Constitution is different. For the dictatorship to survive under a parliamentary guise, two conditions must be fulfilled. In the first place, there must be institutions conceived so as to favour the group that holds executive power in the initial stages. Then there must be a popular power base, a minority if needs be, but nevertheless one which does actually exist, of between a quarter and a third of the electorate. In the absence of these the junta cannot hope to keep power, even under such a Constitution, without resorting to illegalities so gross that all the good effect abroad of 'liberalisation' will be spoilt. Now, although the first of these two conditions is abundantly fulfilled, the second is far from being so. The number of actual supporters of the regime is negligible, and Papadopoulos knows this quite well. Scarcely a month passed between his 92 per cent 'triumph' at the referendum and the gigantic popular demonstration at the funeral of George Papandreou. The junta drew from this the appropriate lesson. It might be argued, of course, that the referendum proves precisely the point that the junta has no need of popular support to assert its authority. What is to stop its holding elections in the same way as it held the referendum?

It is not quite as simple as this. Authoritarian regimes have good reason to prefer referenda and plebiscites to elections. For with elections, if one wishes to convince foreign public opinion that they are being held with even a modicum of honesty, one must permit the opposition to show itself, to organise meetings, to publicise its opinions, to have its representatives at the casting and counting of votes. At elections, opponents will have an alternative —a hope, a rallying point which is absent at a referendum. With its legal and psychological advantages, the junta could still win if it has a genuine 25 or 30 per cent following, but not with the 5 or 10 per cent on which it can now count. This being the case, with a united opposition the political climate will change. The gendarme, the officer even, will hesitate to go beyond a certain point in exercising illegal pressures on an adversary that is numerically so powerful. The opposition could win a large number, if not a majority, of seats and then a parliamentary struggle will commence which will be highly exhausting to the junta and fraught with danger. In extreme circumstances, the junta could lose its grip and find itself forced to fall back on its last refuge, the armed forces. This would result either in confusion, with no one quite knowing who held power, or in a new coup. Certain American circles none the less seem to look with favour on such an evolution, which will assure a democratic façade while leaving the substance of power, with an important right of veto, to the armed forces. And the Pentagon wants to keep the armed forces as a reserve in case civil power falls into the hands of a political force it regards as undesirable.

The junta, on the other hand, does not want any of this. As long as the decision lies with it, it will not apply the Constitution until it is convinced that it has the sincere support of a fairly large segment of the electorate, to assure its uninterrupted enjoyment of total power. For once, we find ourselves in agreement with the junta, albeit for diametrically opposed reasons. Bastard compromises are as repugnant to true democrats as to fascist army officers. If the latter do not want to lose any of their actual power, we can not accept their retaining any power at all. All coexistence with them is politically, psychologically, and morally out of the question.

If the junta decides one day to apply the whole of the 1968 Constitution, this will mean either that it feels itself strong enough to do this without the slightest risk, in which case we will have no reason for playing a walk-on part in its parliamentary farce; or that it is too weak to resist any longer the pressures on it, and then we could demand its total abdication and a return to a true democracy.

2. THE UTOPIA OF THE IDEAL REVOLUTION

One conclusion emerges clearly from the preceding section. The present dictatorship is not capable of evolving gradually towards a true democracy, any more than a leopard can change its spots. To expect such a metamorphosis is not only intellectually unjustifiable but also politically dangerous: to try to make us give up our will to resist in exchange for vain promises is to play the junta's game. There can be no evolution, no compromise. If we wish to be free, we must fight by all means to overthrow the colonels' regime totally, and to undo its work in every sphere, especially in the constitutional and legislative spheres. On this the majority of those in opposition agree.

But who are 'we'? What means of fighting do we possess? And what are our precise objectives? The answers to these questions differ. The opposition to the junta includes all political nuances, from the non-fascist right to the extreme left, but one can distinguish in this great cross-section five principal strands.

Firstly, there is the traditional right, minus those of its former adherents who have made common cause with the regime. We will henceforth call 'the right' that part of the E.R.E. opposition whose spokesmen are Kanellopoulos in Greece, Karamanlis abroad, and who seek the return of the King. Secondly, there are the numerous elements of the Centre Union (E.K.) who are disorganised and without a universally accepted leader. Typical representatives of this group are the former ministers Mavros and Zighdis in Greece and Mylonas abroad. Henceforth we shall refer to these elements as 'the moderates'. A third category is that of the radical wing of the Centre Union, better known by the name 'centre-left'. This is led in exile by Andreas Papandreou with his 'Panhellenic Liberation Movement' (P.A.K.). This group will be referred to as the 'radicals'. Fourthly, there is the 'new left' which issued from the split within the Greek Communist Party in 1968. It calls itself the 'Bureau of the Interior', and relies for support abroad on E.D.A. in Western Europe and within Greece on the 'Patriotic Front' (PAM). Those of its leaders that are known are in prison or abroad. And finally there is the remains of the old Moscow-oriented Communist Party (K.K.E.). Its leader is Koliyannis who lives in Eastern Europe. This will be referred to as the 'Communist Party'.

There is no hope that all five groups will form a common front against the dictatorship. To the right and the moderates, the Communist Party still appears an enemy quite as dangerous as the junta, if not more so. The new left itself, which has not yet sufficiently disowned the totalitarian past of the Communist Party, scarcely appears to them any more respectable, and they are far from being prepared to accept it as an ally, being unused to making subtle distinctions between the different shades of communism. The right is frightened even of Andreas Papandreou's radicalism, and his stand against the monarchy (December 1969) was hardly calculated to make a rapprochement any easier. The right would not shrink from using violent means to overthrow the dictatorship, but it is suspicious of broadly based mass movements. Its ideal solution would be a counter-coup organised by loyal officers, similar to that of 13 December 1967 but more successful. Its object would be to restore the parliamentary system while keeping a firm hold on the armed forces. This would permit it to collaborate with the moderates, without having to fear the left or the radicals.

The moderates themselves are fairly close to the thinking of the right, but they hesitate to say so. Having to compete with the radicals for the voters that constituted the old centre majority, they do not want to appear too right wing in outlook, thus allowing the radicals to claim to be the only true champions of a progressive democracy. Torn between their true convictions and tactical expediency, irresolute, and without a powerful leader able to impose a clear political line, they are not in a position to play an important role. Their principal strength lies in the possibility that they can bargain with the right, which will need the moderate's support to get a broader based backing than that of the conservatives alone.

At the other end of the scale, the Communist Party is lying low, watching and waiting. We have already drawn attention to its conspicuous absence from the struggle waged by resistance activists of all other shades of opinion. The moment has come to try to explain its position as an instrument of Soviet policy.

To Moscow, the Greek dictatorship is a gift from heaven. In the clash of ideologies, propaganda, and influence which the confrontation between West and East has developed into, countries become showcases as well as powers. A Western-oriented Greece, democratic and economically healthy, is scarcely beneficial to Soviet propaganda. Since Greece belongs to a zone in which, for the time being, Moscow must not meddle, it is infinitely preferable from its point of view to see it governed by a reactionary dictatorship. Besides the immediate advantages which this offers to the Eastern bloc's anti-American propaganda, the prolongation of the regime has other long-term benefits.

In the first place the Greek people are becoming gradually estranged from the West. And its resentment against the United States, which is considered responsible for the dictatorship, leads it slowly towards an attitude which, if it is not pro-Soviet—the Czechoslovakia affair has made this difficult—is at least veering towards a neutralism deriving from a double disillusionment.

Secondly, the structures and leadership of a liberal democracy are slowly being destroyed. Little by little, moderate solutions will be discredited, and with them the views of those who advance them. There will be an increasing polarisation between a fascist minority on the one hand and a discontented and anti-American majority on the other. Thirdly, the armed forces are becoming both less efficient and the object of widespread loathing. And finally, the economy is steadily deteriorating, and will acquire an increasingly pronounced neo-colonialist character, thanks to the junta's policy of indebtedness to international financial circles.

These developments could lead, one day, to a revolutionary situation which might be exploited by the Kremlin. Depending upon whether the Kremlin could control the revolutionary element, and according to the prevailing international situation, it might try to wean Greece from the Western camp, or it might negotiate its neutrality, or it might agree once again to abandon the Greek revolutionaries in exchange for gains in other parts of the world.

All this, it is true, will take time, at least several years of dictatorial government. But at the Kremlin, as at the Vatican, they take a long-term view of things. That such a process will entail great hardships for Greece does not repel the Soviet Union. For it matters little to them that a people suffers, if this suffering may one day further their foreign policy. In this they scarcely differ from other great powers with global aims. The essential thing, for the Soviet Union, is that the dictatorship not be overthrown too early, and above all that it be not overthrown by Western-oriented elements not controlled by it. A re-establishment of liberal democracy, that would stop the present disintegration and even partially satisfy popular aspirations, is not at all desirable from Moscow's point of view; only the prolongation of the junta's regime can create a situation where the Soviet Union might possibly gain by its overthrow.

This is why the Communist Party up to now has abstained from any serious participation in the resistance, if one excepts its propaganda, intended mainly to combat the influence of the new left. It allows the new left to expend its strength, along with the other resistance movements, in the fight against the junta. It carefully nurtures itself, hoping that after all the other groups have been weakened or discredited it will be able to present itself as the sole serious contestant as and when it suits Soviet policy.

The policy of the Communist Party is, moreover, fully coordinated with those of the Eastern bloc countries, even in its details, as one saw at George Papandreou's funeral. Party members abstained from the popular demonstration, as the Eastern bloc diplomats abstained from the funeral service which had preceded them. Radio Moscow indulges in verbal attacks on the junta, in the style of the Communist Party's clandestine tracts. But on the diplomatic and economic level the Eastern bloc governments have warmed towards the junta, and send it their commercial delegations, their technicians, and their athletes. These friendly gestures, which Pipinelis publicly praised in December 1969, are reciprocated by the colonels. For if the junta serves the purposes of the Soviet Union and the Communist Party, the latter are wholly indispensable to the junta. The 'red peril' has long been invoked as the principal, if not the only, *raison d'être* of the regime. And when the Western countries put pressure on the junta to end the dictatorship, it replies by pretending to seek rapprochement with the Eastern countries, a tactic which it pursued after its exclusion from the Council of Europe. This behaviour is less contradictory than it might at first sight appear. They hint that after all there are precedents—Nasser locking up Egyptian communists, while being on the best of terms with the Soviet Union.

Again one sees the two political extremes meeting, even giving each other mutual support, each one hoping to exploit the other, just as Hitler and Stalin did in the Nazi-Soviet pact of 1939. All authoritarianism tends to push its opponents towards the other end of the political spectrum. Fascism engenders communists, just as communism engenders fascists; they both tend to eliminate liberals, either by crushing them or by forcing them into one or the other of the extremes; both seek polarisation and gain by it. For this reason the Communist Party cannot be depended upon as an active element in the resistance against the dictatorship.

It remains for us to speak of the sincerely democratic elements of the left-wing opposition, the radicals and the new left. Many affinities exist between these two groups in which youth and a desire for action are dominant traits. The radicals, an offshoot of the centre, seem to incline, if not towards a theoretical socialism, at least to an increasingly marked opposition to everything that smacks of the old right-wing establishment. The new left, which developed from orthodox and Soviet-oriented communism, seems to want a socialism which, if not totally democratic, is at least 'revisionist' and independent, on the Czech or Yugoslav model. It is significant that it protested against the Soviet intervention in Czechoslovakia, and that it is supported by the Rumanians. Both groups distrust the right just as the right distrusts them, and they do not lack grounds for this wariness. To start with, they have much to recall concerning the anti-democratic behaviour of the right in the past. They can plausibly claim that the present dictatorship is a bastard of the right, born of the illicit relations which had long existed between the right and a reactionary, and at times fascist, authoritarianism. It is true that the mother has renounced the child, who has cruelly betrayed her. The right is now also in the camp of the oppressed, alongside its former adversaries, who are not wholly sympathetic. If they are ready to speak well of Kanellopoulos and Helen Vlachou personally, because of the stand they have taken since the coup, they continue to be on their guard against Karamanlis and the right in general. For they sometimes suspect it of being ready to reach an understanding with the junta, and sometimes of plotting to overthrow it for its own exclusive benefit, so as to re-establish its traditional domination. Well aware that the right, like the junta, is under American and capitalist influence, the left tends to emphasise what unites them rather than what divides them. Some of the arguments they most frequently advance run thus:

'First of all, the present regime differs only in degree from that of the 'fifties. All its fascist elements were already germinating then, or were simply better camouflaged. . . . If the colonels hadn't beaten them to it, the King would have carried out the coup with his generals. . . . The quarrel between the traditional right and the junta is not serious, for it is not a class struggle. It is a struggle between two sections of the bourgeoisie, whose essential interests are the same. . . . When the right talks of fighting against the dictatorship, it only wants to substitute one led by the King or Karamanlis. The right proves this by not wanting to collaborate with us in an honest resistance aiming at the re-establishment of a true democracy. . . . Can one seriously believe that the Americans would allow the junta to fall, except to replace it by a regime equally subservient to them? Even if this were to have the external appearances of a democracy, at the least suspicion of an electoral victory by the left, we should have another coup.'

On the basis of this kind of argument, certain left wingers conclude that the right cannot be counted on as a sincere ally in the struggle against the dictatorship; that its actions must be carefully watched and, eventually, denounced; that the only pure and honest form of struggle is that which is not predicated on further conspiracies within the army, but uniquely on the resistance and a mass uprising. This resistance, they firmly believe, will be truly victorious, and will acquire meaning, if it leads not only to the elimination of the present junta but also of such embryonic future juntas as may exist in the traditional right. It is worth waiting, if need be, ten years for this complete and definitive liberation, rather than accept the compromise which a succession of the Karamanlis type would constitute.

Such are the conclusions of some, but by no means of all left wingers. One would expect to find them among the new left. But, curious as it may seem at first sight, it is the radicals instead who argue these views with the greatest intransigence, while the new left often proves to be more moderate. An example of this difference appears in the attitudes of these groups towards the future of the monarchy: the new left does not publicly at least question the future of the monarchy, though Andreas Papandreou does. And when Karamanlis proposed himself, in the autumn of 1969, to head a succession government, the imprisoned leaders of the new left accepted the idea with much less reserve than did the radicals.

The thesis of the radicals, which is of course rarely expressed in the extreme form we have given it, is attractive in a number of ways. Its claims about the past are based on a well-documented historical and sociological analysis. Its critique of the right is mostly justified, despite some over-hasty generalisations. But it can be reproached with not fully realising the former role of the Communist Party. It is fashionable in certain radical circles not to speak of this, to avoid either defending its terrorist past or to appear to be putting it on trial. Again, there is no doubt that the radicals see clearly the necessary conditions for the existence of a full and modern democracy in Greece in the future. Every sincere liberal can only share their hopes, their fears and their ultimate objectives.

Moreover, the radicals have enlisted the support of many energetic young people who are free of the cynicism and weaknesses of the old political parties. They represent a new factor in Greek public life, combining integrity with a passionate will to reform. One cannot but respect their determination to end hypocritical compromises, the humiliating lack of independence, the outdated and reactionary structures. The means of struggle which they envisage are equally attractive. The vision of an entire people rising up against its oppressors, past and present, and gaining its freedom through armed resistance is a splendid and moving one.

In politics, however, it pays to keep a cool head. One must

study the relation between the ends and the means; tactical moves demand calculations for which passionate involvement alone is not enough. The problem is to know whether the means envisaged by the radicals, and the tactics which they adopt, are the most suited to the ends which they pursue. Could this perfect democracy, which they demand and which we all want, be obtained by the masses fighting the junta, without a left-wing totalitarianism being the ultimate beneficiary? In other words, is the radicals' ideal revolution feasible, or is it simply utopian?

Let us analyse it a little. Material power is held by the junta. Only two forces are capable of challenging the regime: army officers who do not support the junta, and the Americans. The first group is almost exclusively right wing, and royalist to boot (for the few officers of centre views have long ago been eliminated from the army). They could not be counted on, any more than could the Americans, to support a fight being waged by the radicals, if these appear to threaten not only the junta but the whole conservative camp. If this were the case, the Americans would support the junta more strongly than ever. Conservatives would at best observe a prudent neutrality, and some would perhaps even back the junta when faced with the spectre of a 'popular front' including communists, of whatever hue.

If such a polarisation occurred, what would the radicals' chances be, even if the new left sided with them? Could they mobilise the people not only to fight but to defeat the combined forces of the right and the Americans? From the indications which we have at present, it would certainly not seem so. The balance of forces is greatly weighted against the left. We are no longer in the age of the barricades, where insurgents armed with rifles could take on the similarly armed royal cavalry. The colonels have tanks, highly armed and motorised units, and telecommunications, and we have nothing at our disposal. One looks in vain at recent history for instances of dictatorships overthrown by popular uprisings. The only apparent exception to this rule is the Hungarian uprising of 1956, but in that case two particular factors should be taken into account: the visible presence of a hated foreign occupier, in the form of the Red Army, coupled with intolerable economic oppression. Perhaps nothing is impossible: a new demonstration like the one at George Papandreou's funeral—assuming that such a demonstration would again be permitted, which is highly unlikely— could turn into rebellion, into general insurrection, and the crowd could overcome the tanks. But all such speculation contains an element of wishful thinking. To found a policy on such a hope would scarcely be responsible.

But, it will be argued, a revolution need not necessarily take the form of a spontaneous and massive insurrection. There is guerilla warfare, on the Chinese, Cuban, or Vietnamese models. All those examples, however, are drawn from obviously underdeveloped countries, where there is little between an obsolete state machinery, serving the interests of a very narrow ruling class on one side, and a miserable proletariat on the other. Besides, these guerilla wars have been led by highly structured communist parties, at least in China and Vietnam. But in Greece, on the other hand, the group that would have to be mobilised are mainly the middle classes. For the workers are largely under the influence of the Communist Party, and the peasantry, most of whom are small landholders, are in no way given to revolution. One can scarcely see, however, middle-class radicals plunging into guerilla war. Circumstances are scarcely propitious for this, both from a technical and a psychological viewpoint. The memory of the civil war alone is a major dissuasive force. And one must remember that guerillas now could not count, as did those of 1946-1949, on any aid from Greece's northern neighbours.

The fundamental error of radical tactics is that their objectives are out of all proportion to the real possibilities of resistance. They tend both to divide the resistance and to push conservatives towards support of the junta. In the phrase of one of our friends, the radicals 'speak the language of the Vietcong without possessing a Vietcong', indulging in a verbal extremism much greater than the actual forces they can mobilise.

There remains terrorism pure and simple—bomb attacks in urban centres. This could well equal and surpass the extent of such attacks in 1969. Can one seriously believe, however, that this alone will be enough to overthrow a dictatorship backed by the Americans, with a right that is either neutral, or even gradually turning against the resistance, through fear of anarchy?

Future developments along these lines are not impossible. A great economic crisis may occur which would lead to a collapse of morale among the middle classes, boosting the ranks of those who 'have nothing to lose but their chains'. A progressive deterioration in the standard of living might result in a vicious circle of violence, of terror and counter-terror, leading one day to the downfall of the dictatorship and with it of American influence and of the old conservative establishment. But what would be the cost of such a process? And would it lead to an ideal democracy, or to a new tyranny? Would Greece find its freedom, or chains of another kind?

Things might one day reach such a state. Despair of any other solution arising might polarise Greek opinion in this way, so that it would be prepared to face merciless war which would reduce the country to ashes, rather than endure the present dictatorship. But surely it is our duty to explore other possible ways before risking such an outcome.

We have admitted that the junta is at present supported by the armed forces and in certain American quarters. The first tactic to explore would therefore be to discover what might lead to this support being withdrawn. As the principal and immediate adversary is the junta, it is a question of isolating it for attack, or better still attacking it in concert with its former allies. What is required for this? It would clearly be necessary to persuade the Americans and conservative officers that they have more to gain by sacrificing the junta than by supporting it. From the moment they are persuaded of this, the end of the junta will be near, and it could be all over with a minimum of bloodshed and disorder.

The crucial question is, what price must be paid for this? The radicals' objection to this type of solution is that to gain the support of Washington and the conservative right, including the royalist officers, concessions must be made which would betray the very meaning of our fight for a democratic and independent Greece. This objection is weighty, and is worth examining in detail. If the radicals' calculations are accurate, they are right: one certainly does not sacrifice the end to the means. Let us return to the arguments cited on p. 175.

Firstly, it is false to claim that there is only a difference of degree between the present dictatorship and the governments of the 'fifties. The difference is enormous, as has frequently been indicated in the present work. There is no need to repeat these arguments. It is enough to re-emphasise that the society of the 'fifties, with the traditional right in power, certainly had many unattractive and illiberal features, but it was essentially an 'open' society. The proof of this lies in the fact that change could, and did, occur by constitutional means.

True, the claim about the 'King's and generals' coup' is difficult to check. But even if it is true, what does it prove? Are we more obsessed with the past than with the future? If we are willing to collaborate, if needs be, with the communists, who previously attacked democratic institutions with armed force, why should we refuse to collaborate with the King and those who are simply suspected of having had anti-democratic designs in 1967? What counts is everyone's present inclination, not their former sins, real or imagined.

The question of defining the class struggle smacks so much of doctrinaire marxism, of simple playing with words, that it is scarcely worth the trouble of refuting it. It could well be that the fundamental interests of the right and the junta are basically identical. But what if they themselves are unaware of it, and are ready to set upon each other? Our business is to profit by their division, not to explain to them that they should make some deal.

The final arguments are the only ones which really carry weight. Will the right and the Americans agree to replace the junta's dictatorship with a truly democratic regime, or only another more or less camouflaged dictatorship? It is a question which cannot be answered quickly or dogmatically. Certain soundings, certain indications allow one to believe that there is a margin of negotiation—that the Americans and the right will be disposed to accept a democratic solution in principle if it incorporates certain guarantees of their essential interests. This is not so surprising. After all, freedom flourishes throughout western Europe, and is not regarded as at all incompatible with 'Atlantic' interests. Why not in Greece?

Certainly the very notion of any such undertakings, which of course represent a compromise, is repugnant to those who insist on holding out for complete liberty and for total independence. But if one cannot obtain this with a single blow, it is not a good tactic to work towards it gradually? Could one not, for example, forgo complete control over foreign policy in exchange for democratic freedoms? Could one not postpone major internal social reforms and content oneself at first with a return to the democracy, with all its faults that we had before the coup, while reserving the right to improve it later? Shouldn't a naked man, trembling with the cold, accept an old patched garment, rather than insist on full evening-dress? 'All or nothing' perfectionism won't lead us very far if we do not have the means of obtaining the 'all'. It is more realistic to aim at a more modest but obtainable objective, than to insist on an uncompromising struggle for immediate perfection.

Some radicals even go so far as to argue that the dictatorship must last ten years, if need be, to ensure that its downfall is followed by a complete victory of the progressive forces in the country. The reply to this is that it is not at all certain that the dictatorship will fall in five, ten or even twenty years' time, but what is certain is that with each passing day the dictatorship brings more suffering to the Greek people, as well as an uninterrupted decline in our institutions and additional difficulties to be surmounted after liberation. It is interesting to note that the most intransigent views are more often to be heard abroad than in Greece itself. They are articulated by men with the best intentions in the world, but who have often little contact with the realities of the Greek situation. They have illusions as to the possibilities of internal resistance, and little realisation of what prolonging the dictatorship means to those who have to live under it.

It is highly significant that the new left, as we have indicated, seems much less inclined to fight 'to the bitter end' than the radicals. Veteran communists now in prison show a much greater sense of reality than those whose left-wing views are of more recent origin, and they are ready to accept any succession government which would guarantee individual liberties and offer the possibility of free elections in the future. Although they have even more reason than the radicals to suspect the right, they are willing to help it overthrow the junta—be it by keeping quiet and not taking the initiative, so as not to frighten American and conservative opinion.

If we criticise the extreme position of certain radicals, it is because we consider it not only unrealistic but also positively dangerous, in so far as by fighting for an ideal and uncertain future they may hinder the adoption of an acceptable short-term solution. At the same time, the language of radical extremism gives many people a comfortable pretext for doing nothing at all: for if the ideal revolution is not realisable at the moment, and any other solution not worth the trouble of fighting for, an attentiste attitude is perfectly justified. The Communist Party also justifies its present inactivity in a rather similar manner.

All this, naturally, plays into the hands of the junta. Let us try to put ourselves in Papadopoulos' shoes and imagine the instructions he might give a clever and trusted agent who is to be infiltrated into radical resistance circles: 'The most dangerous combination for us would be a coalition of the right and the moderates, discreetly supported by the radicals. Such a coalition, with a programme capable of appeasing the Americans, would means that we would forfeit their support. For, as soon as the Americans see a possible solution which would satisfy their own liberals and European democrats, while safeguarding the United States' essential interests, one which would allow the re-establishment of democracy with the minimum of damage, without civil war or anarchy, they will no longer have any reason to support us. Therefore, such a combination and such a programme must be sabotaged at all costs. The radicals must be incited to keep their language as wild and anti-American as possible, to attack the right and the King, to threaten violence and to ally openly with the communists. This would serve a double end: not only would it prevent the formation of a common front against us, but it would frighten the Americans, the conservatives, and even the moderates and make them secretly want our dictatorship to continue.'

These imaginary but entirely plausible instructions of Papadopoulos to his confidential agent coincide remarkably with the postures assumed in certain radical quarters. The radicals, to be sure, have two replies to this argument. First of all, they maintain, what is bad for the junta is not necessarily good for us; if Papadopoulos is frightened of being replaced by the King and Karamanlis, it is because he and his friends will lose power—not because it will mean a return to democracy. Furthermore, it is completely vain to hope that American policy will change. Trying to come to an understanding with them is a waste of time and energy better employed in resistance. Finally, our radical friends could attack us for what amounts to a defence of the 'evolutionary' tactics, dismissed as unrealistic in the preceding section.

Let us clarify our position, starting with this last argument. We have condemned the doctrine of 'evolution', which hopes for a return to democracy through an understanding with the junta, and within the framework of the 1968 Constitution. What we envisage now is a solution founded on the overthrow of the junta and the installation of an 'open society', imperfect but capable of being improved by democratic means.

As for knowing to what extent the traditional right is prepared to create a democratic form of government, albeit with certain guarantees against the extreme left, there is every reason to consider men such as Kanellopoulos as being of good faith. Karamanlis himself has never throughout his career shown any signs of wanting to be anything other than the head of an elected government. He is perhaps authoritarian, but there is a world of difference between an authoritarian leader and a dictator—the difference, say, between General de Gaulle and the colonels of the O.A.S. Without being in the least a partisan of Karamanlis, one is justified in believing that he, probably more than anyone else, has the requisite qualities for the transition period—that is to say an empirical approach, common sense, and the authority necessary to return the army to the barracks. At the same time we consider him too intelligent to want to become a dictator. The only crown which his political career needs is the restoration of Greek liberties.

There is reason to believe that the whole of the right, including the King, has learned a lesson from its terrible experiences under the present dictatorship, and that it will in future respect democratic processes. It is significant, for instance, that Helen Vlachou has publicly made her *mea culpa* for the past. It is not likely, moreover, that the great majority of the left will demonstrate or make extreme demands to upset the right. Whatever its present leaders may say, the rank and file will be far too happy to be freed from the present nightmare to think of provoking dangerous confrontations. For the left also have a lesson to learn on the virtues of moderation and patience, as well as the dangers of verbal braggadocio. The situation will be like that of Austria immediately after the last war. Having experienced Nazism and seen the Red Army at close quarters, the very Catholics and socialists who ten years earlier were shooting at each other in the streets of Vienna co-operated in building a new democracy together. Why can a similar thing not happen in Greece, where the political parties (except the Communist Party) are not divided by memories as bloody as those of the Austrians?

We will perhaps be accused of an excessive, even naïve, optimism. But if the worst comes to the worst, if the King and the right, after their return, show anti-democratic tendencies, there will always be time to take action then. Once the present terror has been broken, it will not be easy to re-establish it on behalf of another group. The fight could begin again in much more favourable conditions than those prevailing today.

There remains the problem of the Americans. It is clearly difficult to predict if, and under what conditions, their policy will change. But none the less, attempts should be made to get them to change it. It is only after having explored these avenues, and failed, that we can make the hesitant understand that there remains only a fight to the bitter end. And in winning them over to our side we would at the same time win over moderate opinion the world over.

We do not suggest that resistance activity should cease or be neglected in the meantime. It is false dilemma to have to decide if one should fight or negotiate. We must fight *and* negotiate, or rather we should fight in order to negotiate from as strong a position as possible. We agree completely with the radicals as to the need for vigorous resistance, in all its forms. The question is, until when? The radical response is that the fight must continue until an ideal democracy is created in a Greece totally independent of external influences. The realistic reply is that we should fight until the moment when we will be given enough democracy to continue the fight by lawful political means. This minimum includes a governmental system where human rights will be respected and where the people will be able to have a voice through honest elections. This presupposes in its turn a Constitution other than that of 1968, either a new one which should be debated and ratified in a democratic manner, or, in the meanwhile, that of 1952. Let us suppose that we have convinced our radical friends to let us attempt negotiation with the provision that we will back them if we are proved wrong, and a 'Western' solution proves impossible. Supposing that we had *carte blanche* to negotiate while continuing to fight. How would we use it?

3. A REALISTIC STRATEGY

We have seen that the chance of overthrowing the dictatorial regime by a popular insurrection or guerilla war is very remote. There remain the means envisaged mainly in conservative and royalist circles: namely an armed military coup, which would be more certain, more rapid, and more economical of human life. This gives rise to two main questions: are there elements now in the armed forces technically capable of overthrowing the junta? If so, what must be done to get them to do it, with the aim of restoring democracy under the auspices, say, of the King, or of a coalition directed by Karamanlis, or both together?

From a technical point of view, there is no doubt that a regime like this, which is based exclusively on the armed forces, can similarly be overthrown by a section of these same forces. The necessary preconditions are that a sufficient number of officers in key posts are involved in the plan for the coup, that the junta's intelligence services do not get wind of it beforehand, and that operations are carried out without the indecision and bungling that characterised the royal coup of December 1967. We do not say that these problems are easily resolved: we do say that they are not insoluble.

According to the circumstances, such a coup could take a number of very different forms. At one extreme, it would mean the revolt of certain units, involving military operations, and perhaps street fighting. At the other, it could take the form of a palace revolution. At a given moment a group of officers (including, possibly, some members of the junta itself) would indicate to Papadopoulos and his lackeys that their dictatorship is finished. All necessary measures would have to be taken to ensure that the key military units obey this group, and Papadopoulos would then have to submit, gracefully or otherwise, and accept the escape offered to him, perhaps in a plane leaving for Portugal or Spain. The next morning, Greece would learn that a provisional government had been formed, and only awaited the arrival of the King and Karamanlis to hand over power to them. Between these two extremes—ninepins or an elegant checkmate—a whole series of variations can be envisaged.

The possibility of enough well-placed officers taking to the idea of a coup depends on psychological factors which are difficult to assess. We know that the junta has gone through the armed forces with a fine-tooth comb to eliminate all the elements which in its opinion were potentially hostile to it, or who simply enjoyed too much prestige. And at the same time it has done everything possible to ensure the loyalty of the remaining officers, by satisfying their career ambitions and material desires. It is difficult at first glance to see why these people should rise up against it. What inducement would be powerful enough to make them rat on the junta, even those who have not dirtied their hands under the present regime, and have nothing to fear from reprisals after its fall?

Firstly, these officers must be convinced that the prolongation of the dictatorship is increasingly dangerous, both for the country and themselves personally, and secondly that its overthrow will hurt neither Greece nor their own interests. These interests, both personal and corporate, must be negotiated carefully, and we clearly cannot go into details here. As for national interests, most officers will not hesitate to entrust power to someone as 'safe' as the King or Karamanlis, especially if they fully understand what the alternative might be. This is that the continuation of the dictatorship may have catastrophic consequences for the country.

Now, if this last proposition is obvious to us, it is by no means so to the majority of officers. Strengthening of the resistance with the threat of internal chaos will perhaps make them ponder, but might result only in their closing ranks behind the junta. One thing alone could turn them against the junta: the Americans. It should be stressed that all Greek officers are conditioned to total faith in their country's attachment to NATO, and even more to the United States. If the Americans were to indicate unambiguously that they have decided to end the Greek dictatorship, and that they are prepared to go as far as to isolate the country politically, militarily, and economically, there is no doubt that a sufficient number of highly placed officers would opt for the American alliance against the junta.

To put it briefly, when the Americans decide to overthrow the junta, they will find the officers necessary to carry it off, as they have found them at other times in many other countries. It is true that the regimes they have overthrown before were generally democracies, but one can hope that for once Washington will utilise its enormous power for freedom and not against it. The difficulty is to get them to do it. Let us not forget, however, that there are many people in Washington: in the State Department, the Pentagon, the C.I.A., the Senate, the White House. Whom should we win over?

Let us approach the problem more simply. Let us admit, and it is not wholly implausible, that certain quarters which influence American policy towards Greece have been won over to the idea of restoring democracy. Let us call these people, who include diplomats, senators, intellectuals, and journalists, the 'blue lobby'. But there are other people, in the Pentagon, the C.I.A., the Senate, and perhaps certain business circles[1] who support the junta, and whom we will term the 'black lobby'. These two lobbies are now battling to influence the administration's decisions. The future fate of Greece depends on the outcome of this struggle. Our business is to help the blue lobby by furnishing it with ammunition to use against the black lobby.

With the black lobby, we are dealing with people who wish to appear 'realistic' to the point of cynicism, so it is only as a matter of form that we will refer to 'the lasting values of the West', 'great American principles', 'the preamble of the NATO Treaty', and so on. The terms 'liberty' and 'human dignity' may simply provoke smiles among those who have hitherto determined U.S. policies towards Latin America for example. So we will turn quickly to the subject of American interests in Greece and the eastern Mediterranean, *realpolitik* alone being capable of moving these Machiavellians. The Americans should logically regard the Greek dictatorship as a calamity, for the very reasons that the Soviet Union welcome it. To recapitulate from the American point of view.

The participation of a military dictatorship in the NATO alliance, whose ostensible role is to safeguard freedom, is as preposterous as would be the presence of a Soho whore in an anti-prostitution league. The fact that the Portuguese dictatorship slipped into NATO at its beginning is an annoying precedent which should serve as neither example nor excuse.[2] The United States' position over this is much more embarrassing than that of the Soviet Union in its relations with its satellites. For the Soviets impose upon their allies the type of regime that the U.S.S.R. aims at openly, and applies at home. The Americans, on the other hand hypocritically speak of democracy and apply it at home, but are ready to abandon it among their allies if their own real or imagined 'strategic interests' appear to be threatened.

Since the great majority of Greeks firmly believe that a hated dictatorship[3] has been imposed on them with the United States' connivance, if not their initiative, a virulent anti-Americanism is developing in Greece. This is a disturbing and wholly new development, for except for the communists the Greeks have always been well disposed towards America. It could still perhaps be reversed, but only if the United States clearly indicates, by deeds rather than mere words, that it has decided to help us restore democracy.

The longer the present regime lasts, the more difficult it will be to replace it by a viable democratic regime. Moderate elements, who could make it work, are gradually losing ground and one day will be completely outstripped by extremists. For this same reason, the transition from dictatorship to constitutional rule will be more difficult, and probably more bloody, the longer it is delayed.

The Greek armed force's declining efficiency should concern even the black lobby in Washington, if it were to look a little further than the next six months. Possibly the Pentagon has never assigned the Greek forces a very important role in its strategic plans. Perhaps they see them mainly as a police force to maintain order around American bases in Greece. But is it intelligent to confide the future and security of the bases to the protection of such a regime, while at the same time alienating the people as a whole? It should not be necessary to stress that before 1967 there were no hostile demonstrations against the American presence in Greece, except for the ritual verbal protests of E.D.A., which represented only 12 per cent of the electorate. It is only under the junta that bomb attacks have been directed at American cars and property. True, the Centre Union, and particularly its radical wing, had wanted to see Greek-American relations established on a basis more acceptable than that of a humiliating dependence. But wishing to reshape an alliance so as to strengthen it is quite a different thing from trying to destroy it. A critical and argumentative friend is often a better ally than a sycophantic hanger-on.

To look now at the contrary arguments of the black lobby. We have seen that, for the first time, official Greece is going through the motions of rapprochement with the Eastern bloc. This innocent flirtation, hinting that the junta can indulge in a little blackmail against the West, is loudly publicised by those same experts in psychological warfare who perhaps counselled it. 'Be careful', they cry, 'Greece is the only country which is wholly loyal to us, in whose ports our fleet can seek refuge in complete security. Let us not risk turning it against us, for it could easily reverse its alliances and go over to the other side.'

All this is pure bluff. We have already seen that the conditioning of Greek officers is marked by a fanatical 'Atlantic bias' and an anti-communism bordering on hysteria. This is what distinguishes them profoundly from their Arab colleagues, for example, whose nationalism has always been strongly tinged with anti-colonialism and distrust of, if not hatred towards, the Western powers. Although a rapprochement with the Eastern bloc was natural for Nasser, it would be an intolerable heresy for most Greek officers. Papadopoulos could not find a more certain means of alienating the officer corps than to push this bluff too far. By so doing he would be signing his regime's death warrant. Consequently, it is puerile to imagine that pressures exercised by Washington could result in the 'loss of Greece' to the Western alliance. On the contrary, if they apply pressure strongly enough, they will accelerate the downfall of the dictatorship.

It is at this point that the other arguments of the black lobby crop up. This is not the moment, they argue, for us to create new difficulties in this region, which already has more than its fair share. We already have the Arab-Israeli conflict, we have the new Libyan regime, we have a Turkey which is becoming increasingly less docile, and an Italy on the edge of anarchy. Greece, in contrast, is beautifully quiet. It would be stupid deliberately to stir up trouble here, to provoke changes with unforeseeable consequences which might add to our present difficulties.

This argument is like that of a man who, because he already suffers from a toothache and stomach ache, refuses to seek treatment for the early stages of cancer. Does Washington not have at its disposal enough officials and agents to deal with a number of problems simultaneously? For it is not a case of creating a Greek problem out of thin air; it is a matter of solving an already existing problem, which is potentially dangerous for the United States. It is not a problem which can be shelved indefinitely. We have given enough evidence that the situation is not static. With each day that passes, the disastrous consequences of the junta's government complicate the problem and make a solution more difficult. The time element is of the utmost importance, for Greece as well as for American interests in Greece, if these last are properly understood.

We will only briefly mention the black lobby's claim that the United States, after its bitter experience in Vietnam, has no inclination to interfere in the internal affairs of other countries. The argument is hypocritical, for it is very well known that the United States government, whether it likes it or not, continues and will continue to intervene in its allies' affairs. Even inaction and abstention are political acts in certain circumstances. Moreover, when it does not shrink from meddling in different regimes, especially when these seem to it too left wing or simply too liberal, as in Latin America, it has no excuse for not intervening against a dictatorship as disgraceful as ours.

Washington's technical ability to overthrow the junta is not in doubt. It is said that the C.I.A. has about eight thousand agents in Greece, and some of them are in high positions. With the practically unlimited financial means at its disposal, it would be child's play for it to overthrow the regime.

This is the case today. One cannot be so sure that it will be so in a few years' time, when the present generation of officers, nurtured on pro-Americanism, will be replaced by another, conditioned by the junta in perhaps another direction. Then a kind of Nasserism may come into fashion, and the C.I.A. as well as the Pentagon will have less influence on the Greek armed forces than they now have.

Very well, replies the black lobby. We admit that we have the ability to overthrow the junta, and also we do not look with favour on it, in so far as it harms our interests and our international image. But what assurance do we have that its downfall will benefit moderate elements, with whom we could reach an understanding, rather than anti-American elements? Do we not run the risk of unleashing a chain of events with unforeseeable consequences, which may be more dangerous for us than a prolongation of the present regime would be?

In the preceding section we have outlined what we think of the chances of a moderate succession able to set American doubts at rest. In this field, it is clearly impossible to speculate with certainty. Freedom always carries with it an element of the unknown, indeed of risk. But present circumstances are more propitious for the restoration of democracy without too many imponderables. Hatreds have not yet been exacerbated to the point of necessarily leading to bloodshed. The left is divided. The great mass of the people only ask to be able to breathe freely and in peace. Moderate leaders and groups still retain a following. The armed forces will regain their prestige in the people's eyes from the moment they dissociate themselves from the small clique of junta officers.

Probably as time passes it is less likely that these conditions will prevail. It is a question therefore of choosing between a calculated and reasonable risk now and a much greater risk later on. In any case, the dictatorship will one day end, and not through 'evolution', as we have shown in a preceding section. It is up to the Americans to decide if we are to be liberated soon, under their auspices, or in a more distant future, against their will. Will our trust in the West be justified? Or will those extremists who think these hopes utopian, and envisage liberation only by means of an intransigent struggle against Washington as well as the junta, be proved right?

And we Greeks? Should we wait patiently for the Americans to decide to hand us our liberty? Can we contribute nothing to it? We can in fact do a great deal. We can and we should resist by all possible means, actively and passively. This is no place to speak of the possibilities of active resistance, save to emphasise that the present apparent calm aids the black lobby's argument that all is for the best in Greece, that an exemplary order reigns there, and that it is pointless to disturb this idyll. On the contrary, there is no doubt that a further outbreak of bomb attacks will hasten a salutary re-examination of American policy. If this does happen, it is to be hoped that new attempts directed at the Americans will once again be against inanimate objects and that there will be no loss of American lives—although such distinctions are not always easy to observe in the heat of action. What is especially important is to emphasise that these attacks are not a reflection of an implacable hatred of the United States, and that members of today's resistance could again become loyal friends of America, as soon as the U.S.A. cease to appear to stand in the way of our freedom. It is essential that the black lobby must not be able to argue that the only true friends of America in Greece are the colonels. At the moment, there is in resistance circles too much anti-American talk and too little action. More decisive action, coupled with more moderate language, would be much more effective.

As for passive resistance, this has been very much neglected. The rare attempts to organise boycotts and mass abstentions have failed. This is at first sight surprising, as passive resistance is the least dangerous and least difficult form of resistance. The reason for this must be sought in the following facts. Firstly, the Greek temperament—impatient, disorderly, and little inclined to co-operation—does not lend itself to a form of resistance which demands organisation, discipline, and patient long-term effort. Secondly, passive resistance has much greater prospects of success under a relatively liberal regime, such as that of the British in their former colonies, than under a regime of terror. What Gandhi's supporters found possible was out of the question for the opponents of Hitler and Stalin. How can one organise a mass movement, give orders and get them carried out, when one has no means of communication and when the penalties, even for a simple strike, are enormous?

Despite all this there are possibilities for a serious, broadly based organisation which would command nationwide respect. The more representative and the less partisan such an organisation appeared, the more likely would its orders be obeyed— particularly if it were to distinguish itself at the same time by active resistance and employ other than purely moral sanctions against traitors and collaborators. All this demands, above all, the greatest possible unity between the different resistance movements, which in its turn entails unity among the different political groups. We will contribute to our liberation not by fighting against each other, even if only with words, but by agreeing a co-ordinated action programme toward a minimum common goal: liberation pure and simple. An immense task could be accomplished in this way. It is no exaggeration to claim that the dictatorship can be thrown off balance, rendered vulnerable, and virtually defeated by a well-organised campaign of passive resistance which would attack the administration, the economy, and the junta's propaganda and would include boycotts of certain newspapers, certain products, certain means of transport. These things can snowball. Once the order 'no one will use the buses today', for example, is followed, one could proceed to 'white strikes', strikes of over-enthusiasm, etc., in the civil service and large public utility organisations.

It is equally important that all future resistance be organised on a long-term basis. It may be necessary for a number of years. Patience and systematic effort should replace amateurism and a taste for spectacular and immediate results. While not ruling out an understanding with the Americans, and a 'conservative' path to liberation under their auspices, we must prepare for a generalised resistance of long duration such as that pessimistically envisaged by the radicals, in concert with people of as many shades of political opinion as possible.

4. THE ROLE OF EUROPE

On the international front, Greece during the period 1967-1970 has been unlucky. Almost everything that has happened in the world—and in our era the destiny of various nations is intertwined—has reinforced the position of the dictatorship in one way or another. The Arab-Israeli conflict, the May 1968 'events' in France, the invasion of Czechoslovakia, the assassination of Robert Kennedy, Nixon's presidential victory, the Italian troubles, and the Libyan revolution: all this could not have been better timed for the Greek colonels and their black lobby in Washington.

Let us confine ourselves here to events in Western Europe. How, for example, have the French and Italian troubles helped the Greek junta? The link is indirect but none the less clear. When any democratic regime seems incapable of ensuring order, when anarchic demonstrations threaten to paralyse the life of the nation, a good segment of opinion in all countries takes fright and cries out for some kind of order, even if fascist in tendency. The average citizen, when frightened, veers towards extremes, and extremist movements afford each other mutual aid. When Paris seems on the verge of anarchy many Frenchmen think more highly of the Greek dictatorship, which knows how to control this sort of thing. Likewise, some Greeks who scarcely like dictatorship, but who like disorder even less, think if only temporarily that the junta is perhaps the lesser of two evils. In Washington the black lobby exults at seeing the trend towards 'strong' governments growing. When French students chalked on walls 'de Gaulle-Pattakos', they rendered no service to freedom. For although they persuaded no one that de Gaulle was an illiterate petty dictator, they may have made many of their compatriots think that Pattakos is perhaps not so bad as all that if he really is like de Gaulle.

The extremist new left in Western Europe, however generous its motives may be, runs the risk of sounding the death knell of democracy. For in a final confrontation between it and a terrified right, backed by fascist military men, it will always be the tanks of the latter which will carry the day. In 1968 France escaped, thanks partly to the moderation of the French Communist Party, with a mere electoral swing to the right, which was entirely predictable. Things could have been worse, as we know only too well.

It is almost laughable to have to repeat in 1970 basic principles such as 'liberty cannot survive without respect for the law', or 'the greatest enemy of democracy is anarchy'. Some young Western Europeans who are lucky enough to live in free countries, can afford to sneer at all this. It is none the less profoundly true, and it is deeply upsetting for those of us who have lost our liberty to see these young people profiting from their liberty, as well as from the leisure and comfort of the consumer society they despise, in order to open the road to reactionary dictatorship, however unconsciously.

Europeans can do a great deal to help in the liberation of our country, or at least in alleviating certain of its present effects.

On a purely humanitarian level, the victims of the dictatorship (prisoners, deportees, those who have lost their jobs) or their families desperately need money. We might mention Amnesty International and the Greek Relief Fund as two of the serious organisations concerned with such appeals. Those who have had to flee abroad to escape persecution also need help. Helping them find suitable employment which would allow them to live in exile without having to beg for charity is a considerable moral encouragement to our resistance.

Every member of a trade union or professional organisation can help by mobilising his colleagues on behalf of the Greek resistance. Whether it is a matter of boycotting official Greece, of protesting against the fate of political prisoners or of journalists, or of lobbying for government action against the regime, all kinds of organisations could play an important role. Fortunately for us, the colonels are sensitive to foreign opinion. Foreign protests have often contributed to alleviating the lot of a prisoner, or avoiding an execution (as was the case with Panagoulis), or ending some particularly objectionable measure. When a number of well-known lawyers were arrested during the summer of 1969, their Greek colleagues appealed to legal associations abroad. Some of these, particularly in West Germany, took action which affected the treatment of the detainees. If this reaction had been more widespread the results would probably have been even more significant, and especially more rapid. For every minute counts for those being tortured.

The junta exploits to the full the propaganda value of foreign public figures, artists, sportsmen, etc., visiting Greece. Papadopoulos never loses a chance of being photographed shaking hands with English M.P.s, French actors, or German scholars passing through, to demonstrate to the Greeks that the regime is respected by the élite of Europe. It is difficult to argue with those vain, naïve and sometimes greedy enough to agree, in exchange for a free trip at the expense of the Greek taxpayer, to lend themselves to a vulgar propaganda effort by participating in congresses, festivals, or sporting events in Greece. If they knew, however, that such behaviour would be criticised by their fellow-countrymen, their colleagues, and their own press, perhaps they would hesitate more before so compromising themselves.

Individually or collectively, Europeans can help Greece by exercising pressure on their governments, encouraging them to adopt an openly hostile policy towards the dictatorship. This pressure can be applied in various spheres, political, economic, and cultural, as well as through their government's membership of international organisations such as the E.E.C. and especially NATO.

European member states of NATO can exercise considerable pressure on Washington to modify its policy towards the junta. The American black lobby invokes NATO's strategic interests to justify the support given to the colonels' dictatorship. It is up to the European members of the Alliance, who after all have a say in the matter, to reject the sophistry according to which the defence of Western democracy entails propping up an anti-democratic regime. The American administration may well be influenced by the black lobby, but it cannot afford to allow its relations with a good number of European countries to deteriorate. That would be too high a price to pay for the love of four colonels. In the final analysis, those European countries which are intransigent over the Greek question are performing a service to the United States, by helping it adopt a policy more in keeping with its true interests. It is also a way of helping the blue lobby, that is to say honest and intelligent Americans, of making their opinions prevail, opinions which would certainly have been shared by the great liberal presidents such as Roosevelt and Kennedy.

If one looks at the free countries of Europe one by one, one sees that there are individuals and groups working for Greek liberty in almost all of them. At the official level, however, things are much less clear cut. Only the Scandinavian countries and Holland have adopted an openly hostile line towards the Greek regime. Most of the others have become more indecisive, blowing hot and cold towards the junta. The most disappointing attitude has been that of the French, who have not shown any scruples in dealing with the colonels. France's Greek friends have been grieved to see the French government alone go so far as to invite Makarezos on a official visit to Paris, solely in order to sell him some French goods. And Gaullist French deputies were the only ones, at the Consultative Assembly of the Council of Europe, to oppose the censure motions, proposed by their colleagues, against the regime which had destroyed parliamentary democracy in Greece. (There have also been deliveries of French military equipment, French investment, a visit by the French Radio Orchestra to the Athens Festival, and also the refusal of a French residence permit to Brillakis, the exiled representative of E.D.A.)

Despite this manœuvring, however, the Council of Europe finally forced the regime to withdraw. This was the most damaging blow which it had received up till then, and was greatly due to the pressure of European public opinion.

Although there is no doubt that free Europeans can help us overthrow the dictatorship, many of them perhaps question whether they should. Morally speaking, such doubts have no substance. For the obligation to help of all those who still believe in liberty and in the dignity of the individual, whether they be of the right or the left, is manifest. Man's duty to his fellow-man does not stop at a country's frontiers. As for those who claim to act only according to the military and political interests of their country, or those of the West in general, we refer them to what we have said to the Americans. There remains another category, for whom economic considerations are of primary importance. Their attitude can be summarised in the following way: 'We need markets to sell our products, and profitable investments for our capital. Provided that we can do profitable business with Greece, her form of government is of little concern. Besides, if we don't do business with the junta, others will.'

To these people, who see themselves as cool realists, we would point out that even from a strictly economic point of view the best business is ultimately based on the people's good-will and co-operation. To seek only quick profits obtained from a clique of tyrants is short-sighted. There will come a day when a free Greece will look closely at economic agreements signed by the junta, and will remember who have been her true friends in difficult times, and who have exploited her. But there are considerations of a different type which may carry weight with 'realistic' foreign businessmen: namely, the danger which Greece runs of proving to be a very poor investment risk in the future if the regime lasts for a long time. . . .

There are, however, more important considerations, even for businessmen who have not ceased to be human, than these sordid calculations. I would point to the following text:

'The conscience of the people condemns the cowards, the moles who work in the obscurity of anonymity . . . the vulgar whisperers, those who write anonymous letters. They are mentally unbalanced, completely dishonest rascals, for they have not the courage to emerge into the light of day and to speak in a responsible manner, instead of indulging in calumnious whispering. The only way to treat them is as enemies in the pay of our country's enemies, as a fifth column, directed from abroad as the paid instruments of foreign propaganda. It is the duty of every Greek . . . to close his ears to these whisperings and to silence the whisperers by subjecting them to public contempt.

and *by delivering them into the hands of the law*. These whisperers are earthworms who gnaw at the roots of the tree of national unity. Treat them as worms.'

Does this sort of language, worthy of George Orwell's *1984*, emanate from Peking, Cairo, Nazi Germany, or the depths of Africa? Not at all. It is merely an extract from a broadcast made on the Armed Forces Radio, the second national radio network, at 9.00 p.m. on 10 February 1970.

For all Europeans who believe that the word 'Europe' has more than a merely geographical significance, and that it is linked to certain human values; for all free men who are disturbed to see the world divided into two totalitarian protectorates, each using similar methods—for all these Greece is a test case. If the military dictatorship succeeds in establishing itself for good—if the experiment 'succeeds', as certain American quarters would put it—other countries will inexorably follow suit. If the first flames are not extinguished in time, the fire will spread. Hatred and obscurantism will be propagated by other European radio networks: concentration camps will rise to the west and north of Greece. Almost everywhere there are officers with Bonapartist fantasies who dream of 'saving' their country; being incapable of becoming Napoleons, they will gladly agree to be Papadopouloses.

Liberty is indivisible. Blows struck against freedom in Czechoslovakia or in Greece should be felt as immediately in Britain as in West Germany, in France as in Italy. For unfortunate Czechoslovakia, Western Europe could do little, but for Greece it can do all. And the help which Europeans are able to give to the cause of Greek freedom will not only be indirect help to the cause of Czech, Spanish, Polish and Portuguese freedom—it will also be an insurance policy safeguarding their own future freedom.

Notes

Author's Preface

1 (p. 14). It is disappointing to find certain right and left wing circles apparently agreeing that the present regime does not notably differ from earlier ones in the country's history. It is interesting to compare, for instance, the article by N. Svoronos in the issue of *Les Temps Modernes* devoted to Greece (1969) with the *Times* leader of 13 December 1969. It is time that the democratic left realised the harm which such imprecise claims do to the cause of liberty, and how easily this kind of argument plays into the hands of the reactionaries.

2 (p. 14). Such analyses, of uneven quality, may be found in the issue of *Les Temps Modernes* referred to in the previous footnote.

PART ONE

Section 6

1 (p. 55). And with good cause. It has since been ascertained beyond any doubt (although it is not yet possible to produce the evidence) that the most violent of these incidents were deliberately engineered by army and police *agents provocateurs*.

2 (p. 56). N. Cassandras, *Zwischen Skylla und Charybdis: Griechenland unter der Diktatur*. Vienna 1968, p. 78.

Section 7

1 (p. 64). See p. 49.

2 (p. 67). Colonel Ladas candidly told a German journalist that not more than fourteen officers were in on the secret.

3 (p. 69). The suspension of heavy arms shipments was lifted by the State Department on 29 September 1970. (Translator's note.)

4 (p. 70). The American Ambassador Talbot almost certainly advised the King on that day to accept the *fait accompli*. But this begs a number of questions.

PART TWO

Section 1

1 (p. 73). On the various conspiratorial groups within the army at this time see C. L. Sulzberger's revealing article 'Greece under the Colonels', *Foreign Affairs* 48 (2), January 1970. (Translator's note.)

Section 2

1 (p. 76). By means of decree laws, which we shall refer to simply as 'laws'.

2 (p. 78). Since becoming Prime Minister Papadopoulos has held at various times the ministries of Defence, Foreign Affairs, Education and the Prime Minister's Office. He is currently (April 1971) Prime Minister, Minister of Defence and Minister of Foreign Affairs. (Translator's note.)

3 (p. 78). Almost £625. Papadopoulos receives almost £830.

4 (p. 78). A minister used to receive £65 a month, to which was added, if he was a deputy as well, his parliamentray salary of £345. The displacement allowance, to meet the cost of travelling, was calculated at £3 per day.

5 (p. 78). See p. 41.

Section 3

1 (p. 83). Now appointed by the junta to direct the State Electricity Corporation.

2 (p. 83). It is worth remembering that the Metaxas dictatorship did not interfere with justice.

3 (p. 83). At the same time Kamberis, a member of the High Court, was made Vice-President in return for services rendered when he had presided over the ASPIDA trial (see p. 52).

4 (p. 84). Law No. 192 of 29 May 1969. This was repealed at the end of 1970.

5 (p. 87). The *coup de grâce* may be delivered by a new law, the draft of which was published at the beginning of 1970. This requires the certificate of 'civic reliability' for all lawyers, meaning of course that in the future their professional careers will be dependent on the good will of the police.

Section 4

1 (p. 88). This law does not seem ever to have been implemented. (Translator's note.)

Section 5

1 (p. 102). Liberal newspapers are also subject to a form of economic blackmail. This takes the form of arbitrary fiscal measures, and the forbidding of all advertising on the radio and in public places. State controlled organisations are also forbidden to place advertisements or paid notices. As a further bait, preferential tariffs with 30 per cent rebates are granted to pro-government papers for broadcast advertisements.

Section 6

1 (p. 105). The 'national interest' appears to coincide remarkably frequently with that of a certain engineer and businessman who has been awarded a large number of public works contracts since he became Pattakos' son-in-law.

2 (p. 105). Let us give another example, on a smaller scale, but none the less instructive. A group of American businessmen have just founded a printing concern in Greece which has already obtained a monopoly of all state publications, a concession which will ruin a number of Greek firms.

3 (p. 106). According to the official figures, which have certainly been doctored. An estimate of about 2 per cent is probably more accurate. (By 1970 the annual growth rate was about 7·2 per cent, approximately the rate of the years immediately before the coup. (Translator's note.)

4 (p. 106). The regime cannot claim the credit for monetary stability. Between 1956 and 1966 the index of consumer prices increased annually by an average of 2 per cent. Between 1967 and 1969 the increase was 1·5 per cent. But before the junta it was a case of stability accompanied by expansion, notoriously more difficult to achieve than the stability of stagnation as in 1967-68.

5 (p. 106). A deep distrust of the drachma has led to an incredible increase in industrial share prices, which have increased roughly sixfold within three years, although their yield is significantly less than that of treasury bonds.

6 (p. 107). The fact that by 1969 they had almost regained the 1966 level is scarcely a triumph. There are still three lost years to make up. Given the previous rate of growth, tourist receipts would have doubled between 1966 and 1969.

7 (p. 107). The slight increase claimed is simply the result of a gross accounting fiddle. Included in the official reserves are, firstly, a large part of the special gold reserve which was formerly retained to control market prices and, secondly, the reserves of the commercial banks.

8 (p. 107). These operations are highly secret and details are not known.

9 (p. 108). The agreement between Litton and the Greek regime was terminated by mutual agreement in October 1969. (Translator's note.)

10 (p. 108). These interest rates are often nominal, and the cost of the loan much higher. When contracts are awarded without being put out to tender, their terms are virtually dictated by the successful contractor, who is thus in a position to assure himself a substantial profit margin, besides the interest.

11 (p. 109). More exactly, that of its lackeys with pretensions to economic expertise. The degree of Papadopoulos' own knowledge of economic matters can be judged by the fact that, speaking to journalists on the announcement of the 1970 budget, he inadvertently revealed that he did not know the difference between the budget and the balance of payments: he mentioned the receipts from tourism and migrants' remittances as sources of income that would help reduce the budget deficit.

12 (p. 109). Fiscal charges, which had been 17·7 per cent of the gross national income in 1966, represented 20·8 per cent in 1968.

13 (p. 109). Another fiscal measure, minimal from the point of view of yield, severely hurt intellectuals by reducing by a half their exemption from tax on royalty payments.

14 (p. 110). One such is *Alkimoi*, a version of the Boy Scouts for older children, which is becoming a paramilitary organisation. The state pays for their uniforms and jackboots, and headmasters have been told to 'guide' young boys to become members. It is scarcely necessary to add that they do not share the naïve but sympathetic, humanitarian, and public spirited ideology of the Boy Scouts.

15 (p. 110). According to Androutsopoulos, the junta's Minister of Finance, defence expenditure should be considered 'productive'. (See *Eleftheros Kosmos* of 24 October 1969.) He failed to specify precisely what it produces, except the well-being of the military. The military's pay, together with that of the security forces has entailed, during the first quarter of 1969, an increase in expenditure of 63 per cent over that of the first quarter of 1967. The credits advanced for the salaries of civil servants have increased only by 21 per cent during the same period.

16 (p. 110). Especially in view of the upward swing in economic activity from 1969 onwards, following the end of the recession of 1967-68.

17 (p. 111). One evening in a night club a customer loudly demanded that a piece by Theodorakis be played. A deathly silence followed, and then the head waiter murmured that it was forbidden. The customer curtly revealed his identity: 'Brigadier K.'. The piece was duly played.

18 (p. 111). The more officers are feared, the more their support seems to be prized in certain petit-bourgeois circles. To judge from the small advertisements by those seeking marriage partners, kinship with members of this privileged class is highly regarded. 'Young girl, 29, irreproachable morals, school leaving certificate, daughter of a colonel . . .'. 'Businessman, 42, own car, brother of a major . . .'.

19 (p. 112). What we have said applies to officers as a whole, and not just to the ruling élite. The ex-colonels who have become the secretaries-general of ministries officially receive some 26,000 drachmas monthly, as well as the use of a car. During the epoch of 'parliamentary corruption', a civilian secretary-general received only 6500 drachmas.

20 (p. 112). Purists will reproach us with the alternate use of 'class' and 'caste' in talking of the military. Essentially it is a class which intends to become a caste, as the privileges accorded to officers' sons who are candidates for entry into the Military Academies indicate.

21 (p. 112). American sources have calculated that the army has lost about 47 per cent of officers of these ranks who were on active service on 20 April 1967, the navy 52 per cent, and the air force 95 per cent.

Section 7

1 (p. 113). This section contains a number of references to sources, for much of it might otherwise appear scarcely credible.

2 (p. 113). Those who may object that it is not a separate species but a sub-species of *homo sapiens* evidently do not know the Greek colonels.

3 (p. 114). *Creed*, I, 131. In this and the following quotations the author and translator disclaim all responsibility for style.

4 (p. 114). Notably in *Eleftheros Kosmos* on 16 March and 20 April 1969.

5 (p. 114). This is all part of a cult of personality which Papadopoulos scarcely seems to repudiate, judging by the slogans 'Papadopoulos—Greece', which began in 1969 to appear 'spontaneously' in the provinces.

6 (p. 115). *Creed*, IV, 86

7 (p. 115). *Creed*, I, 168.

8 (p. 115). *Creed*, II, 188. There is no question here of plagiarism, for Papadopoulos has never read Pascal.

9 (p. 115). *Creed*, II, 184.

10 (p. 115). *Creed*, II, 184.

11 (p. 115). *Creed*, I, 110.

12 (p. 115). *Creed*, I, 116.

13 (p. 116). *Creed*, I, 164.

14 (p. 116). This slogan gave a great deal of pleasure to educated Greeks. For it reminded them of a character in one of George Theotokas' novels, which had appeared before the last war—the general leading a putsch who cried to his men, 'Strike up, lads, it's an historical necessity!'

15 (p. 116). The leaking of this secret text, and the reproduction of substantial extracts from it in the international press at the end of November 1969, greatly annoyed the junta.

16 (p. 117). This was 'Civics' (*Politiki Agogi*) by Theofylaktos Papakonstantinou, for a time Minister of Education under the junta. Papakonstantinou claims that 'hundreds' of Cypriots were subjected to 'bestial tortures' by the British, but explains Greece's withdrawal from the Council of Europe in December 1969 simply as due to the Council's 'one-sided anti-Greek stance'. He also vouchsafes the information that the regime's expenditure on state security rose by 51 per cent between 1967 and 1970 and that women with unsatisfactory sex-lives make natural fellow-travellers. (Translator's note.)

17 (p. 117). Speech of Papadopoulos of 15 December 1969.

18 (p. 117). In the text of a speech printed by the papers on 11 June 1968, in capital letters.

19 (p. 117). Because they are ghost-written, some by the quasi-fascist pseudo-intellectual D. Tsakonas, who was appointed to a chair of sociology by the regime.

20 (p. 117). Speaking on 29 October 1969, the junta appointed Mayor of Athens, Ritsos, summoned the shades of Metaxas: 'Rest assured, John Metaxas, that . . . the valiant second lieutenants of 1940, colonels in 1967, continuing your work, have saved Greece. . . .'

21 (p. 119). In fact, there was every reason to believe that he encouraged the murder. Sartzetakis, the examing magistrate who had indicted him as a suspect, was one of the first victims of the purge of the judiciary; he was subsequently arrested at Christmas 1970 and held incommunicado until being charged in May 1971 with sedition under Law 509.

22 (p. 119). A passage in a speech of a visiting American general which referred to this preamble was censored in the version given to the Greek press.

23 (p. 119). *Creed*, II, 194.

24 (p. 120). This elevated thinking is matched by the man's manners. When Karamanlis severely criticised the regime's policy in the autumn of 1969, Makarezos replied by indirectly threatening to stop the pension which he received as a former Prime Minister.

25 (p. 120). When we say that the speeches of Pattakos are clearer than those of Papadopoulos, we make an exception of the philosophic parts which an admirer of Jarry has described at 'Pattakophysics'.

26 (p. 120). *Creed*, I, 149.

27 (p. 121). See the textbook of experimental physics and chemistry for the fifth year of primary school, published in 1969, p. 28.

28 (p. 121). It was in the same speech, which is rich in extravagant metaphors, that Papadopoulos asserted that 'as the human organism rejects old cells and replaces them by new, so we must lead the young in the right direction, so that there will exist an organism capable of creating a society which will lead to its great destiny'.

29 (p. 123). Papadopoulos' frequent use of biological metaphors is interesting. These have been the trade mark of all reactionary ideologies from Plato onwards.

Section 8

1 (p. 124). Pipinelis died in July 1970, whereupon Papadopoulos assumed the portfolio of Foreign Affairs. (Translator's note.)

2 (p. 125). In June 1969 he was fired, as Onassis considered him a supporter of his rival Niarchos.

3 (p. 125). He is the only person closely associated with the regime capable of writing the purist language correctly.

4 (p. 126). Constantine Thanos, an economist who occupied important posts in the Ministry of Co-ordination and at the Bank of Greece, and who has now been found officially to have plagiarised his thesis, also deserves mention.

5 (p. 129). This can work both ways. An employee dismissed for laziness, incompetence, or drunkenness has only to complain to the military authorities, making a point of his loyalty to the regime. Very often they will intervene and force the employer to take him on again.

6 (p. 130). In the summer of 1970, Pattakos, the Minister of the Interior, announced that in future passports would not be arbitrarily withheld. However, a number of Greeks continued to be refused passports on vague grounds such as that they constituted 'a threat to national security'. (Translator's note.)

7 (p. 132). Sometimes the demands of the junta's propaganda services assume tragi-comic proportions. When, for example, it was decided to organise the customary flood of 'spontaneous protests' against the award of a foreign literary prize to a Greek resistance hero, the Under Secretary for the Press, Vovolinis, summoned the directors of various literary associations, including the Union of Writers which had been dissolved in 1967. 'But we no longer have any legal existence,' they replied. 'For the purposes of this protest, you do exist,' was the answer.

Section 9

1 (p. 133). By April 1971 the only Centre Union deputy still detained was Alevras. (Translator's note.)

2 (p. 134). Theodorakis was allowed to leave Greece in April 1970 following the personal intervention of the French radical politician Jean-Jacques Servan-Schreiber. (Translator's note.)

3 (p. 135). For once, the Faculty of Law of the University of Athens, generally a very timid body, showed a collective courage in protesting against the judges' dismissal.

4 (p. 135). As most writers refuse to collaborate with the State Radio, the junta has been obliged to find a way of overcoming this difficulty. Law No. 451 of March 1970 allows the State Radio and Television network to broadcast any musical or literary work without the author's consent, thus directly contravening all previous legislation and all international agreements on authors' rights to which Greece is a party.

5 (p. 136). Dealing with clandestine tracts is a highly dangerous activity, which has led to prison sentences of up to twenty years.

6 (p. 137). His novel *The Dam* has recently appeared in French translation.

7 (p. 137). Filinis is now in prison, while Leloudas escaped abroad where he works along with Brillakis. Not all those arrested and tried in connection with the *Patriotic Front* belonged to the left. One of them was Mrs Sylva Akritas, widow of the Minister of Education under the Centre Union.

8 (p. 137). This was the figure given by the American weekly *Newsweek* in an article (19 January 1970) whose conclusions were generally favourable to the junta.

9 (p. 138). An ironic allusion to the farcical referendum on the new Constitution, which had taken place a little over a month before, and to which we shall return.

10 (p. 138). Signed 'Democratic League'.

11 (p. 140). See Introduction.

12 (p. 140). At the trial of the group which included Zannas, the presiding judge said to him, 'After all, all you have done is to translate these texts from the English.' Refusing to grasp the lifeline that was being held out to him—perhaps because the regime would have rather not had to convict a respected figure, descended from such a well-known family which had greatly distinguished itself in the service of the nation—Zannas proudly replied, 'Yes, but I also assume full responsibility for everything which my friends have done.' The tribunal, infuriated by this reply, sentenced him to ten and a half years in prison.

13 (p. 140). These lines were written in January 1970.

14 (p. 143). In early 1971 an important step towards unity was achieved by the signing of an agreement between representatives abroad of several major resistance groups, ranging from royalists to non-Moscow leftists. The one notable exception was Andreas Papandreou's organisation P.A.K., which refused to participate because it insisted on a provision questioning the future of royalty in Greece.

Section 10

1 (p. 144). A provincial gendarmerie officer, sent to arrest a former army officer, said to him, deeply upset: 'General, how my men and I prayed that we would not find you at home.' Another summoned a man exiled in a village and said, 'Yesterday, sir, you were speaking out against the government in the café. This puts me in a very difficult position, because informers have just reported the incident to me. Don't do it again, I beg of you. When you want to let off steam, come and see me, and together we will curse the bastards who rule us.'

2 (p. 146). In April 1971, just before the fourth anniversary of the coup, Papadopoulos announced the closure of the two detention camps at Partheni on the island of Leros and Skala Oropou. The remaining detainees were released with the exception of about fifty judged to be 'dangerous and unrepentant communists'. These were exiled to villages. Papadopoulos in a speech of 19 December 1970 had promised to release all detainees by the fourth anniversary of the coup provided that the existing conditions of internal security prevailed. (Translator's note.)

3 (p. 146). The International Red Cross protested several times against these conditions; some of its reports have been published.

4 (p. 146). The conversation was reported in fasc. no. 12 of *Socialist International Information*, 23 June 1967.

5 (p. 147). Following the escape of George Mylonas, the desire to keep detainees isolated was outweighed by considerations of security. For greater efficiency and economy, the authorities grouped most of the deportees in three villages.

6 (p. 147). The well-known left-wing poet, Ritsos, was firstly interned at Leros, and then was in enforced residence on Samos, despite the state of his health which required the care of specialists not to be found on a small island.

7 (p. 147). To quote from a letter from a deportee. '. . . While out walking yesterday, I came across old Michael. He is a simple man, almost the village idiot. Desperately poor, he barely manages to scrape a living by running errands and doing odd jobs for a few

pennies. He came up to me and said, "I want to ask you a favour, sir." I thought he wanted money, which was embarrassing because I was broke myself. Not at all. "Don't do it, sir, do me the favour of not losing hope. All this will pass." And his sweeping gesture indicated that "all this" was the dictatorship, my deportation, all our country's troubles. . . .'

8 (p. 148). This was the source of a joke that enjoyed a considerable vogue in Athens. Woken up in the middle of the night by violent knocking, a trembling citizen opens his door to find himself face to face with threatening policemen. 'There must be some mistake, gentlemen,' he stammers, 'I am a communist, the royalists are on the third floor.'

9 (p. 148). These have now either been released or exiled. (Translator's note.)

10 (p. 149). Starakis was subsequently sentenced to eighteen years' imprisonment at the Trial of the Thirty-Four. He was released shortly afterwards following the intervention of the French Government. (Translator's note.)

11 (p. 149). We know of a case where an educated detainee suffered the refined torture of being allowed to read only Papadopoulos' *Creed*.

12 (p. 149). In courts-martial in Greece the public prosecutor is called a 'Royal Commissioner', but to simplify matters we will use the ordinary term.

13 (p. 150). It was Karapanos who, when presiding over another trial in February 1970, replied to a young man on trial who had invoked human rights: 'Human rights are of no interest to us.'

14 (p. 150). Professor George Mangakis, who has been mentioned several times. He should not be confused with his cousin, also George, mentioned on p. 87. The fact that both are called George and that both have shown, in very different fields, an exemplary courage only adds to the confusion.

15 (p. 152). The following case deserves mention. In November 1969 a bus narrowly escaped colliding with a military vehicle travelling at high speed. Playing on the initials on the truck E.S. (Ellinikos Stratos—Greek Army) a passenger repeated a current joke: 'Ellinikes skotostres' (Greek killers). A police informer denounced him. He was sent before a military court, and condemned to a year in prison for 'insulting the army'.

16 (p. 152). Despite this discrimination, political prisoners are not allowed to refer to themselves as such in their letters; the word 'political' is struck out by the prison censor.

17 (p. 153). These figures were no longer accurate in April 1971. Those actually sentenced numbered rather less than 400,

those in exile about 70, while 150 to 200 were being held pending trial, most of them without having been charged. Some prisons, notably Corfu and Thessaloniki, are far worse than others. The Corfu prison dates from 1830 and has never been modernised. Those serving their sentences in Corfu are kept in cold, damp, unheated, underground cells for nineteen hours a day, during which time they are in total isolation, not even being allowed to visit the prison canteen. They included until recently the 70 year-old retired General Iordanidis, a former NATO staff officer. (Addendum 1971.)

18 (p. 154). See p. 151. Besides the other tortures that have been inflicted on him, Panagoulis was kept handcuffed day and night for several months. He was reduced to begging to be executed. However, his death sentence appears unlikely to be carried out. After worldwide protests the junta postponed his execution indefinitely. This has allowed his torturers to continue to satisfy their sadistic instincts on this human wreck.

19 (p. 154). This character maintained in 1963 that Lambrakis had died accidentally. It has been said of Kapsaskis that had he been employed by Pontius Pilate he would not have hesitated to certify that Christ had died of natural causes.

20 (p. 155). The police did this to Theodorakis in 1967.

21 (p. 155). It is noteworthy that this dictatorship, reviled by all Greek democrats, appears in retrospect almost idyllic in comparison with that of the junta.

22 (p. 156). None the less, the leader writer on *Eleftheros Kosmos* has on a number of occasions praised Papadopoulos for his great magnanimity in not shooting Andreas Papandreou immediately after the putsch, as though he had every right to do so.

23 (p. 156). Other names of victims may be found in the *Livre Noir de la Dictature en Grèce*, and in Nos. 10-11 of the *Greek Report* of London. But these alleged cases are not as certain as that of Tsarouchas. The case of the lawyer Mandilaras, for instance, is still dubious. It is not known if he was killed by the police or if he died while diving from the small fishing-boat in which he was trying to escape. Possibly the terrified boat crew did away with him when they learned that the authorities knew of his presence on board.

PART THREE

Section 1

1 (p. 158). The concept popularised by Karl Popper, *The Open Society and its Enemies*, London 1962.

2 (p. 159). Law No. 346 of 1969. We will refer to it henceforth by the initials P.L.

3 (p. 159). Art. 191 of the Penal Code, as it has been modified by Law 372 of 1969, known as the 'Law on Rumour-mongering'.

4 (p. 160). Law 790 of 31/12/70 has made things even worse, for it forbids *any* sentence for a press offence to be converted into a fine, even in the case of a first offence (art. 3, para. 2).

5 (p. 162). See, on this whole issue, the excellent articles of Phaedon Vegleris and George Cateforis in *Les Temps Modernes*.

6 (p. 162). Law No. 58 of 1968, to whose articles the following quotations refer.

7 (p. 162). Moreover, no appeal can be made to the Council of State against the decisions of these officers' committees on the promotions, retirements, etc., of their colleagues (Const. Art. 131, para. 4).

8 (p. 163). Art. 135 of the Constitution expressly provides that the first elections will be held by the 'National Revolutionary Government'. Moreover, the first *two* elections will be held in accordance with its own electoral law.

9 (p. 165). Normally, in Greece, a judge or lawyer. At this referendum the judicial observer was often replaced by a civil servant, regarded by the junta as 'safer'.

10 (p. 165). As well as the provisions guaranteeing the independence of the Council of State and the tenure of its members, which the junta rode roughshod over a few months later.

In April 1970 article 10 of the 1968 Constitution which forbids arrest without warrant and provides that the accused must be brought before the examining magistrate within twenty-four hours was activated. It has been breached on numerous occasions since then, notably during the two large waves of arrests in November 1970 and March 1971. (Translator's note.)

11 (p. 167). *Ethnos* ceased publication in April 1970 after its proprietors and editors had been sentenced to terms of imprisonment. The pretext for the trial was an article written by the former Centre Union minister John Zighdis calling for a government of national unity to deal with the Cyprus problem. Zighdis was sentenced to four and a half years imprisonment and fined. (Translator's note.)

Section 3

1 (p. 186). Mr Tom Pappas, a Greek American and a great meddler in the affairs of the two countries is a friend of the Greek colonels as well as of Vice-President Agnew, whose political campaigns he appears to finance.

2 (p. 186). Perhaps age is thought to give an aura of respectability to dictatorships as to prostitutes. The Spanish regime, of a more recent vintage than the Portuguese, has not been considered mature enough for NATO. On this score, the Greek junta is even less acceptable, being only a beginner in the profession.

3 (p. 186). The champions of the black lobby who dispute that it is hated should consider what sort of regime needs to impose martial law for four years, and not only fears elections but does not dare even to tolerate criticism in the press.

Index